OUTCASTS FR(

Ideas of Landscape in British Poetry
since 1945

LIVERPOOL ENGLISH TEXTS AND STUDIES
General editors: JONATHAN BATE and BERNARD BEATTY

This long-established series has a primary emphasis on close reading, critical exegesis and textual scholarship. Studies of a wide range of works are included, although the list has particular strengths in the Renaissance, and in Romanticism and its continuations.

Byron and the Limits of Fiction edited by Bernard Beatty and Vincent Newey. Volume 22. 1988. 304pp. ISBN 0-85323-026-9

Literature and Nationalism edited by Vincent Newey and Ann Thompson. Volume 23. 1991. 296pp. ISBN 0-85323-057-9

Reading Rochester edited by Edward Burns. Volume 24. 1995. 240pp. ISBN 0-85323-038-2 (cased), 0-85323-309-8 (paper)

Thomas Gray: Contemporary Essays edited by W. B. Hutchings and William Ruddick. Volume 25. 1993. 287pp. ISBN 0-85323-268-7

Nearly Too Much: The Poetry of J. H. Prynne by N. H. Reeve and Richard Kerridge. Volume 26. 1995. 224pp. ISBN 0-85323-840-5 (cased), 0-85323-850-2 (paper)

Outcasts from Eden: Ideas of Landscape in British Poetry since 1945 by Edward Picot. Volume 28. 1996. 344pp. ISBN 0-85323-531-7 (cased), 0-85323-541-4 (paper)

A full list of titles available in this series is available from Liverpool University Press.

OUTCASTS FROM EDEN

Ideas of Landscape in British Poetry since 1945

EDWARD PICOT

LIVERPOOL UNIVERSITY PRESS

First published 1997 by
LIVERPOOL UNIVERSITY PRESS
Senate House, Abercromby Square, Liverpool, L69 3BX

British Library Cataloguing-in-Publication Data
A British Library CIP Record is available for this book
ISBN   0-85323-531-7 *cased*
          0-85323-541-4 *paper*

Printed and bound in the European Union by
Bell & Bain Limited, Glasgow

Contents

Preface

In this book, firstly, I have attempted to re-examine five of the more important British post-war poets, in terms of their contributions to the British tradition of landscape poetry. Secondly, I have also attempted to identify some of the ideas and myths which have dominated that tradition, right down to the present day. Thirdly, I have tried to set my discussion in the context of the modern environmental debate, not only because I believe that environmentalism is certain to have a profound effect on the ways in which our poets describe their landscapes, but also because a good understanding of our landscape poetry may well serve as a key to some of the iconography deployed by environmentalists, in their attempts to depict the relationship between Man and Nature.

If the relevance of poetry to environmentalism seems rather tenuous, then it ought to be remembered that environmentalism began as an aesthetic movement rather than a scientific one. Wordsworth and the other Romantics certainly inspired a new veneration for the natural world in Britain; but they also inspired such American Romantics as Emerson, Thoreau and Muir; and probably the Americans should be credited with founding the modern environmental movement, through their struggle to establish the great National Parks, the first of which was created at Yellowstone in 1872. John Muir and his supporters, when they launched their campaign to preserve the natural grandeur of the Yellowstone area, were not fighting to avert a scientifically-quantifiable crisis, but a spiritual and aesthetic one. They were not worried about what might happen to the atmosphere if all the trees were cut down and industrialism continued at an unsustainable rate, but about what might happen to the human spirit if all the natural grandeur of the world was plundered and spoilt by Man. And the same aesthetic and spiritual values have been close to the heart of the environmental movement ever since.

Outcasts from Eden was originally a thesis, submitted for the degree of Doctor of Philosophy in English Literature at the University of Kent in 1991, but it has been substantially revised since then. At the time when I began to work on it, in 1987, the field of post-war British landscape poetry was virtually unexplored by literary critics. There seemed to be a widespread academic belief that the landscape genre had either died out or become unworthy of attention during the period of the Georgian poets. Modernism and modern industrial society had put paid to it. This view was strongly reinforced by a number of books about the landscape genre, all of which appeared within a span of ten years: John Barrell's *The Idea of Landscape and the Sense of Place* (1972); Raymond Williams's *The Country and the City* (1973); *The Penguin Book of English Pastoral Verse* edited by John Barrell and John Bull (1974); James Turner's *The Politics of Landscape* (1979); and John Barrell's *The Dark Side of the Landscape* (1981).

Excellent though some of these books were, they all took the same broadly-Marxist view that representations of the landscape, whether in writing or in paint, ought to be analysed in terms of what they had to say about the social realities of rural life. They all assumed that aesthetic responses to the landscape were heavily influenced by practical, social and economic considerations. If writers and artists chose to concentrate on certain aspects of the countryside, it was argued, then it must have suited their purposes to do so, even if those purposes were sometimes unconscious ones. The charming unrealities of pastoral convention, for example, provided a convenient way of writing about life in the country without facing up to the unpleasant harshness of rural labour. Thanks to such conventions, the cultured and fortunate few were able to play their philosophizing games, contrasting the worthy (but sometimes dull) simplicities of rural life with the gay (but often corrupt) elegance of the town, in accordance with the best literary traditions, without ever confronting the poverty and drudgery suffered by the lower classes in the country and the city alike.

This kind of evasion of the truth, argued the Marxists, was particularly striking during the late eighteenth and early nineteenth centuries, the period of enclosure and agrarian reform. And although, from the end of the eighteenth century onwards, the Romantics abandoned some of the most obviously artificial aspects of pastoralism, they still could not bring themselves to depict rural society as it really was. Their picturesque cottagers, woodland hermits, scholar–gypsies, heroic simpletons, and what have you, scarcely came closer to the everyday conditions of rural labour than had Corin and Phyllis with their oaten pipes and their flocks of well-behaved sheep. In any case, argued the Marxists, the attention of the audience was constantly being drawn away from the habitations of men, towards the more wild and untamed areas of the landscape, because here questions of social structure and cohesion could be avoided, in favour of an untrammelled confrontation between the individual and the inspiration of Nature.

The Marxist critics certainly made a valuable contribution to our appreciation of pastoralism and landscape, in both literature and the visual arts. It can be a chastening and eye-opening experience to read a well-researched comparison, of the kind that John Barrell makes, between poetic descriptions of rural contentment and the historical facts about life in the countryside during the same period. But in the final analysis the Marxist approach was too narrow. It always seemed to be taking the writers and artists of former centuries to task, for failing to analyse and represent social structures in the proper (Marxist) manner. It sometimes laid such emphasis on what the poets and painters *ought* to be saying, that it failed to pay any real attention to what they actually *were* saying. Aesthetic, philosophical and religious questions tended to be either pushed to one side, or treated brusquely as the inevitable products of a given set of social circumstances.

The Marxists saw no intrinsic aesthetic or spiritual difference between a streetlamp and a star, and they assumed that writers who claimed to prefer the star only did so because it so obviously stood beyond the awkward everyday world of social injustice and downtrodden poverty. By gazing admiringly at the star, the artist and his audience could temporarily forget the problems of real life: but the natural world was not of itself any more beautiful than the man-made world, and rural life was not of itself any more inspiring than urban life. The idea that God made the country but Man made the town was simply hokum. It was certainly easier to imagine that an isolated rural labourer might be contented with his lot, than to believe the same thing of the festering crowds that lived in the city slums; but that ought not to blind us to the fact that the country and the town were not intrinsically different from one another at all; they were only different aspects of the same system, embodying the drama of ownership and subjugation in slightly different forms.

If this were granted, then it must follow that in the ever-more-urbanized society of the twentieth century—a society where Marxist analysis should have made an impression on anyone capable of rational thought—writers and artists ought not to be still harping on about the grandeur of the natural world and the supposed nobility of rural life, but turning their attention more and more to the towns and the cities. Any poet who still insisted on churning out the same old nostalgic nonsense about fields and mountains was probably avoiding the important issues of the day, and did not deserve to be taken very seriously, unless he could be claimed as the representative of a disenfranchised rural minority. The pastoral myth had been exploded, and landscape poetry, which had enjoyed a tremendous vogue from Wordsworth to Hardy, was now over and done with. That was what the Marxists thought; and by and large the same verdict has been tacitly accepted by the critical establishment as a whole, throughout the post-war period—or at least up until very recently.

With the emergence of the environmental crisis, however, landscape poetry has begun to look surprisingly 'relevant' again. When we look at landscapes, after all, we can see the evidence of either the power of Man or the power of Nature. Frequently we can see both; and for this reason, landscape descriptions reflect our feelings about the relationship between Man and Nature in a peculiarly intense manner. The environmental crisis has served to focus attention on this relationship as never before, and as a result the genre of landscape poetry is rapidly regaining its old importance. And once we begin to look at it again, it soon becomes apparent that it never really went out of fashion at all. Landscape poems have been appearing with great frequency throughout the century, and I hope my book will show that the tradition has continued to flourish in the post-war period.

Not only has the landscape genre never really gone out of fashion, but a whole body of attitudes which were associated with it in the eighteenth and nineteenth centuries has been carried forward into the post-war period. The old idea that God made the country but Man made the town, for example, still seems to persist, even in the work of poets who would not describe themselves as religious. The natural world is still often represented as divinely formed, spiritually uplifting and serene, whereas the man-made world is shown as flawed, ugly and riddled with unsolved problems. It comes as a surprise to find that these attitudes have survived the advent of Darwinism and the celebrated 'death of God' at the end of the last century, but their survival is an undeniable fact. If the evidence of our literature is to be believed, then it would seem that our view of the relationship between Man and Nature is often still mythological and pseudo-religious, rather than rational and scientific.

But we do not have to rely on the evidence of English literature alone. When, in the course of my research, I began to

read the works of modern environmentalist writers, I found
the same tendency to describe the relationship between Man
and Nature in mythological language. In the following pages I
have discussed only four environmentalist works at any
length—*Only One Earth* by Barbara Ward and René Dubos
(1972); *Gaia* by James Lovelock (1979); *The End of Nature* by
Bill McKibben (1990) and *The Rebirth of Nature* by Rupert
Sheldrake (1990)—but I believe them to be representative of
the *oeuvre* as a whole. All of these books are attempting to
redefine the relationship between Man and Nature in the light
of recent scientific research, especially research into the
impact of human beings on the environment, and into the
interdependence of different parts of the biosphere. Yet all of
them, at crucial points, slide away from scientific discourse
and towards what Philip Larkin once called 'a common myth-
kitty'. It is this use of the 'myth-kitty' which eventually
provided me with the main theme of my book.

I mention Larkin's name at this point for a particular
reason. Once I had noticed the recurrence of mythological
references in the material I was studying, I soon started to
wonder if they might be connected to one another by any
underlying pattern. It was while I was reading Blake
Morrison's excellent book *The Movement* (1980) that such a
pattern was suggested to me. Morrison makes a detailed
analysis of Larkin's poem 'MCMXIV', which I had been examining myself, because its subject is the English landscape and
the way in which it was affected by the outbreak of the First
World War. Morrison asserts that Larkin's apparent interest in
social and historical circumstance really goes no deeper than
the surface of the poem. Beneath that surface, what he is actually up to—despite his declared aversion to the 'myth-kitty'—
is a bit of concealed mythmaking:

> What, exactly, is the myth articulated in 'MCMXIV'?
> Possibly, it is a new version of the myth of the Fall.
> The Great War is the equivalent of the serpent,

enticing man from his paradisal home amongst the 'flowering grasses' of England, and depriving him of his 'innocence' (a key word in the poem): Larkin's pity is for a race of innocents about to be exposed to experience...[1]

For me, the significance of Morrison's argument here lies, not in what he has to say about the Great War, but in what he has to say about 'the myth of the Fall'. As soon as I read this passage, it occurred to me that 'MCMXIV' is not the only poem in which Larkin surreptitiously recirculates the Fall-myth; and before very long, I began to notice how often the other poets I was studying did the same thing. Eventually, I came to realize how central the Fall-myth is, not only to our whole tradition of landscape poetry, but to our cultural assumptions about the relationship between Man and Nature itself.

Before I begin my argument in detail, I had better say a few words about the limitations of my book. First of all, it is not in any sense a catalogue. I have not been exhaustive in my reading of post-1945 poetry; I have made no attempt to track down (let alone mention) every poet who has published a poem about the landscape since the war ended; and nor have I attempted to list (let alone discuss) all the different ways of writing about the landscape which have been used by poets of the period. I browsed fairly widely, I decided what I thought were the dominant ideas, and I set out to discuss them. Furthermore, in pursuit of my argument I have felt free to analyse poems which are not ostensibly about the landscape at all. Skyscapes and seascapes make frequent appearances, and my chapter on Charles Tomlinson examines a poem about a barometer.

I have chosen to write about only five poets, because I wanted to discuss each one at some length. Obviously there was bound to be a trade-off between the number of poets I could discuss and the depth in which I could discuss them. I am aware that my final list might be criticized as unrepresentative. Readers may feel entitled to suspect that I have chosen only the writers who happen to suit my argument, at the expense of all the others who do not. I can only urge readers to decide for themselves whether the same ideas recur in landscape poems by other hands. It is my belief that they do. The five that I have chosen are all fairly 'mainstream' poets, and their merits have been widely recognized by 'mainstream' critics. This in itself might be decried as a form of bias, but I think it indicates a certain degree of cultural centrality. I would argue that the ideas and myths embedded in the works of these writers are both relevant to our literary traditions, and of some importance to our culture as a whole. Again, readers must decide for themselves whether they find my argument convincing.

Let me say a word about the manner in which I have organized my material. As my research progressed and certain dominant themes began to emerge, I was tempted to arrange my discussion under a number of headings, such as 'The Eden-myth', 'Primitivism and Rationalism', 'Style' and 'Time'. But this would have meant jumbling the works of my five poets together and then reordering them in accordance with my own ideas. I preferred to meet each poet in turn on his own ground, as it were, and thus to allow the aspects of his work which interested me to emerge more naturally from the context of his output as a whole. I have therefore chosen to devote a separate chapter to each poet in turn: a scheme which has the added advantage of user-friendliness. Any student who wishes to read what I have to say about a particular poet, without having to bother himself with the rest of my argument, can simply read the relevant chapter and ignore the rest of the book. It would be nice to think that such students will be few and far between, but I have been a student myself, and I am a realist.

The advantage of writing about the post-war period is that the ground is relatively unexplored, leaving each critic comparatively free to arrive at his own conclusions. The disadvantage is that the earth keeps shifting beneath your feet. At the time of writing, all of my poets except Philip Larkin are still alive and publishing (and long may this state of affairs continue). Since *Outcasts from Eden* was submitted as a thesis, an alarming amount of new material has appeared. Anthony Thwaite has published an edition of Larkin's letters, and Andrew Motion has published a biography. R. S. Thomas has published two new collections entitled *Counterpoint* and *Mass for Hard Times*, and brought out his *Collected Poems*. Charles Tomlinson has also published two new collections, called *Annunciations* and *The Door in the Wall*. As for Ted Hughes, he has brought out a new collection entitled *Rain-Charm for the Duchy*; he has reissued *Remains of Elmet, Cave Birds* and *River* in a single volume under the title *Three Books*, with numerous revisions; he has published two story-books entitled *Tales from the Early World* and *The Iron Woman*; he has also published a lengthy study of Shakespeare entitled *Shakespeare and the Goddess of Complete Being*; and very recently he has issued *Winter Pollen*, a collection of literary essays. And this is to say nothing about academics, besides myself, who are always likely to bring out new books and essays about the five poets I have chosen, or about the subject of landscape poetry, or about the impact of the environmental crisis on modern writing. By the time my book appears, in other words, it will be partially out of date. But if my argument is a valid one, it should survive the advent of a few new publications.

I want to end this Preface by extending my thanks to those people who have helped me to get *Outcasts from Eden* written. My supervisors at the University of Kent were Martin Scofield, Graham Clark and Mike Irwin. I owe a great deal to all of them, but especially to Mike Irwin, who supervised me throughout the three years of my course. And the person who deserves my gratitude more than anyone else is my wife Sarah, who enabled me to get this book finished by not nagging me to go out and get a proper job.

NOTE

1. Morrison, *The Movement* (Oxford University Press, 1980), p. 195.

Acknowledgements

Extracts from *Pig Earth* by John Berger reprinted by permission of Random House UK Ltd (world rights except USA) and Random House Inc. (USA rights).

Extracts from *I and Thou* by Martin Buber (trans. Ronald Gregory Smith) reprinted by permission of T. & T. Clark Ltd (world rights except USA) and Scribner, a division of Simon & Schuster. Copyright © 1959 by Charles Scribner's Sons, Renewed (USA rights).

Extract from *Collected Poems 1970–1983* by Donald Davie reprinted by permission of Carcanet Press Ltd.

Extract from 'See, and Believe' by Donald Davie reprinted by permission of the author.

Extract from *Purity of Diction in English Verse* by Donald Davie reprinted by permission of Routledge & Kegan Paul.

Extract from 'The Poetry of Charles Tomlinson' by Michael Edwards reprinted by permission of *Agenda*.

Extract from 'Ted Hughes and *Crow*: an interview with Ekbert Faas' reprinted by permission of *The London Magazine*.

Extract from 'Ireland since 1870' by David Fitzpatrick, taken from *The Oxford History of Ireland* (ed. R. F. Foster), reprinted by permission of Oxford University Press.

Extracts from *Modern Ireland* (copyright © 1988) by R. F. Foster reprinted by permission of Sheil Land Associates.

Extracts from *The Bog People* by P. V. Glob (trans. R. L. S. Bruce-Mitford) reprinted by permission of Faber and Faber Ltd.

Faber Ltd (world rights except USA) and Farrar, Straus & Giroux Inc. (USA rights).

Extract from *Answer to Job* by Carl Jung (trans. R. F. C. Hull) reprinted by permission of Princeton University Press.

Extracts from *The Less Deceived* by Philip Larkin reprinted by permission of The Marvell Press, England and Australia.

Extracts from *Collected Poems* by Philip Larkin (ed. Anthony Thwaite) (copyright © 1988, 1989 by the Estate of Philip Larkin), *The North Ship* and 'Introduction to *The North Ship*' from *Required Writing: Miscellaneous Pieces 1955–1982* by Philip Larkin (copyright © 1982, 1983 by Philip Larkin) reprinted by permission of Faber and Faber Ltd (world rights except USA) and Farrar, Straus & Giroux, Inc. (USA rights).

Extract from 'Philip Larkin' by George A. Plimpton, taken from *Writers at Work, Seventh Series* (ed. George A. Plimpton) (copyright © 1986 by The Paris Review), reprinted by permission of Viking Penguin, a division of Penguin Books USA Inc.

Extracts from *Jill* (copyright © 1946, 1976 by Philip Larkin) and *A Girl in Winter* (copyright © 1947, 1976 by Philip Larkin) by Philip Larkin reprinted by permission of Faber and Faber Ltd (world rights except USA) and The Overlook Press, Woodstock, NY 12498 (USA rights).

Extracts from *Apocalypse* by D. H. Lawrence (Introduction Richard Aldington) (copyright © 1931 by the Estate of D. H. Lawrence, renewed © 1959 by the Estate of Frieda Lawrence Ravagli) reprinted by permission of Laurence Pollinger Ltd and the Estate of Frieda Lawrence Ravagli (world rights except USA) and Viking Penguin, a division of Penguin Books USA Inc. (USA rights).

Extracts from 'Introduction to *Pansies*', 'Climb Down, O Lordly Mind' and 'Only Man' by D. H. Lawrence, taken from *The Complete Poems of D. H. Lawrence, Vols 1 & 2* by D. H.

Extracts from *Collected Poems 1945–1990* by R. S. Thomas reprinted by permission of J. M. Dent & Sons Ltd.

Extracts from *The Echoes Return Slow* by R. S. Thomas reprinted by permission of Macmillan General Books.

Extract from *Some Americans* by Charles Tomlinson reprinted by permission of the author.

Extract from *Eden* by Charles Tomlinson reprinted by permission of Redcliffe Press Ltd.

Extract from *Poetry and Metamorphosis* by Charles Tomlinson reprinted by permission of Cambridge University Press.

Extract from the Introduction to *Marianne Moore: A Collection of Critical Essays*, edited and introduced by Charles Tomlinson, reprinted by permission of Prentice Hall, a division of Simon & Schuster.

Extracts from *Collected Poems* and *The Return* by Charles Tomlinson reprinted by permission of Oxford University Press.

Extracts from *Only One Earth* by Barbara Ward and René Dubos (copyright © by Report on the Human Environment, Inc.) reprinted by permission of Curtis Brown Ltd.

Extract from *Ted Hughes* by Thomas West reprinted by permission of Methuen & Co.

Extract from *In the American Grain* by William Carlos Williams (copyright © 1933 by William Carlos Williams) reprinted by permission of Laurence Pollinger Ltd (rights in UK and Commonwealth, except Canada) and New Directions Publishing Corporation (rest of world).

Extract from 'The Lake Isle of Innisfree' by W. B. Yeats, taken from *The Collected Poems of W. B. Yeats*, reprinted by permission of A. P. Watt Ltd on behalf of Anne and Michael Yeats.

Chapter One
Introduction

I

So far as the circumstances in which we live are concerned, the most significant challenge and influence for the modern landscape poet must be the environmental crisis. When we look at the landscape today, we are more inclined than ever before to read it in terms of the damage being done to Nature by Man. And since much of this damage is something we have learned about, rather than something which can easily be observed by the naked, untrained eye, this must mean that we are more and more inclined to see the landscape in a scientific way—specifically, from the point of view of the modern ecologist. The scars made by new roads and the rubbish swept up on our beaches are plain enough, but many of us now read the landscape in terms of absences, too: the absence of hedgerows, of wild flowers, of insect-life, of certain native trees, and so forth. And we worry about the invisible things: the pesticides which we know are being used on the land, the poisons leaking out of buried landfills, nuclear waste in the Irish Sea, exhaust pollution in the air, ozone depletion...

As the environmental crisis deepens, so it becomes apparent that the myths and images, by which we in the West have traditionally sought to characterize the natural world, are inadequate to our new situation. It no longer makes sense to think of Nature as an alien force which lies beyond us and exists independently from us—a bestower of gifts and a bringer of destruction, inexhaustible, inscrutable, unpredictable and all-powerful. The following lines from the Book

1

of Job exemplify the extent and depth of the change that has taken place:

> Canst thou draw out leviathan with an hook? or his
> tongue with a cord which thou lettest down?
> Canst thou fill his skin with barbed irons? or his
> head with fish spears?
>
> *(Job 41:1, 7)*

No modern reader can contemplate this ancient challenge without realizing with a slight shock that the answer is different now to what it was when the lines were first written.

The author of Job meant to imply that Man was too puny either to threaten or to comprehend the wonders of God's creation, and in a universal sense of course this is still true; but within the biosphere of our own Earth there is no longer any doubt that Man is the master in terms of physical power. He *can* fill leviathan's skin with barbed irons, and he *can* pierce the hide of behemoth. What he cannot do is escape the consequences of his own actions. Our growing awareness that the exploitation of the natural world can never be free from such consequences is one thing that separates our attitudes towards Nature from the attitudes of our forefathers.

In the first chapter of Genesis, when God has finished creating the natural world, his decision to establish human beings as the rulers of the new Earth is presented in these words:

> And God said, Let us make man in our image, after
> our likeness: and let them have dominion over the
> fish of the sea, and over the fowl of the air, and over
> the cattle, and over all the earth, and over every
> creeping thing that creepeth upon the earth.
>
> *(Genesis 1:26)*

From the outset Man is thus granted absolute power to exploit the natural world as he will. The manner in which God blesses Adam and Eve reflects this:

> And God blessed them, and God said unto them, Be
> fruitful, and multiply, and replenish the earth, and
> subdue it...
>
> *(Genesis 1:28)*

After the Flood, Noah and his family are blessed in virtually
the same terms:

> And God blessed Noah and his sons, and said unto
> them, Be fruitful, and multiply, and replenish the
> earth.
> And the fear of you and the dread of you shall be
> upon every beast of the earth...
> And you, be ye fruitful, and multiply; bring forth
> abundantly in the earth, and multiply therein.
>
> *(Genesis 9:1, 2, 7)*

There is no word of warning here about the dangers of over-
population or over-exploitation of the environment. The
unspoken assumptions are that the riches of the natural world
are inexhaustible, that the task of subduing the wilderness will
never fully be accomplished, and that there can never be too
many human beings.

It is true that there is an apparent contradiction between
God's declaration to Noah and his sons that 'the fear of you
and the dread of you shall be upon every beast of the earth',
and his ironical challenge to Job, 'Canst thou draw out
leviathan with an hook?' Genesis seems to assure us that we
are the rightful masters of the whole natural world, whereas
Job implies that some of God's creatures are completely
beyond our control. In fact, however, these two attitudes are
not as contradictory as they may seem. They both arise from
the idea that the natural world is a self-sufficient realm that
stands apart from Man and can never be completely used up or
tamed by him, even though he has been given power over it.

When God reminds Job that he is too puny either to understand or to grapple with leviathan, he is not contradicting his

earlier instruction than Man should seek to subdue the natural world. He is reminding Job that there is a difference between the power of dominion and the power of creation. Man is entitled to subdue and exploit the natural world to the best of his ability, but his ability is limited. There are vast tracts of wilderness where Man will never penetrate, and which must therefore be looked after by God:

> Who hath divided a watercourse for the overflowing
> of waters, or a way for the lightning of thunder;
> To cause it to rain on the earth, where no man is; on
> the wilderness, wherein there is no man;
> To satisfy the desolate and waste ground; and to
> cause the bud of the tender herb to spring forth?
>
> *(Job 38:25–27)*

The Bible describes a natural world which is ultimately inscrutable and inexhaustible; a world that can never be fundamentally affected by Man's efforts to tame it or plunder it; a world that showers him with gifts, but which also brings forth weeds and serpents to punish him for his sinfulness. Within this Biblical image there lurks the ghost of a more ancient conception of Nature as a fickle goddess, bountiful one moment and destructive the next, who exercises the power of life and death over Man rather than yielding to his dominion.

But both these versions of the natural world insist on its separateness as the keynote. Because it is separate from us it can never be changed or used up or spoilt by us. It soaks up our actions without returning them to us in the form of consequences (with the one exception of Original Sin, which I shall examine later). And it is this power to remain untouched by us which, paradoxically, allows us to assume that we are in some way superior to it or outside its laws. As long as our exploitation of Nature is without consequences, we are allowed to think that Nature has been created for our benefit, to give us something to exploit. But once the natural world begins to show signs of being fundamentally changed by our actions—worse still, once the wealth of food and materials that we have always regarded as inexhaustible begins to run out—it becomes evident that the natural world and the human world cannot be separated after all. They are interdependent: they are parts of a single all-embracing system. Nature is no longer capable of defying us, but equally we are now obliged to admit our own subservience to natural laws.

It follows from all this that our perceptions and descriptions of the landscape are bound to change as our awareness of the environmental crisis becomes more acute and obliges us to reassess our relationship with the natural world. Images of separation will be replaced by images of interdependence. In particular, the traditional assumption that life in the country is somehow separate and different from life in the town—that a rural lifestyle embodies a different set of values from an urban one—seems likely to be called into question. In a modern Western country such as Britain, where almost every part of the landscape has been thoroughly domesticated for hundreds of years, this distinction already seems artificial. It would be more accurate to describe what we call the 'countryside' as a series of extended suburbs and outdoor food-factories, decorated here and there with recreational parkland and artificially-preserved 'wild' habitats. By continuing to refer to this as the 'countryside' we are allowing ourselves to separate it mentally from the towns and cities in which most of us live. We are preserving the illusion that the 'countryside' shares some of the properties of an untouched wilderness and that therefore, by visiting it or even going to live in it, we will be able to 'get away from it all'.

What we seem to be in search of, when we pay our visits to the countryside in order to 'get away from it all', is a temporary escape from ourselves and the consequences of our actions, into a world where it always seems possible to make a fresh start. We are looking for an alternative to the man-made complications and problems of modern life. But we can only enjoy the natural world and the countryside in these terms once we have drawn a dividing line to separate them from ourselves—a line which seems to separate the natural or God-given things from those which are unnatural or man-made— and a dividing line of this sort is illusory.

For one thing, the modern British countryside is as much the work of Man as it is of Nature. If towns and cities are unnatural, then our countryside is unnatural too. By thinking of it as natural, by which we mean self-sufficient, we are misrepresenting to ourselves the kind of care with which it must be treated if it is to be preserved in a healthy state. Leaving it to itself is not the answer: it must be tended, like a garden. Many ancient heathlands, for example, have only come into existence as a result of deforestation and constant grazing. These habitats can certainly be destroyed by Man's interference, but they would also be destroyed by his complete withdrawal, which would cause reforestation. Secondly, even if the landscape in question were a more obvious example of 'untouched wilderness' than our own countryside—such as a desert, a piece of Arctic tundra, or a stretch of equatorial rainforest—we would still be wrong to think of it as self-sufficient and separate. There is now no corner of the globe secluded enough to have escaped entirely the impact of Man's presence, either in the form of global warming or of ozone depletion—developments which are now changing the patterns of the weather, the currents of the oceans, the structure of our atmosphere and the levels of radiation which reach us from the sun.

As long ago as 1972, Barbara Ward and René Dubos were emphasizing in their book *Only One Earth* how deeply Man's influence could penetrate the living structures of the planet, without any conscious intention on his part that it should do so:

> There is still some uncertainty concerning the mode of transportation of DDT, but it is a striking mani- festation of the interrelatedness of things on a

global scale that this insecticide, used in temperate
and tropical countries, has turned up in the fatty
tissue of penguins.[1]

Their book is subtitled 'The Care and Maintenance of a Small
Planet', and the implication of this subtitle is plain: we must
not think of Nature as something that can be left to look after
itself. The world is smaller than we imagine, and it must be
cared for and maintained if it is to be kept in good condition.

The environmental crisis cannot be usefully considered as a
failure on Man's part to leave the natural world alone. Human
beings cannot survive if they separate themselves from
Nature, let alone enjoy the comparatively comfortable,
disease-free lives that Western societies have come to expect as
a right. The environmental crisis arises from our failure to
achieve a balanced relationship with the natural world, and if
this crisis is to be negotiated then we must learn to see Nature
as something with which we are constantly involved. In order
to do so, however, we will be obliged to change some deep-
lying cultural assumptions, and since these assumptions are
generally held at an unconscious rather than a rational level,
the task of changing them may not be an easy one.

The kind of mental upset which can be caused when our
ideas about the natural world are threatened is exemplified by
Bill McKibben's recent book *The End of Nature* (1990).
Ostensibly it deals with Man's impact on the earth's atmosphere and weather patterns; but in fact McKibben is less
concerned with the practical consequences of the 'greenhouse
effect' than he is with the change that it has brought about in
our relationship with the natural world. Throughout the book
he insists that by changing the weather we have effectively
abolished the barrier which once separated us from the natural
world; and in this way, he claims, we have put an end to
Nature itself:

> By changing the weather, we make every spot on
> earth man-made and artificial. We have deprived

nature of its independence, and that is fatal to its
meaning. Nature's independence *is* its meaning;
without it there is nothing but us.[2]

Of course, McKibben is jumping from the idea that the
human race is increasingly responsible for the health and
maintenance of the biosphere, to the idea that Nature can no
longer be thought of as independent at all. Granted that
Man may now have to 'doctor' the atmosphere in order to
keep the weather within tolerable limits; granted that genetic
engineering (as McKibben argues) may to a certain extent
replace wild species, or their selectively-bred descendants,
with new creatures and plants designed by Man; and granted
that we will have exterminated a large range of the flora and
fauna that once graced the earth before the environmental
crisis has been negotiated; yet it still does not follow that the
independence of Nature will have been brought to an end. The
world is already full of examples of wild things leading their
independent lives in man-made contexts. Wild flowers grow
on roadside verges, just as they once grew in meadows and on
heathlands cleared and maintained by Man. Foxes and pigeons
live and breed very successfully in cities. Certain types of ant
can infest air-conditioning systems; and the rat population of
Britain, largely resident in man-made sewers and drains, now
exceeds the human population. The task of exterminating all
wild species from the face of the earth, and replacing them
where necessary with genetically-engineered substitutes,
would be beyond human patience, even if it lay within human
power.

   McKibben's argument on this level is less interesting than
his underlying theme, that Nature must be separate from us in
order to be of value. It may help to remember that he is an
American, and that he lives (as he keeps reminding us) in the
Adirondacks, a comparatively uninhabited and unfarmed area
of the USA. In other words, he is used to real wilderness. The
British idea that you can 'get away from it all' by going out

into the countryside and looking at the fields, or even by digging in your own garden, will not do for him: the least sign of human control, or even of previous human visitation, is enough to spoil things for him. What he demands is a self-sufficient natural world which will afford him a complete release from any sense of human interference. If this cannot be found any more, he insists, then Nature is really at an end.

But why is Nature, in this sense, so valuable to him? Evidently what he wants from Nature is a chance to escape into another world which is completely free of man-made things. But why should a human being be so anxious to refresh himself by turning away from all traces of human activity? And what sort of refreshment does he hope to gain by doing so? Why should he find the experience invigorating, rather than terrifying? What is it that we sometimes find oppressive about the world we have created for ourselves?

If we were to reverse McKibben's insistence that Nature must be separate from Man in order to be natural at all, another question we might ask is this: Why do we find it so difficult to recognize ourselves as belonging to the natural world? Why do we insist on seeing the man-made world as something unnatural? After all, evolutionary theory is supposed to have put paid to the idea that Man is anything more than just another animal. So why should we think man-made towns and cities any more unnatural than termite-hills or coral reefs? The fact that McKibben, who is supposed to be arguing his case from a scientific point of view, seems full of praise whenever he describes the work of Nature, whereas he is overcome by a sense of moral repugnance whenever he turns to the works of Man, seems to indicate the almost-buried presence of an unscientific structure of ideas.

And it gradually becomes apparent that he is unable to think of Man as an integral part of Nature, because to him Man is what pollutes the natural world. He speaks of Bob Marshall, founder of the Wilderness Society, in the following terms:

> Marshall was very nearly the last to see surroundings
> unpolluted even by the knowledge that someone
> had been there before.[3]

Man does not merely cause pollution: he *is* the pollution. The only perfect landscape is a landscape unvisited by human beings, and the most blessed human being is the first one to set foot in a tract of untouched wilderness. Hand-in-hand with this attitude goes the idea that the natural world is *better* than the human world: more beautiful, more spiritually-uplifting, better designed, and more virtuous:

> Most of the glimpses of immortality, design and
> benevolence that I see come from the natural
> world—from the seasons, from the beauty, from the
> intermeshed fabric of decay and life, and so on.[4]

There follows from this a sense that Man has somehow fallen away from the perfection of Nature, and that individuals such as McKibben yearn for occasional contact with uncontaminated wilderness, because it will afford them glimpses of how things ought to be. If the natural world passes entirely under human control, then it will be as degraded as we are. It will become the province of Man, rather than of God. The underlying myth here, of course, is the myth of Man's expulsion from Eden:

> Our actions will determine the level of the sea, and
> change the course and destination of every drop of
> precipitation. This is, I suppose, the victory we have
> been pointing to at least since the expulsion from
> Eden...[5]

The natural world is better than the human world because, unlike us, it has not rebelled against the will of God. This is the unexamined myth which underlies all of McKibben's arguments; and the considerable confusion of ideas in his book arises from the fact that he is constantly passing from the

realm of scientific discourse to the realm of mythology
without seeming to realize that he is doing so.

From my limited experience of the field, it would seem that
this confusion of scientific and mythological ideas is not
untypical of environmentalist writing. It is true that many of
the most convincing arguments for 'green' policies are practical ones, which make a direct appeal to our sense of self-
interest: global warming could cause terrible droughts, storms
and floods which would wreck our houses and spoil our crops;
ozone depletion could give us all skin cancer and cataracts;
traffic emissions seem greatly to aggravate the symptoms of
asthma, which is an extremely expensive, unpleasant and
sometimes fatal illness; and so on. But arguments of this kind
are only a part of the environmentalists' armoury. They also
seek to convince us that the natural world is worth preserving
for its own sake, and that human life could be a much more
rewarding experience if we would only learn to adopt a more
receptive, less rapacious attitude towards our planet.

This line of thought, however, opens a path into some
rather difficult philosophical territory. Any discussion of
Man's relationship with Nature tends to lead on automatically
to assertions about spiritual values, which in turn must be
justified and backed up by appeals to the generality of human
experience; and those appeals themselves, being rather numi-
nous by definition, can easily become garbed in pseudo-religious, quasi-philosophical and mythologizing language. Thus
Barbara Ward and René Dubos, for example, in their book
Only One Earth, feel compelled to flesh out their scientific
facts with a few remarks about ancient philosophy:

> The philosophers told us we were one, part of a
> greater unity which transcends our local drives
> and needs. They told us that all living things are
> held together in a most intricate web of interdepen-
> dence. They told us that aggression and violence,
> blindly breaking down the delicate relationships of

existence, could lead to destruction and death. These were, if you like, intuitions... What we now learn is that they are factual descriptions of the way in which our universe actually works.[6]

A few sentences later, they follow up with a stampede of mythological references:

It is in the Western tradition that we find the most urgent warnings against arrogant and unheeding power. For the Greeks it is Prometheus, stealer of fire, who is chained to the rock. Nemesis in the shape of shrieking, destroying harpies follows the footsteps of the overmighty. In the Bible, it is the proud who are put down from their seats; the exalted are those of humble spirit. At the very beginning of the scientific age, in the Faustian legend, it is the man of science who sells his soul to secure all knowledge and all power.[7]

Rupert Sheldrake's book *The Rebirth of Nature* is a more extreme example of the same tendency. To do him justice, he goes some way towards justifying his confusion of styles, since the gist of his argument is that science, by persuading us to look at the natural world in purely mechanistic terms, has spoilt our relationship with Nature:

From the time of our remotest ancestors until the seventeenth century, it was taken for granted that the world of nature was alive. But in the last three centuries growing numbers of people have come to think of nature as lifeless. This has been the central doctrine of orthodox science—the mechanistic theory of nature.[8]

Since he is setting out to chronicle the drawbacks of this coldly rational view, we can hardly expect him to do so in coldly rational language. Nevertheless, it is undeniable that at times he flies to the other extreme; and by the end of the book it becomes clear that his solution to the environmental crisis is nothing less than a form of religious conversion:

> The recognition that we need to change the way we live is now very common. It is like waking up from a dream. It brings with it a spirit of repentance, seeing in a new way, a change of heart. This conversion is intensified by the sense that the end of an age is at hand.[9]

James Lovelock, in his book *Gaia*, adopts a more cautious and reasonable tone, but the mythologizing tendency is if anything even more deep-rooted. It gives him his title, and it gives his book its appeal, which has proved to be considerable. His hypothesis, in a nutshell, is that the whole of life on earth can be viewed as a single living creature, which actively controls the biosphere (the mixture of gases in the atmosphere, the saltiness of the seas, the alkalinity of the soil, and so on) in order to perpetuate its own existence.

> The concept of Mother Earth or, as the Greeks called her long ago, Gaia, has been widely held throughout history and has been the basis of a belief which still coexists with the great religions. As a result of the accumulation of evidence about the natural environment and the growth of the science of ecology, there have recently been speculations that the biosphere may have been more than just the complete range of all living things within their natural habitat of soil, sea, and air. Ancient belief and modern knowledge have fused emotionally in the awe with which astronauts with their own eyes and we by indirect vision have seen the Earth revealed in all its shining beauty against the deep darkness of space. Yet this feeling, however strong, does not prove that Mother Earth lives. Like a

religious belief, it is scientifically untestable and
therefore incapable in its own context of further
rationalism.[10]

Lovelock hedges his bets. He touches the mythological well-
springs, and then he almost denies having done so. There is
also more in the way of scientific evidence and reasoned
hypothesis in his book than there is in the others I have
mentioned. In spite of all this, however, Lovelock's book is
really mythology dressed up as science, whereas the others
might at least claim to be science dressed up with mythology.

There is an argument to be made about the standards by
which we classify living things as self-contained individuals. It
would be possible to show that what we regard as separate
entities are often really colonies or groups of organisms, living
together in symbiotic or parasitic relationships; and that in the
same way, it makes sense to regard the life of our biosphere as
a single organism, instead of as a bewildering collection of
innumerable separate ones. But Lovelock never makes this
argument. He simply asserts that life on earth is a single
entity, christens it Gaia, and then sets out to show how it
controls the environment of our planet. Whether deliberately
or not, his book makes a powerful appeal to our desire to see
life as something more than the by-product of purely mechanical forces. The fact that *Gaia* has started a kind of cult, and
that its hypothesis is now regurgitated unquestioningly (in a
greatly simplified form, and without any of the bet-hedging
on which Lovelock himself insists) by other writers such as
McKibben and Sheldrake, seems to indicate that he has
touched a kind of nerve in the environmentally-aware reading
public.

The environmentalist debate, then, is by no means being
conducted in purely scientific terms. Here and there it
touches on what are known as 'eternal questions', and at these
points it is characterized by mythological references and religious or pseudo-religious language. If these departures from

strictly factual discourse seem confusing rather than enlight-
ening in their effect, they do nevertheless share some common
features which merit further investigation. Even from the few
quotations I have given, there emerges a pervasive sense that
'our forefathers' were wiser and more sensitive in their attitudes towards the natural world than we are today. They
recognized its divinity and beauty, they acknowledged that it
had a life of its own, and they treated it with proper respect.
What follows from this is the sense that at some stage there
has been a fall from grace, which has brought us to our current
state of estrangement from Nature.

As we have already seen, this notion that our forefathers
lived in harmony with the natural world, or at least treated it
with greater respect than we can manage today, is contradicted
by the evidence of the Bible, the first chapters of which seem
to have granted our ancestors licence to exploit the natural
world for their own purposes just as much as they liked. All
the same, the sense of a fall from grace, which emerges from
the writings of modern environmentalists, is based on a
Biblical model, namely the myth of Man's fall from Eden. This
myth frequently lies behind representations of Man's relationship with Nature, not only in modern environmentalist
writing, but in modern landscape poems too; and not only in
modern landscape poems, but in the landscape poetry of the
Romantic period, and in the literary traditions stretching back
for centuries before that. It is a myth which teaches us that
Man and Nature were once in harmony, because they were
once both content to live in accordance with the divine will.
But Man rebelled and fell from grace. Since the Fall, he has
been obliged to rely on his own flawed intelligence, instead of
on God's guidance and support, and he has always been at
odds with the natural world. The results are the ugly, man-
made muddles that we see all around us today. The Eden-myth
thus encourages us to believe that the natural world is closer
to God than we are; and that, as a consequence, it possesses a
moral purity and aesthetic beauty which we have lost. And

these same ideas are often still expressed, as we shall see, in environmentalist writings and in landscape poetry alike.

I am aware, of course, that the relationship between Man and Nature does not have to be seen or represented in Judaeo-Christian terms. There are other traditions and other bodies of belief available, which might well encourage quite different approaches to the natural world and the environmental crisis. Buddhism, Hinduism and the religions of various native American ('Indian' and 'Eskimo') tribes come immediately to mind as alternatives; not to mention more recent feminist critiques of both Christianity and Western science. I am not particularly well-qualified to discuss any of those, but in any case they would not be germane to my argument. The environmental crisis has to some extent been aggravated by the exploding populations of the 'undeveloped' countries, but on the whole it must still be regarded as a crisis manufactured in the West, arising from Western scientific ideas, Western financial and trading systems, Western industrialism, Western consumerism and Western assumptions about how life on this planet should be lived. The Judaeo-Christian tradition is central to the whole body of Western thought and culture, and however mistaken or limited it may be, it is inextricably intertwined with the emergence of the environmental crisis, with the development of the environmental movement, and with the way in which environmentalist themes have been interpreted by modern British literature.

II

The keynote of the Eden-state, it would seem, was an absolute acceptance of God's law. The desire to question, to seek alternatives and to make improvements was absent. The original sin was not pride, wrath, envy, lust, gluttony, avarice or sloth—which were later defined as the seven deadly ones—but *disobedience*: in other words, Man fell when he first chose to make his own decisions instead of simply doing as he was told. Eden can therefore be taken to represent Man's primitive origins, the period when he was still at one with the beasts, before he began to use his intellect to exploit and reshape the natural world to suit his own preferences. In this way, the myth is connected with ideas about noble savages, which became common currency in the eighteenth century and are still very much in circulation today; and it has helped to form a host of cultural assumptions about the spiritual superiority of old-fashioned or primitive ways of life, assumptions which probably underlie the environmentalists' claims that 'our fore-fathers' were more in sympathy with the natural world than we are. But besides dealing with the primitive origins of our species, the Eden-myth also represents the pre-rational stage in the life of each one of us. It reminds us of the period of early childhood, when we soaked up experiences without questioning or categorizing them. Like all powerful myths, this one is personal as well as universal.

At its feeblest, the Eden-myth is merely a form of nostalgia—a feeling that things were better when we were children, or even before we were born. Dissatisfaction with our own era, and pessimism about the future, can easily lead us into the mental laziness of supposing that former ages must have been more blessed than our own. When we apply these feelings to the landscape, we soon begin to feel that towns and cities represent the evils of modernity, whereas the 'country-side' represents a simpler, happier, more old-fashioned way of life. These ideas are certainly present in both the environmen-talist debate and modern landscape poetry, but they do not by any means exhaust the significance of the Eden-myth. Beyond the nostalgic prejudice in favour of old-fashioned things, there is also an undefined but powerful moral discrimination at work, in favour of lifestyles which accommodate themselves to the universe, instead of demanding that the universe be rebuilt to make room for them.

We are all aware of the shortcomings of man-made things.

They seem to create three new problems for every one that they solve, and in the end they are powerless to protect us from the things we fear most: old age, suffering, indignity and death. Every now and then we find ourselves thinking that the luxuries of modern life make things worse rather than better. We get tired of the nine-to-five existence, of our petty responsibilities, and of the constant struggle for money and possessions. We start to hanker after a simpler, more spiritually fulfilling way of life, and we assume that a life in the country would fit the bill. People who live in old-fashioned or primitive ways strike us as less materialistic, less self-obsessed, and more conscious of eternal things. If towns and cities, with their meaningless hustle and bustle, represent the folly of Man's self-obsession, then the countryside must represent a more humble state of existence: an implied acceptance of the laws of Nature, which equate with the laws of God.

To some extent, of course, these attitudes will change as times change. Today, we are sometimes inclined to associate Eden with complete wilderness, as we have seen from the writing of Bill McKibben. To us, the countryside may be only a second best, especially since the advent of pesticides and factory-farming. To the early Christians, on the other hand, wilderness itself could be seen as a form of man-made pollution. They believed that Eden was a garden, supremely domesticated and fashioned for Man's delight. The danger and hostility of untamed Nature had only arisen since the Fall, as a result of Original Sin. It was part of Man's punishment for his disobedience that he could only recreate the Eden-state of orderliness and harmony through an effort of unceasing labour. Wild Nature was therefore a reminder of sinfulness, and only areas that were farmed or gardened represented virtue. But this should not be taken, as it sometimes is, to mean that the appreciation of untamed Nature is a purely modern phenomenon. Certainly we have been able to find more beauty in the wilderness as its dangers have grown more distant; and certainly the modern taste for such phenomena as towering mountains and uncultivated woods can be traced back to the cults of enthusiasm for the Sublime and the Picturesque, which both indicated and helped to bring about a profound change in aesthetic values at the very beginning of the Romantic era.

But because Nature was always seen as guiltless of Original Sin, even though spoilt by it, the natural world was always in a sense closer to God than any man-made environment could be. And the most mysterious and grand aspects of the natural world—such as behemoth and leviathan, oceans, rainbows, the sun, the planets and the stars—were always interpreted as evidence of the majesty and harmony of God's creation. Thus the psalmist writes:

> When I consider thy heavens, the work of thy fingers, the moon and the stars, which thou hast ordained;
> What is man, that thou art mindful of him?
> *(Psalm 8:3–4)*

and again:

> The heavens declare the glory of God; and the firmament sheweth his handywork.
> *(Psalm 19:1)*

Aesthetic judgements can change as circumstances and societies change, and Eden has been a different kind of place at different times. But whether we see it as a garden or a wilderness, we always seem to see it as an alternative to city life. The urban environment is by definition the province of Man rather than God, since it is man-made rather than natural in origin. Towns and cities are not automatically corrupt and sinful places—in fact celestial cities are fairly common in religious iconography. But being man-made, they do tend to reflect the flaws of human nature—and certainly, if we grow tired of Man and his works, then we are always likely to turn our backs on city life and look towards non-urban environments as the first stage in our search for an alternative.

The Eden-myth and the Fall-myth are virtually one and the same thing, since it is only through our belief that we have undergone a fall that we are able to look back and retrospectively identify the unspoilt state which we think of as Eden. Our feelings about Eden are therefore very closely intertwined with our feelings about what caused the Fall; and if we are to understand how the Eden-myth affects our ideas about Man and Nature, we must first understand that in one of its aspects it deals with our uncertainty and guilt about the sinful power and independence of our own rational minds.

The opening of Genesis can be read as an account of how Man's discovery of rational thought brings about his banishment from the state of unconscious contentment which he previously shared with the rest of the natural world. It is also an account of how we each learn to think for ourselves, and thus become aware of ourselves as individuals. We are all born as innocent, unconscious infants, but we all grow up into rational, self-aware adults. In the process, we become conscious of our mortality and our separateness from the rest of creation. We are therefore inclined to attribute our mortality and our separateness to our rational self-awareness: before we grew up and became aware of ourselves as individuals, we seemed to be immortal. This idea is reinforced by the way that we become more absorbed in our own thoughts as we grow older. Our minds are more taken up with thinking and remembering; less open to new perceptions and experiences. Correspondingly, the days and years seem to be passing more and more quickly. Rational thought, which has detached us from the external world, now seems to be hurrying us towards death, too. But because the denizens of the natural world seem less self-aware than we are, we suspect that they may also be unaware of their own mortality, and we therefore attribute to them an unselfconscious serenity—a satisfaction with their fate—which Man has lost. In some ways, as we shall see, the natural world seems immune to the effects of Time: a fact which only increases our sense of separateness.

The Eden-myth thus conflates the history of the human race with the history of every human individual, in a manner which encourages us to think of children as unspoilt primitives, of primitives as unspoilt children, and of the whole natural world as supremely childlike. Sin comes in with rational thought, and anyone who has not yet learned to think for himself—whether he is a noble savage, a child, an animal or a tree—has not yet rebelled against God.

In Genesis, God sets the mark of sinfulness and guilt on rational thought by forbidding Adam to eat from the Tree of Knowledge:

> And the Lord God commanded the man, saying, Of every tree of the garden thou mayest freely eat:
> But of the tree of the knowledge of good and evil, thou shalt not eat of it: for in the day that thou eatest thereof thou shalt surely die.
>
> *(Genesis 2:16–17)*

Knowledge and mortality are thus associated with one another. Man can only remain immortal by resisting his urge to find out about things. But the serpent persuades Eve:

> And the serpent said unto the woman, Ye shall not surely die:
> For God doth know that in the day ye eat thereof, then your eyes shall be opened, and ye shall be as gods, knowing good and evil.
>
> *(Genesis 3:4–5)*

Although they seem to contradict one another, both the serpent and God are telling the truth. The knowledge of good and evil and the gift of conceptualization are the same, and when Man begins to conceptualize he becomes like the gods, in that he is more self-aware than the animals and more capable of controlling his environment and his destiny. But at the same time he becomes conscious both of his separateness from the natural world, and of his mortality. He awakes from semi-consciousness, loses his innocence and begins to die, all in the same moment.

Adam and Eve, having eaten the fruit, immediately become aware of their nudity and clothe themselves in fig-leaves. Conceptualization, in other words, leads directly to sexual self-awareness and the formation of sexual taboos. This is no false association of ideas: sexual conduct is one area where Man's separation from Nature is plainly apparent. Adam and Eve's fig-leaves symbolize the way in which conceptualization encourages us to reinterpret our experiences according to what we understand to be true, rather than what our senses tell us at any given moment. Thus we understand the genitals to represent lust even when they are not tumescent, and we hide them to prevent them from displaying our feelings indecorously. The penis attracts the strongest taboo of all since its tumescence is the most obvious. Once the genitals are hidden we are no longer at the mercy of our sexual feelings: we can pretend not to feel lust when we do, or to feel it when we do not. Our sexuality is thus removed from the realm of pure feeling and transferred into the realm of social behaviour, governed at least partially by the operation of the rational mind. Humans conceal their genitals in order to demonstrate an ability to control their power; we have become less interested in what they are than in what they mean; and in this way we separate ourselves from the beasts, who are only conscious of the sexual functions of their genitals when they are ready to copulate, and who make no attempts to conceal or overmaster their sexual instincts. So Adam and Eve's fig-leaves represent the self-awareness of the Fall, and the way in which this self-awareness separates them from the natural world. 'Who told thee that thou wast naked?' demands God when he finds them dressed (Genesis 3:11). Their expulsion from Eden follows as a matter of course.

In the outside world, a world where Man has been separated

from Nature, Adam and Eve are no longer able to take the fruits of the earth for granted. Instead, they are obliged to struggle to stay alive:

> cursed is the ground for thy sake; in sorrow shalt thou eat of it all the days of thy life;
> Thorns also and thistles shall it bring forth to thee; and thou shalt eat the herb of the field;
> In the sweat of thy face shalt thou eat bread, till thou return unto the ground; for out of it wast thou taken; for dust thou art, and unto dust shalt thou return.
>
> *(Genesis 3:17–19)*

The bitterness of Man's postlapsarian existence lies in the fact that his attempt to rise above the mindlessness of Nature has merely increased his awareness of his own subservience to natural laws. Separateness has not brought freedom. Unlike the other animals, he now makes his own conscious decisions instead of slavishly obeying the promptings of his instincts and appetites; but this only seems to mean that his life has become a constant struggle to survive ('In the sweat of thy face shalt thou eat bread'), whereas the other animals are apparently fed and cared for by the very laws which they obey so mindlessly. And although Man has separated himself from Nature sufficiently to become aware of himself as a spiritual being rather than a merely physical one, the drawback of his self-awareness is that, unlike the other animals, he is now haunted by the prospect of his own death. The spiritual and self-aware part of him is tortured by the limitations of the mundane flesh in which it is housed: 'for dust thou art, and unto dust shalt thou return.'

Man's separation from Nature and from God is confirmed and reinforced by his increasing preference for urban ways of life rather than rural ones. Our modern prejudices about urban life are inextricably intertwined with ideas about the Industrial

Revolution and modern capitalism, but the association of
cities (and human inventions) with sinful arrogance actually
predates the Industrial Revolution by thousands of years. The
story of the Tower of Babel, again from Genesis, demonstrates
as much: it tells how the invention of bricks leads men to
build a city which is intended to reach up to heaven and thus
to challenge God:

> And they said one to another, Go to, let us make
> brick, and burn them thoroughly. And they had
> brick for stone, and slime had they for mortar.
> And they said, Go to, let us build us a city and a
> tower, whose top may reach unto heaven; and let us
> make us a name, lest we be scattered abroad upon
> the face of the whole earth.
> And the Lord came down to see the city and the
> tower, which the children of men builded.
> And the Lord said, Behold, the people is one, and
> they have all one language; and this they begin to
> do: and now nothing will be restrained from them,
> which they have imagined to do.
> Go to, let us go down, and there confound their
> language, that they may not understand one
> another's speech.
> So the Lord scattered them abroad from thence
> upon the face of all the earth: and they left off to
> build the city.
> Therefore is the name of it called Babel; because the
> Lord did there confound the language of all the
> earth...
>
> *(Genesis 11:3–9)*

It may seem odd that the Bible attributes the advent of separate languages to an incident that brought men together and
united them in a single task, rather than to the spreading-out
of the tribes and the evolution of different ways of life in
different places. But the Tower of Babel represents the sin of

conceptualization run wild, and the message of the story is that conceptualization separates men from one another just as it separates them from Nature.

The more we think and learn, the more we acquire specialist knowledge and individual opinions, and the less likely we become to agree with one another. If each man relies for his wisdom upon his own rational mind and his own fund of experiences, then no two men will ever see things the same way; and if we rely instead on communal experience, then the community at large will soon subdivide into smaller groups, each with its own common history or common bond of interest, and these smaller groups will separate out and tend to go their separate ways. Complete unity can only be maintained through unthinking quiescence: thought creates gaps between us. Once again the Biblical narrative is full of irony: men build the Tower of Babel in order to make a name and avoid being scattered, but their actions result in their dispersal 'upon the face of all the earth', and the possibility of all men being united by a single name is destroyed by the advent of separate languages. The only name that the men actually create stands for disunity: 'Therefore is the name of it called Babel; because the Lord did there confound the language of all the earth...'.

Not all cities in the Bible are sinful, but those that are not are generally idealized spiritual centres, rather than everyday places where people can live and die, work and play, or buy and sell. Jerusalem in her more sublime moments, especially as the rebuilt Holy City in the Book of Revelation, is an example. On the other hand, there are plenty of more recognizably mundane cities that are denounced as dens of sin and blasphemy: Babel, Sodom and Gomorrah, Babylon, Nineveh and (at times) even Jerusalem herself. The tradition that the Bible establishes, one which has persisted down to the present day, is that although cities are potentially places of great virtue, in practice they generally turn out to be characterized by sinful arrogance. One of the functions of an urban environment, after all, is to shield us from the natural world: and therefore, although it may also serve to bring together and promote the finest human achievements in scholarship and the arts—and even though it may be a religious centre, or even a place of pilgrimage—a city must always enshrine the sin of conceptualization and confirm our separation from Nature. It represents an extreme of the fallen state.

III

If the urban environment represents sinfulness, then the non-urban world—whether this means wilderness or domesticated countryside—will come to represent virtue, and into it will be projected all the values that we deem to be absent from urban life. Descriptions of non-urban life must therefore be considered not only as depictions of rural or wild environments, but as oblique commentaries on the shortcomings of life in the towns and cities. The Biblical prophet who goes to live in the wilderness does so as much because he is rejecting the hypocrisies and compromises of city life as because he is choosing an inherently virtuous existence:

> John did baptize in the wilderness, and preach the baptism of repentance for the remission of sins.
> And there went out to him all the land of Judaea, and they of Jerusalem, and were all baptized of him in the river of Jordan, confessing their sins.
> And John was clothed with camel's hair, and with a girdle of a skin about his loins; and he did eat locusts and wild honey.
>
> *(Mark 1:4–6)*

But this tradition is not simply a Biblical one: it also comes into our literature via the Latin poets:

Happie is he, that from all Businesse cleere,
As the old race of Mankind were,
With his own Oxen tills his Sires left lands,
And is not in the Usurers bands
                    (*Horace*, Epodes II, *trans. Ben Jonson*)

Or again:

Climb at Court for me that will
Tottering favors Pinnacle;
All I seek is to lye still.
Settled in some secret Nest
In calm Leisure let me rest;
And far off the public Stage
Pass away my silent Age.
Thus when without noise, unknown,
I have liv'd out all my span,
I shall die, without a groan,
An old honest Country man.
                    (*Seneca*, Chorus from Thyestes Act III,
                    trans. Andrew Marvell)

In the Latin poems translated above, we are more concerned
with a quiet life on a country estate than with the self-imposed
exile of a prophet in the wilderness; but in the Latin and
Christian extracts alike, we are being asked to admire isolated
individuals who are prepared to turn their backs on the
corruption of the city in order to seek out a better way of life.

Having said this, the differences between the two traditions
are worth examining. John lives in the wilderness in imitation
of Moses, and the people go out to him in recollection of the
forty years that the tribes of Israel spent in the wilderness
under Moses' leadership, after the escape from Egypt. In
those days they were looked after by God: they ate the manna
which he sent for them in the mornings, and they drank the
water which Moses conjured for them by striking a rock.
From Moses onwards, the Bible is full of leaders and prophets
who summon the people away from the corruption of the

cities and into the wilderness, where they will be looked after
directly by God. The people who flock to John are therefore
seeking a return to a more inspired way of life, a more direct
relationship with God. Later, of course, when Jesus feeds the
five thousand in another echo of Moses, their hopes are
fulfilled. But for the Latin poets, life in the country represents, not a setting-aside of practical considerations for the
sake of divine guidance and protection, but a return to the
stoical patrician virtues on which a healthy society should be
founded; virtues which are all too often corrupted or
forgotten in the self-seeking environment of the city. For the
Latin poets, in other words, life in the country is not a radical
alternative to life in the city: it is a purified version of it.

I am not suggesting that Hebrew culture favours divine
inspiration, whereas Latin culture favours stoicism and self-
reliance: such a conclusion would be too sweeping, and doubtless both ethics are available within both traditions. What I am
trying to do is distinguish between possible alternatives to the
life of the city, once that life has been identified as corrupt. In
the fallen world, there are two virtuous alternatives to the sins
of human arrogance. One is to use rational thought as carefully as possible, with a constant sense of its dangers and limitations; and this alternative equates with the sober country life
recommended by Horace and Seneca in the extracts above.
The other is to abandon practical considerations entirely and
live the life of faith, hoping to recapture something of the
Eden-state; and this course of action equates with the self-
exile of the prophet in the wilderness. Both of these alternatives, in other words, start from an acknowledgement that our
fallen state has its drawbacks and our separation from Nature
(or God) is a regrettable state of affairs; but the first alternative involves an acceptance of things as they stand, whereas
the second involves an attempt to put matters right.

Those in the first camp, whom I shall call rationalists,
believe that although Man can never reunite himself with the
natural world, he must never turn his back on it either.

Likewise, they view rational thought as a necessary evil without which Man would be unable to survive, since he has lost the instinctive behaviour patterns that preserve order in the natural world and prevent it from degenerating into a state of formless chaos. Humans must rely on their rational minds to tell them how to act or they will not be able to act at all: but they must also always remember the flaws and limitations of rationality, or their behaviour will soon become arrogant and self-destructive. The best way to steer a course between these two extremes is to stay close to the natural world. Nature reminds Man of his smallness, his mortality, and the feebleness of his conceptualizing way of thought. City-dwellers choose to ignore the natural world as completely as possible rather than acknowledge these uncomfortable truths, but the rationalists insist that we must confront Nature and allow ourselves to be chastened by her into a state of proper self-awareness. This is one of the lessons of the Book of Job. At the beginning of the story Job behaves righteously because he believes that his righteousness will be rewarded with happiness and material wealth; but at the end, after God has destroyed his wealth and his children and reminded him of the hugeness and mystery of the natural world, he behaves righteously out of a proper sense of awe and duty.

Another example of rationalism is the account of the Eden-myth that Milton gives in *Paradise Lost*. Milton portrays the natural world as a hierarchy with Man at the top. The earth was created for Man's benefit, and can only retain its Edenic tranquillity and beauty while Man retains his virtue. Adam and Eve are not merely the rulers of the natural world: they are the keystones that hold the entire structure together. So when they fall they do not fall alone: the whole natural world is spoilt too. Milton's universe is constructed on a Ptolemaic basis, with the earth in the middle. It is also constructed on a basis of perfect symmetry, so that the day and the night are of equal length, the sun and moon are never in the sky at the same time, the earth does not tilt on its axis, and there are no

seasons. All this symmetry is spoilt as a result of the Fall, as
we hear at the end of Book X:

> the creator calling forth by name
> His mighty angels gave them several charge,
> As sorted best with present things. The sun
> Had first his precept so to move, so shine,
> As might affect the earth with cold and heat
> Scarce tolerable, and from the north to call
> Decrepit winter, from the south to bring
> Solstitial summer's heat.
>
> *(Milton,* Paradise Lost, *Bk. X, ll. 649–56)*

Later, Milton describes the effects of these disruptions on the
earth:

> These changes in the heavens, though slow,
>   produced
> Like change on sea and land, sideral blast,
> Vapour, and mist, and exhalation hot,
> Corrupt and pestilent.
>
> *(Bk. X, ll. 692–95)*

The implication is that sickness and disease, which did not
exist before the Fall, arise from these new 'corrupt and pesti-
lent' exhalations and vapours, which result from the 'changes
in heaven', which in turn are part of the punishment for
Original Sin. Later again, Milton describes how the same
disruption spreads to the beasts:

> Beast now with beast gan war, and fowl with fowl,
> And fish with fish; to graze the herb all leaving,
> Devoured each other; nor stood much in awe
> Of man, but fled him, or with countenance grim
> Glared on him passing.
>
> *(Bk. X, ll. 710–14)*

The words 'to graze the herb all leaving' refer to the idea that
meat-eating was unknown prior to the Fall: Adam and Eve's

sin has thus set the natural world at odds with itself, as well as creating antagonism between the natural world and the human race. This new strife between Man and Nature is exemplified by the actions of the beasts in the lines above, either fleeing from Man or glaring at him grimly.

In Milton's scheme of things, therefore, there is never any prospect of an individual casting off the burden of sin, reversing the Fall, and reuniting himself with the natural world in a new Eden. The natural world has been irredeemably spoilt, and the separation between Man and Nature is permanent. These things can only be rectified by God himself; in the meantime the best that any human individual can do is reconcile himself as thoroughly as possible to the fallen world in which he has been placed.

But the alternative school of thought—which I shall call primitivism—teaches that such an acceptance of the fallen state is in itself sinful: instead of accepting the sin of conceptualization as an integral part of postlapsarian human nature, we should be seeking to reject that sin, to re-enter the bosom of the natural world, and thus to recapture the Edenic state. The primitivists argue that rational thought is at the root of all our problems, and that we should abandon both it and the forms of social organization it engenders, in order to reproduce as closely as possible the simplicity and purity of our previous existence in Eden.

The archetypal statement of these beliefs is given in the Sermon on the Mount, where Jesus recommends that we should abandon rational thought in favour of faith, in order to recapture the direct relationship with God still enjoyed by the denizens of the natural world:

> Ye cannot serve God and mammon.
> Therefore I say unto you, Take no thought for your life, what ye shall eat, or what ye shall drink; nor yet for your body, what ye shall put on. Is not the life more than meat, and the body than raiment?

> Behold the fowls of the air: for they sow not,
> neither do they reap, nor gather into barns; yet your
> heavenly Father feedeth them. Are ye not much
> better than they?
> Which of you by taking thought can add one cubit
> unto his stature?
> And why take ye thought for raiment? Consider the
> lilies of the field, how they grow; they toil not,
> neither do they spin:
> And yet I say unto you, That even Solomon in all his
> glory was not arrayed like one of these.
>
> *(Matthew 6:24–29)*

One implication of these lines is that the fowls of the air and
the lilies of the field are still in Eden: God feeds them and
clothes them without any effort on their part being necessary.
Only Man, who insists on 'taking thought' and who puts his
faith in Mammon rather than in God, is obliged to labour to
keep himself alive. It is Man's rational determination to take
care of himself, to plan for the future rather than living for the
moment, which separates him from Nature.

This kind of primitivism is plainly at odds with the views of
a rationalist such as Milton. Milton believes that the natural
world was as much spoilt by the Fall as was Man himself, and
that Man and Nature can never be reunited by any effort on
Man's part. But in St Matthew's Gospel, Jesus, on the
contrary, insists that Man could reunite himself with the
natural world, and thus with God, at any moment, if only he
would abandon his rational obsession with taking care of
himself.

But there are other English poets who are more in
sympathy than Milton with the primitivism of the Sermon on
the Mount. One example is William Wordsworth. In Wordsworth's account of the Fall, Man is not literally banished from
the Garden of Eden; nor is the natural world physically spoilt
as a consequence of Original Sin. Instead, Man loses his

visionary powers, and thus loses the sense of union with God that still inspires the rest of creation. This version of the myth is voiced by the Wanderer in Book IV of *The Excursion*:

> Upon the breast of new-created earth
> Man walked; and when and wheresoe'er he moved,
> Alone or mated, solitude was not.
> He heard, borne on the wind, the articulate voice
> Of God; and Angels to his sight appeared
> Crowning the glorious hills of paradise;
> Or through the groves gliding like morning mist
> Enkindled by the sun...
> From those pure heights...
> Fell Human-kind—to banishment condemned
> That flowing years repealed not...
> (*Wordsworth,* The Excursion, *Bk. IV, ll. 631–48*)

Wordsworth conceives of the unfallen state in terms of Man's undamaged ability to find God through Nature: 'He heard, borne on the wind, the articulate voice/Of God'. In other words, unfallen Man lived permanently in that state of visionary communion with God through Nature which Wordsworth's most sublime poetry strives to recapture. When Man fell, he exiled himself from this state of communion; but the natural world is still just as much interfused with God's presence today as it ever was.

Wordsworth's poetry itself is a testament to his belief that individuals can release themselves from the fallen state—at least partially and temporarily—and recapture the visionary powers that were theirs in Paradise. But in order to do so they must subordinate rationality to a more impulsive and receptive mode of thought and feeling:

> One impulse from a vernal wood
> May teach you more of man,
> Of moral evil and of good,
> Than all the sages can.

Sweet is the lore which Nature brings;
Our meddling intellect
Mis-shapes the beauteous forms of things:–
We murder to dissect.

Enough of Science and of Art;
Close up those barren leaves;
Come forth, and bring with you a heart
That watches and receives.
          (Wordsworth, 'The Tables Turned', ll. 21–32)

These stanzas are from one of the poems in the *Lyrical Ballads*. Wordsworth is not merely reminding us of the limitations of human rationality here, but suggesting that there is a better alternative—an impulsive communion with Nature which teaches truer wisdom than any form of scientific investigation or book-learning. He also indicates how the two modes of perception differ from one another: one is associated with the heart, the other with the intellect; one is impulsive, watchful and receptive while the other is 'meddling'; and one 'murders to dissect' while the other accepts the 'beauteous forms of things' as it finds them. Furthermore the rational way of life is associated with hard work, forward planning and self-advancement, while the primitivist is content to take life as it comes and accept whatever gifts the natural world may present him with.

The previous poem from the *Lyrical Ballads* makes this clear. In the poem, a friend of Wordsworth's takes him to task for spending half the day sitting dreamily on an old grey stone:

'Why, William, on that old grey stone,
Thus for the length of half a day,
Why, William, sit you thus alone,
And dream your time away?'

But William replies:

'Think you, 'mid all this mighty sum
Of things for ever speaking,
That nothing of itself will come,
But we must still be seeking?'
                    *(Wordsworth, 'Expostulation and
                    Reply', ll. 1–4, 25–28)*

The resemblance between this and Christ's instruction to
'Take no thought for your life, what ye shall eat, or what ye
shall drink' is plain.

The essential difference between rationalists and primitivists, then, is that primitivists believe it is possible for us to
reverse the fallen state and reunite ourselves with the natural
world, even if we can only do so partially and temporarily;
whereas rationalists believe that the conceptualizing habit is
now too much a part of us ever to be discarded. But this single
difference has several implications. So far as poetry is
concerned, the different philosophies of the two groups are
reflected in two distinct styles of writing. Since primitivists
put their faith in impulse, instinct and intuition rather than in
rational self-control or long and rigorously-sustained trains of
logical thought, their work naturally tends to be less formal,
less syntactically strict, more spontaneous and more unself-
consciously subjective than that of the rationalists.

In our own century, when a wider range of poetic styles has
become available to the writer and acceptable to his public,
primitivists have been drawn towards 'free' verse-forms
whereas rationalists have tended to experiment with different
formal disciplines. Rationalist descriptions also tend to
combine clinically accurate observation of external data with
fastidiously structured rational discussion of the same. The
poet stands back from his subject, observing it and thinking
about it carefully, but always aware of his own separation from
it—of the shortcomings and limitations of his own subjective
viewpoint. Primitivists, on the other hand, seek to merge
themselves with whatever they describe. Their descriptions

are typically more effusive, more excited, full of assertions that are not rationally argued-out, of spontaneous reactions to the subject, and of imaginative sympathy with that subject's 'inner life'. Rather than emphasizing their separateness from the things they describe, they seek to conjure up a state of communion or visionary inspiration: to convince us that they are able to see inner truths which are hidden from more quotidian minds. Furthermore the primitivist, relying as he does on his own imagination and his own instincts, puts his faith in his own personal vision at the expense of everybody else's. The rationalist is more likely to write his poems as conscious continuations of the traditions of English Literature.

A comparison between D. H. Lawrence and Donald Davie will illustrate some of these points. Lawrence is the quintessential primitivist, who feels that Man's fallen state ought to be corrected rather than endured. Like Wordsworth, he believes that the natural world is still suffused with the spirit of God, and that only Man has separated himself into self-awareness and isolation:

> Only man can fall from God
> Only man.
>
> No animal, no beast nor creeping thing
> no cobra nor hyaena nor scorpion nor hideous
>   white ant
> can slip entirely through the fingers of the hands
>   of god
> into the abyss of self-knowledge,
> knowledge of the self-apart-from-god.
>   *(Lawrence, 'Only Man')*[11]

He associates this state of separation and self-awareness with modern Man's excessively cerebral attitude towards experience; but he believes that the error can be corrected. He preaches a kind of mental revolution, and looks forward to a time when the instincts and intuitions of Man will reassert themselves against the tyranny of the intellect:

> Climb down, O lordly mind!
> O eagle of the mind, alas, you are more like a
> buzzard.
>
> Come down now, from your pre-eminence,
>   O mind, O lofty spirit!
> Your hour has struck
> your unique day is over.
>   (*Lawrence*, '*Climb Down, O Lordly Mind*') [12]

It is therefore appropriate that he should favour a very free poetic style which mimics the abruptness and directness of impulsive utterances and flashes of insight. He wishes to give his readers the impression that his poems have been dashed off in the heat of the moment rather than coldly considered. As he writes in his Introduction to *Pansies*:

> Each little piece is a thought; not a bare idea or an opinion or a didactic statement, but a true thought, which comes as much from the heart and the genitals as from the head. [13]

The poet and critic Donald Davie, on the other hand, never seeks to conceal the fact that his poems are as much the products of his intellect as of his imagination. They embody carefully worked-out trains of thought rather than sudden exclamations or spontaneous insights. An extract from his poem 'Townend, 1976' will give a flavour of his poetic style:

> When does a town become a city? This
> That ends where I begin it, at Townend
> With Wright the Chemist (one of the few not
>   changed),
> Grows citified, though still my drab old friend.

Thanks therefore for the practical piety
Of E. G. Tasker, antiquarian;
His *Barnsley Streets*. Unshed, my tears hang heavy
Upon the high-gloss pages where I scan

What else, though, but remembered homely
    squalor?...

Of cities much is written. Even Scripture
Has much to say of them, though mostly under
The inauspicious name of 'Babylon'.
What a town is, one is left to wonder.

Is homely squalor, then, its sign and function?
Is it a swollen village? If it is,
Are swellings lanced? Have towns a size or shape
More than villages and less than cities?

I think of the Irish, or perhaps the Celtic
'Townland'. (Also, 'township' might provoke us.)[14]

The signs of Davie's rationalism are everywhere in these
stanzas. He begins with an abstract question—'When does a
town become a city?'—and instead of using this as a mere
rhetorical device to focus our attention on his subject, he
actually sets to work reasoning out an answer. This reasoning
process provides the poem with both its forward momentum
and its broad structure. Furthermore, rather than seeking to
take his question by storm and provide us with the answer in
a flash of personal insight, Davie attempts to back up his
arguments with references to other authorities. He begins
with a book of photographs by E. G. Tasker, and although
he provides the poem with its 'personal touch' by making it
plain that these photographs record a world that he once
inhabited himself ('remembered homely squalor'), he does
not dwell on this personal aspect of his subject-matter,
moving on instead to a learned declaration ('Of cities much is

written'), a reference to 'Scripture', and a consideration of the etymologies of 'townland' and 'township'. And whereas Lawrence's syntax is typically very straightforward, consisting largely of bald statements and exclamations, Davie's is much more convoluted, pausing in mid-flow for the sake of a piece of extra information—'Wright the Chemist (one of the few not changed'—or for a correction—'I think of the Irish, or perhaps the Celtic'. The end result is fastidious to the point of fussiness. Lawrence's language seems to aspire to a Biblical munificence ('No animal, nor beast nor creeping thing'), but Davie's poem sounds at one moment like a book-review ('Thanks therefore for the practical piety/Of E. G. Tasker') and at another like an academic essay ('Of cities much is written').

Yet if Davie's writing sometimes seems hidebound and uninspired, long on effort and short on inspiration, its virtue is that it never loses touch with the human scale of things. It never attempts to burst the bounds of normal human experience. In fact Davie ends his poem with a warning about the superhuman scale of modern towns:

> And now what will befall?
> Concourse and complex, underpass and precinct,
> The scale not human but angelical...
>
> The end of a town—however mean, however
> Much of a byword—marks the end of an age,
> An age of worn humility. Hereafter,
> The Prince of Darkness and his equipage![15]

'Humility' is the keyword. The hallmark of rationalist writing is stoicism about the fallen world as we find it. Davie does not feel inclined to sweep away ordinary life and replace it with a more inspired state of existence. For that reason, he might well be just as suspicious of visionary primitivists such as D. H. Lawrence as he is of unrestrained town planners.

IV

I am conscious that by now I may appear to have contradicted myself. I began this Introduction by arguing that the environmental crisis must eventually force us to recognize the interconnections between the human world and the natural world, as well as those which bind together the country and the city. But I have ended by examining in some detail a system of ideas which can only make sense once a dividing-line has been drawn between Man and Nature, so that the two can be seen as alternatives to one another. So far as the environmental debate is concerned, such a dividing-line can sometimes be unhelpful, since it ignores the existence of some extremely important cross-connections between the two realms, and thus tends to cloud our ideas about both. Yet the image of Eden and the myth of our fall from grace nevertheless deserve investigation. They are, after all, pervasive enough to have found their way into the works of the environmentalist writers themselves. For good or bad, they are already part of the environmentalist debate. They are also, as we have seen, a part of our literature. And since every powerful myth embodies a psychological truth of some kind, we should do our best to decipher this one's message, before we make any rash attempts to discredit or discard it.

NOTES

1. Ward and Dubos, *Only One Earth* (André Deutsch/Penguin, 1972), p. 81.
2. McKibben, *The End of Nature* (Penguin, 1990), p. 54.
3. *Ibid.*, p. 49.
4. *Ibid.*, p. 66.
5. *Ibid.*, p. 78.
6. Ward and Dubos, *Only One Earth*, p. 85.
7. *Ibid.*, p. 86.

8. Sheldrake, *The Rebirth of Nature* (Ebury, 1990), pp. xii–xiii.

9. *Ibid.*, p. 175.

10. Lovelock, *Gaia* (Oxford University Press, 1979), p. ix.

11. D. H. Lawrence, *The Complete Poems* (ed. V. de Sola Pinto and F. W. Roberts; Penguin, 1977), p. 701.

12. *Ibid.*, p. 473.

13. *Ibid.*, p. 417.

14. Davie, *Collected Poems 1970–1983* (Manchester: Carcanet, 1983), pp. 80–81.

15. *Ibid.*, pp. 82–83.

Chapter Two
Philip Larkin: 'Such absences!'

I

Janice Rossen, in her book *Philip Larkin: His Life's Work*, has noticed how often the speakers in Larkin's poems find themselves indoors on their own, aware of the natural world outside, but isolated from it just as they are isolated from other human beings.[1] The speaker in 'Friday Night in the Royal Station Hotel' is one example:

> Isolated, like a fort, it is—
> The headed paper, made for writing home
> (If home existed) letters of exile: *Now*
> *Night comes on. Waves fold behind villages.*[2]

Likewise, the speaker in 'Mr Bleaney' reacts to the drabness of his rented room by staring out of his window at the sky, and wondering if Mr Bleaney, the room's previous inhabitant, ever did the same:

> But if he stood and watched the frigid wind
> Tousling the clouds, lay on the fusty bed
> Telling himself that this was home, and grinned,
> And shivered...
>
>   ...I don't know.[3]

The same pattern recurs in 'High Windows',[4] where Larkin begins by commenting, both enviously and ironically, on the sexual emancipation of the young—'When I see a couple of kids/And guess he's fucking her/...I know this is paradise'—but ends by presenting us with his own idea of happiness.

This takes the form of a lofty isolation which brings him face to face with the simplicity and emptiness of the blue sky (simplicity and emptiness, as we shall see, are often associated with the natural world in Larkin's verse):

> Rather than words comes the thought of high
>   windows:
> The sun-comprehending glass,
> And beyond it, the deep blue air, that shows
> Nothing, and is nowhere, and is endless.

In the same way, the speaker in '*Vers de Société*', rather than accept an invitation to a party, would prefer to spend the evening on his own:

> Under a lamp, hearing the noise of wind,
> And looking out to see the moon thinned
> To an air-sharpened blade.[5]

This image of someone isolating himself from human companionship, and turning his attention instead towards Nature, appears over and over again in Larkin's poetry. It seems to arise from a feeling that the natural world possesses a simplicity and perfection which are missing from human life.

Yet although Larkin's protagonists yearn towards the purity of Nature, in his mature poetry they are never allowed to achieve a state of spiritual union with it. In 'Mr Bleaney', as we have seen, the speaker chooses isolation in order to watch 'the frigid wind/Tousling the clouds'; but the word 'frigid', which suggests the clean separateness of the natural world, also emphasizes its soulless inaccessibility to the human observer. If the 'frigid' skyscape stands for clarity and freedom, then it is a clarity and freedom which the observer cannot share; and the poem ends, accordingly, on an untranscendent note, with the speaker wondering whether he is really any different from his predecessor Mr Bleaney, who probably never bothered himself with the natural world at all. The image at the end of 'High Windows' seems more transcendent, but it retains a sense of separation between the natural and human worlds nevertheless: the 'sun-comprehending glass' separates the speaker from the sunshine and the deep blue air, at the same time as it makes them available to the person behind the glass. And in 'Vers de Société' the speaker, who initially reacts to an invitation to pass the evening with a 'crowd of craps' by claiming he would rather spend his time alone 'Under a lamp, hearing the noise of the wind', eventually changes his mind because 'Only the young can be alone freely', and he is at the age when 'sitting by a lamp more often brings/Not peace, but other things'. He decides to go to the party after all.

In Larkin's poetry, the beauty and simplicity of the natural world are compared with the shallowness and inadequacy of the human world to expose the tawdriness of the latter, and this gives rise to an impulse to break away from human society and move into an isolation from which Nature can be contemplated more freely. But this impulse is balanced by an awareness that individuals cannot shake off the limitations of their own humanity by an act of will, no matter how thoroughly they cut themselves off from the rest of mankind. Larkin's references to the natural world are therefore often characterized by an urge towards transcendence held in check by a feeling that such transcendence is an impossibility. It is this deliberately sustained conflict of feelings which gives his natural descriptions their characteristic note. His wry refusal to accept any escape route from the difficulties of human existence lends both toughness and poignancy to the more transcendent moments in his poetry, when such an escape route seems to be exactly what he is straining towards. We are left with the impression that he is refusing to allow himself to take an easy way out.

One reason why Larkin's early poetry lacks the air of ironic wisdom which characterizes his later work is that here the movement towards transcendence is not checked in the same way. The early poems also make it clear that for Larkin, hermit-like isolation and contemplation of the natural world

represent not only the contemplative life itself, but also the
poetic vocation and the poet's lonely devotion to his art.
Isolation, awareness of Nature and poetic creativity are all
closely associated with one another. In his later work, Larkin's
insistence on the impossibility of any transcendent union with
Nature is linked to an insistence that the poetic vocation will
not allow the individual to transcend his limitations either; but
in the early poems, the romantic figure who stays awake and
lonely while other people are asleep in bed with their lovers, is
both a poet who refuses to be distracted from his devotion to
the muse, and a lover of Nature who wants to be at one with
the cold clarity of the natural world for its own sake.

The feeling that such a cold clarity is desirable, and that the
way to achieve it is to abandon or rise above normal human
relationships, is exemplified by the poem 'Dawn', written in
1943–44 and first published in *The North Ship*:

> To wake, and hear a cock
> Out of the distance crying,
> To pull the curtains back
> And see the clouds flying—
> How strange it is
> For the heart to be loveless, and as cold as these.[6]

The heart is 'as cold as these' by virtue of the fact that it is
'loveless'. Having managed to stay free of any human
entanglements, the poet has been able to achieve a kind of
inhumanity, so that when he wakes in the morning he feels
more akin to the distant cock and the flying clouds than to
other people. But there is no real sense that anything has been
sacrificed in order to achieve this transcendent state; nor is
there any real sense of what the transcendent state feels like.
Life without love is simply 'strange' and 'cold'.

The word 'cold', which might seem to indicate despair or a
sense of loss, actually stands for the kind of deliberately willed
detachment from emotion which is suggested by W. B. Yeats's
epitaph:

Cast a cold eye
On life, on death.
Horseman, pass by!

Larkin admitted in his Introduction to the 1966 reprint of *The North Ship* that many of the poems in the book were composed when he was 'trying to write like Yeats',[7] and several of them certainly show signs of Yeatsian influence—the use of refrains, the rather antiquated diction, the mythological imagery, and the references to horses and horsemen. The chilly, unemotional transcendence which Larkin evokes in 'Dawn' is another Yeatsian characteristic.

The same attitudes are on display again in 'One Man Walking a Deserted Platform',[8] another poem from *The North Ship*:

Who can this ambition trace,
To be each dawn perpetually journeying?

What lips said
Starset and cockcrow call the dispossessed
On to the next desert, lest
Love sink a grave round the still-sleeping head?

The poet does not lie comfortably in bed as other people do, 'lest/Love sink a grave' round his head: he chooses to be 'dispossessed' instead, 'perpetually journeying' 'to the next desert', away from human entanglements. And his isolation brings him closer to the natural world: he responds to 'starset and cockcrow', whereas other people simply sleep through them. Again, however, these assertions of freedom and transcendence seem unconvincing, partly as a result of the pretentious language of the poem, and partly because of its apparent lack of feeling about the human normality from which the poet-figure claims to have separated himself.

Even this early in his career, however, Larkin sometimes pictures his isolated protagonist as lonely and frustrated

rather than heroic and transcendent. Here is the second half
of another poem from *The North Ship* called 'Ugly Sister':

> Since I was not bewitched in adolescence
> And brought to love,
> I will attend to the trees and their gracious silence,
> To winds that move.[9]

'Ugly Sister' works better than either 'Dawn' or 'One Man
Walking a Deserted Platform' because the girl's isolation and
closeness to Nature seem forced upon her as much as chosen.
Larkin is suggesting that she would rather have been loved
than obliged to seek comfort from Nature; and it is this sense
of rejection and disillusionment which gives the description of
'the trees and their gracious silence' its poignancy. The ugly
sister has been cut off from the joys of human society by her
looks, and the natural world therefore appeals to her as a kind
of refuge, a longed-for and 'gracious' alternative to the pain
and frustration of human life. But there is a price to be paid
for this alternative. She can only align herself with the
'gracious silence' of Nature once she has given up hope of
being 'bewitched' by human love.

In a 1982 interview with the *Paris Review*, Larkin, when
asked what he had learnt from various different poets, replied
that Yeats had taught him 'the formal distancing of emotion',
whereas from Hardy he had learnt 'not to be afraid of the
obvious. All those wonderful *dicta* about poetry: "the poet
should touch our hearts by showing his own"....'.[10] It seems
from these remarks that, to his mind, Yeats stood for
emotional detachment, whereas Hardy stood for emotional
honesty. As I have already mentioned, in the Introduction to
The North Ship Larkin blames some of the book's inadequacies on the fact that he was 'trying to write like Yeats', and he
attributes his cure to the counter-influence of Hardy. This
transfer of allegiance from Yeats to Hardy has been argued
over on a number of occasions (notably by Andrew Motion in
his book *Philip Larkin*), but it is worth mentioning again

because it illuminates the manner in which Larkin's attitudes towards Man and Nature change between *The North Ship* and his next collection, *The Less Deceived*. In both volumes the poet–protagonist characteristically stands apart from the rest of humanity, and this isolation makes him more aware than other people of the presence of the natural world; but in *The North Ship* his isolation is voluntary and painlessly achieved, and he seems coldly confident of his own ability to attain a transcendent union with Nature; whereas in the mature poems from *The Less Deceived* onwards, he seems much more aware of what he has lost, and much less certain of what he has gained. The Yeatsian emphasis on the triumph of the individual's will is replaced by a Hardyesque interest in the awkwardness and pathos of human affairs.

'Spring',[11] written in 1950, illustrates the more mature style of *The Less Deceived*. In this poem, Larkin describes himself passing through a springtime scene without belonging to it— contemplating the festival of rebirth from the outside, as it were—'Threading my pursed-up way across the park,/An indigestible sterility'. The terms 'pursed-up' and 'indigestible' cleverly (or perhaps unconsciously) hint at the underlying reasons for his detachment: the compulsion for self-hoarding, and the fear of losing himself by being digested. His description of the season is half-resentful in places—'Spring, of all seasons most gratuitious'—yet he finishes by claiming that his status as an outsider confers upon him a clearsightedness which is denied to anyone who allows himself to be sucked in:

> those she has least use for see her best,
> Their paths grown craven and circuitous,
> Their visions mountain-clear, their needs immodest.

The 'gratuitous' fertility of the natural world in this poem seems quite different from the 'gracious silence' by which it was characterized in 'Ugly Sister'. This difference of tone arises from the fact that 'Spring' is one of the few poems where Larkin fully acknowledges the sexual aspect of

Nature—and, because sexuality is a dominant force here, it follows that for once closeness to Nature seems to involve a surrender to the human entanglements of love and sex, rather than a move away from them and towards paradisal emptiness. It also follows that the paradox of sexual and emotional frustration, which underlies so much of Larkin's mature work, is particularly close to the surface here. He seems to be longing for involvement and yet rejecting it—running away from the very thing he wants the most—and compensating himself for his own cowardice by telling himself that it makes him more clearheaded than other people. But the poem works precisely because it traces this paradox with such accuracy, thus making plain the price which Larkin must pay for his privileged position as a detached onlooker. No longer does he seem merely dismissive or unfeeling about the human happiness he has chosen to make do without. The protagonist here is an anti-Romantic figure, 'pursed-up', 'indigestible', sterile, 'craven' and 'circuitous'. He is unable to share the excitement of spring either as a human being or as a part of the natural world—he can only contemplate it from the outside. He seems to be caught halfway between humanity and Nature, belonging properly to neither, and with only his sense of artistic perspective and accuracy to show for it.

In some respects Larkin never really outgrew or discarded the Yeatsian poses of his early poems. Instead, he refashioned the heroic, isolated, cold-hearted protagonist of *The North Ship* into the 'pursed-up', sterile figure of the later poems, by using the example of Hardy to bring a much-needed sense of particularity, irony and pathos into his work. The poet-figure of *The North Ship* seems shallow and self-congratulatory because he fails to describe with any particularity either the human world he has sacrificed or the lonely, cold-hearted world he has now attained. The pursed-up protagonist of the later poems is just as much an outsider, and his sense of himself as a poet arises from the same clear-eyed isolation as before: there is still a feeling that we can only be as clear-eyed as this if we are prepared to live outside the 'normal' world of human entanglements. But now the protagonist is less boastful of his powers of insight and more acutely aware of the everyday world from which he has excluded himself. At times he is reduced to wondering if his isolation is really heroic and not merely cowardly.

Larkin's two novels, *Jill* (1946) and *A Girl in Winter* (1947), can be interpreted as his fullest investigations of the theme of isolation: how the individual becomes isolated, what he gains in the process, and what he loses. Neither John Kemp (the hero of *Jill*) nor Katherine Lind (heroine of *A Girl in Winter*) deliberately chooses an isolated way of life, as does the poet–hero who appears throughout *The North Ship*. Instead they struggle to make themselves at home in the social milieux in which they find themselves. The status of outcast is forced upon them: John Kemp is a lower-class boy from a provincial town who finds himself stranded amongst snobbish students at Oxford, while Katherine Lind is a refugee from an unspecified European country who is similarly stranded in a large city in the Midlands, where everybody treats foreigners with suspicion. Both books are love-stories, but the object of John's affection rejects him, while the object of Katherine's destroys her illusions by sleeping with her without feeling anything for her.

In both cases, isolation brings disillusionment, but with this disillusionment comes a certain clarity of understanding—and in both books, this clarity is expressed through images of the natural world. John Kemp, lying alone, ill and rejected in the college sick-room, stares out through the window at some trees:

> He was watching the trees, the tops of which he could just see through the window. They tossed and tossed, recklessly. He saw them fling this way and that, throwing up their heads like impatient horses, like sea waves, bending and recovering in the wind.

> They had no leaves. Endlessly, this way and that,
> they were buffeted and still bore up again to their
> full height.[12]

Clearly these lines are intended to express something about
the inevitability of suffering and the resilience of life. They
also seem to develop the closing images from 'Ugly Sister'.
But they describe a quintessentially Larkinesque situation too:
an isolated protagonist, who feels himself to be cut off from
normal human society, stares out of a window and loses
himself in contemplation of the natural world.

The images at the end of *A Girl in Winter* are symbolic
rather than realistic, but the indoor–outdoor contrast is still
essential. Katherine Lind is lying in bed with her cold-hearted
lover. Their conversation lapses into silence, and they both
become aware of the snow outside:

> There was the snow, and her watch ticking. So many
> snowflakes, so many seconds. As time passed they
> seemed to mingle in their minds, heaping up into a
> vast shape that might be a burial mound, or the cliff
> of an iceberg whose summit is out of sight... Icefloes
> were moving down a lightless channel of water.
> They were going in orderly slow procession, moving
> from darkness further into darkness, allowing no
> suggestion that their order should be broken, or
> that one day, however many years distant, the dark-
> ness would begin to give place to light.
>
> Yet their passing was not saddening. Unsatisfied
> dreams rose and fell about them, crying out against
> their implacability, but in the end glad that such
> order, such destiny, existed.[13]

Despite its symbolic style, this passage (which seems to have
been partly inspired by the ending of James Joyce's famous
short story 'The Dead') still tells us something about Larkin's
attitudes towards the human and natural worlds. The indoor,

human world is associated with 'unsatisfied dreams', and with feeble protests against the immutable order of things; whereas the outdoor, natural world equates with 'implacability', 'order', 'destiny' and—unmistakably, despite the fact that this point is never made explicit—death. As we shall see, Larkin's depiction of the natural world continues to carry all of these associations in his later poetry.

The sense of grim comfort that emanates from the snowy weather at the end of *A Girl in Winter* does not always play such a prominent part in Larkin's later descriptions of the natural world, however. More often, Nature serves to chasten the protagonist. It puts his problems into perspective by giving him a disconcerting reminder of his own mortality. In 'Dockery and Son', for example (1963, first published in *The Whitsun Weddings*), the protagonist is contemplating the difference between his own solitary existence and the family life which his old college compatriot Dockery has chosen for himself; but he breaks off from this contemplation for long enough to give us the following description of his actions on a railway station in Sheffield:

> I changed,
> And ate an awful pie, and walked along
> The platform to its end to see the ranged
> Joining and parting lines reflect a strong
>
> Unhindered moon.[14]

The 'joining and parting' railway lines represent different possible paths through human life; whereas the moon represents the clean, transcendent reality of Nature, which exists beyond all human difficulty and muddle. The line-break between 'strong' and 'unhindered' serves to emphasize both words; and the gap between stanzas seems to allow a fractional pause, during which the protagonist's eye is travelling upwards from the gleaming tracks below to the moon above; yet when his gaze reaches its target, he finds himself rebuffed by the moon's serene otherness. He is attracted and rejected at one and the same time. The moon is 'unhindered' because human considerations do not apply to it; it is unhindered by us, its mortal admirers; it represents a state of existence which we yearn for but cannot achieve.

None of this is explicitly stated in 'Dockery and Son', but the description of the moon and the railway lines is the point on which the poem pivots. It leads on to the untranscendent final lines, in which the poet gloomily emphasizes the limitations of mortal existence:

> Life is first boredom, then fear.
> Whether or not we use it, it goes,
> And leaves what something hidden from us chose,
> And age, and then the only end of age.[15]

This is exactly the same pattern as in 'Mr Bleaney', where the protagonist's observation of 'the frigid wind/Tousling the clouds' leads on to his gloomy admission that he is probably no different from Mr Bleaney after all. Awareness of the natural world serves to chasten the individual, to remind him he is incapable of sharing Nature's clarity and strength, and thus to force him to admit his own human weaknesses.

The same sequence of ideas occurs again in 'Sad Steps' (1968, first published in *High Windows*), which I give here in full:

> Groping back to bed after a piss
> I part thick curtains, and am startled by
> The rapid clouds, the moon's cleanliness.
>
> Four o'clock: wedge-shadowed gardens lie
> Under a cavernous, a wind-picked sky.
> There's something laughable about this,
>
> The way the moon dashes through clouds that blow
> Loosely as cannon-smoke to stand apart
> (Stone-coloured light sharpening the roofs below)

High and preposterous and separate—
Lozenge of love! Medallion of art!
O wolves of memory! Immensements! No,

One shivers slightly, looking up there.
The hardness and the brightness and the plain
Far-reaching singleness of that wide stare

Is a reminder of the strength and pain
Of being young; that it can't come again,
But is for others undiminished somewhere.[16]

The moon reminds the speaker of 'being young' not only because its stare seems to combine the 'strength and pain' of youth, but because only the young feel self-confident enough to claim kinship with it, and to greet it with exclamations of the type caricatured in the fourth stanza: 'Lozenge of love! Medallion of art!/O wolves of memory! Immensements...'. Larkin is probably thinking of himself here, and of the early poems in which he wrote similar invocations to the moon and other aspects of the natural world. But he has now outgrown the assumption that a human individual can ever really share 'the hardness and the brightness and the plain/Far-reaching singleness' of the moon. He checks the excited exclamations of the fourth stanza with a flat 'No', and the stanza-gap which follows seems to stop the poem in its tracks, until it starts up again with a line emphasizing the smallness and weakness of the human observer: 'One shivers slightly, looking up there.'

All the way through the poem, the phrases which describe the moon stress its inhuman strength and clarity: 'the moon's cleanliness', 'stone-coloured light', 'High and preposterous and separate'. Contrastingly, the 'thick curtains' and 'wedge-shadowed gardens' suggest a rather lumpen earthly existence; and the first line, 'Groping back to bed after a piss', which may seem needlessly coarse, actually serves the same purpose. The moon 'stands apart' from all this. It *is* like youth in some respects: its strength, its singleness, and its freedom from entanglements. And like youth, it is also 'laughable' and 'preposterous'. But what makes the observer shiver is the fact that the moon is 'undiminished', whereas his own youth has been taken away from him and passed on to 'others... some-where'.

Another poem which gives a variation on the same theme is 'The Trees' (1967, first published in *High Windows*), in which Larkin describes trees putting on their new leaves in spring-time.[17] He observes that 'Their greenness is a kind of grief', and he asks himself:

> Is it that they are born again
> And we grow old? No, they die too.
> Their yearly trick of looking new
> Is written down in rings of grain.

The trees grieve us because they seem immune to the effects of time, yet in reality they are just as mortal as we are. What they are immune to is not time, but the terror which passing time inspires in human beings. Unlike us, they are strong enough to put the past behind them and make a new start every year, without regretting the way in which their life-spans are being used up. 'Last year is dead, they seem to say', as Larkin observes at the end of the poem: 'Begin afresh...' But these lines only serve to remind us that we are incapable of shrugging off the past and starting all over again in the same way. The trees exist in a timeless state not because they are immortal but because they are unconscious. Human beings cannot 'Begin afresh' as the trees do without discarding their own humanity. So although the trees seem to be setting us an example and saying something to us, their example is impos-sible for us to follow, and their message can only be heard, not obeyed. The end result of the poem, once again, is a sharpened awareness of our own limitations, as compared with the strength and simplicity of Nature.

This insistence on the otherness and separateness of the natural world is one feature of Larkin's poetry that identifies

him as a rationalist rather than a primitivist. As we shall see
when we come to examine the poetry of R. S. Thomas and Ted
Hughes, the primitivists believe that Man has cut himself off
from Nature by repressing the emotional and instinctive parts
of his character and putting his faith in rational thought
instead. They also believe that Man could reunite himself with
Nature by abandoning rationality and returning to a way of
life governed by the imagination. These ideas give rise to a
style of description in which the poet attempts to enter into
sympathy with whatever he is describing. He evokes its inner
life rather than its surface appearances, and his language seeks
to suggest that his imagination has allowed him to penetrate
the barrier which separates the human observer from the non-
human world. In Larkin's early poetry there is, as we have
seen, an attempt to achieve union with Nature, and in these
poems his language is correspondingly heightened. But from
The Less Deceived onwards he begins to suggest that the most
important thing about the natural world is its separateness,
and his descriptive style becomes more quotidian as a means
of enacting this belief. Like Hardy's, Larkin's mature poetry is
much concerned with mortal limitations, and the impossibility
of transcending them. But this is not to say that he denies the
strength of our desire to transcend.

II

The strength and peculiar character of Larkin's urge to find
release in the natural world are perhaps most clearly expressed
by a poem which does not deal directly with Nature at all—
namely 'Wants' (1950, first published in *The Less Deceived*).
The poem[18] is in two sections of five lines, the first of which
begins and ends with the line 'Beyond all this, the wish to be
alone', while the second begins and ends 'Beneath it all, desire
of oblivion runs'. Sandwiched between these gloomy declara-
tions come two short lists of 'normal' human activities—

'invitation-cards', 'the printed directions of sex', 'tabled fertility rites' and other activities of the kind from which Larkin's 'pursed-up' protagonists either deliberately stand aside or feel themselves to be excluded—all of which Larkin sombrely dismisses as no more than a 'costly aversion of the eyes from death'. Death, he seems to be suggesting, is what we spend our lives running away from; yet death (in the form of 'the wish to be alone' and 'desire of oblivion') is also what we secretly long for.

It is an oddly clumsy poem—in some ways hardly a poem at all—more of an abrupt and awkward declaration of feeling. There is little attempt either to explain this feeling or to evoke it in a manner which would encourage our sympathy. There are no rhymes, and the repetition of phrases at the beginning and end of each stanza seems selfconscious and unnatural, a stylistic trait left over from the Yeatsian era. The air of mingled clumsiness and theatricality might indicate that Larkin is simply posing, voicing a death-wish which he does not really feel, because it fits with the aloof and world-weary stance he likes to adopt; but it might equally well indicate the presence of a personal truth which he has not yet learned how to digest and convert into poetic subject-matter. For anyone who is familiar with Larkin's *oeuvre* as a whole, in fact, this awkward little poem seems to grow in resonance. It expresses a desire to be alone so intense that it amounts to a desire to discard the self; and the loss or forgetfulness of the self is a type of freedom which Larkin associates very strongly with the natural world.

One very clear example of this association of self-forgetfulness and Nature is 'Absences' (1950, first published in *The Less Deceived*), a poem[19] in which Larkin first describes the surface of the ocean, and then the sky above, finishing with the abrupt and startling exclamation: 'Such attics cleared of me! Such absences!' This is a description, in fact, which insists on the absence of an observer. Instead of referring to our most common experience of the sea, as a body of water crashing against a shore, it describes the middle of the ocean, 'Where there are no ships and no shallows'. The sky above is 'yet more shoreless': and the purpose of this insistence on the absence of shores or ships is to make it clear that there is no human onlooker at hand.

Nevertheless the poem describes the sea, and a description implies an observer; and a protagonist does appear at the end, to voice the exclamation with which the poem ends—an exclamation which paradoxically draws attention again to the absence of human life. Larkin makes no attempt to resolve this paradox, because it embodies his feelings about the non-human world—that its value lies in its separateness from human beings, and that the only way they can share this separateness is to leave their humanity behind, which means ceasing to be themselves. Like 'Wants', 'Absences' is a statement of death-wish. All the same, the exclamations at the end seem euphoric rather than despairing, suggesting that Larkin has been able to achieve a measure of escape from himself simply by contemplating the non-human world and turning the contemplation into a poem.

Another piece in which the natural world seems to offer an escape from human limitations is 'Here' (1961, first published in *The Whitsun Weddings*). It is easy to overestimate the extent to which this poem[20] describes an individual managing to 'get away from it all'—in fact, it is much more ambiguous in this respect than it may seem at first glance. It begins with a very long first sentence that seems to describe a train journey to Hull:

> Swerving east, from rich industrial shadows
> And traffic all night north; swerving through fields
> Too thin and thistled to be called meadows,
> And now and then a harsh-named halt, that shields
> Workmen at dawn; swerving to solitude...

Altogether, this first sentence goes on for twenty-four-and-a-half lines, taking in a description of 'a large town' (presumably

Hull, where Larkin had settled by this time) complete with
'raw estates', shops with 'plate-glass swing doors', and 'A cut-
price crowd' which lives and shops there. The sentence only
finishes once this town has been left behind, and the poem has
pushed on again into the empty countryside beyond:

> And out beyond its mortgaged half-built edges
> Fast-shadowed wheat-fields, running high as
>   hedges,
> Isolate villages, where removed lives
>
> Loneliness clarifies. Here silence stands
> Like heat.

The bewildering length of this first sentence, and the ease
with which we can identify the 'large town' as Hull, Larkin's
home, both encourage us to assume that we are following the
journey of one man (Larkin himself), and thus distract our
attention from the fact that the sentence is never actually
supplied with a subject: we never find out *who* is doing the
'swerving', if indeed anybody is. This ambiguity recurs at the
end of the poem:

> Here silence stands
> Like heat. Here leaves unnoticed thicken,
> Hidden weeds flower, neglected waters quicken,
> Luminously-peopled air ascends;
> And past the poppies bluish neutral distance
> Ends the land suddenly beyond a beach
> Of shapes and shingle. Here is unfenced existence:
> Facing the sun, untalkative, out of reach.

Is it the poet who is 'Facing the sun, untalkative, out of reach',
or is it the 'unfenced existence' he describes? Are the leaves
'unnoticed' and the waters 'neglected' by everybody except
the poet, or simply by everybody? Are we to read these lines
as a description of a human individual making an escape into
the natural world, or as a reassertion of the natural world's

separateness from all human life? As in 'Absences', the attitude is paradoxical: Nature is at its most valuable when it is empty of all human presence, even the presence of the poet. So the poet describes the natural world as if he wasn't there; and in doing so, he achieves the release from self which he desires.

But 'Here' also exemplifies another paradox of which Larkin seems less fully aware and which he is therefore less well able to control. Clearly what he values about the countryside is its emptiness—yet when he describes the land instead of the sea or the sky he uses pastoral images, images of domesticated countryside rather than untamed wilderness. The 'fast-shadowed wheat-fields' imply human attendants and human activity, but Larkin does his best to ignore this implication by dwelling on the least domesticated parts of the landscape—'Hidden weeds', 'neglected waters', the poppies, the bluish distance, the 'shapes' on the beach and the air 'peopled' with luminous, non-human creatures. At the same time he also suggests that the isolation of the humans who inhabit this landscape confers on them a kind of simplicity which the cut-price crowd in the city does not share—'removed lives/ Loneliness clarifies'. As we shall see, Larkin believes that traditional, pastoral ways of life allowed human beings to achieve a kind of unselfconscious dignity which the modern urban population has generally lost; and this belief seems to be partly derived from the simple feeling that people are better living few and far between in a rural setting than coming together in large numbers in towns or cities—'loneliness clarifies'.

These examples show that natural descriptions in Larkin's poetry do not invariably serve to chasten the observer into a renewed awareness of his own mortal limitations; they sometimes provide him with a sense of release from those limitations; but only if he is able to forget himself, and thus, in a sense, to free himself momentarily from his own humanity. But there is another group of poems in which Larkin deals with men as social creatures rather than as isolated individuals; and these poems indicate his belief that whole communities can sometimes behave in an unselfconscious and unified manner which enables them to respond positively to the natural world, even to share its patterns of timeless self-renewal.

'To the Sea',[21] for example (written in 1969 and first published in *High Windows*), describes 'the miniature gaiety of seasides'. The word 'miniature' is a key to the poem: the huge, flawless sky that overarches the seaside on a day of perfect weather reduces the visiting humans and all their activities to 'miniature gaiety', and thus emphasizes their mortality and frailty. 'Everything crowds under the low horizon' begins Larkin; and he goes on to mention 'The small hushed waves' repeated fresh collapse', transistor radios 'that sound tame enough/Under the sky', 'uncertain children... grasping at enormous air' and 'the distant bathers' weak protesting trebles'. Throughout his description, in other words, individual details, especially details of human activity, are made to seem small and frail against the hugeness of the scene as a whole. Larkin goes on to observe that one purpose of a visit to the seaside is to 'wheel/The rigid old along for them to feel/A final summer', and this reference makes explicit the contrast between the immortality of the scene and the mortality of its human inhabitants. Larkin recalls how he 'searched the sand for Famous Cricketers' when he was a boy, and how 'farther back' his parents 'first became known' to each other at the seaside.

Human individuals grow old and die, but the human response to the scene is as timeless as the scene itself. It represents what Larkin sees as a properly humble and therefore admirable response to the challenge of the immortal natural world as a whole:

> If the worst
> Of flawless weather is our falling short,
> It may be that through habit these do best,

Coming to water clumsily undressed
Yearly; teaching their children by a sort
Of clowning; helping the old, too, as they ought.

The landscape and the weather have taught the adults who respond to them an awareness of their own weaknesses, and a humility which encourages them to remember their responsibilities towards the young and the old. The action of undressing—'Coming to water clumsily undressed'—symbolizes the holiday-makers' acknowledgement of their own frailties. There are no bronzed musclemen or bikini-clad nymphettes on this beach: for Larkin, undressing in the sunshine is an act of clownish self-abasement rather than a piece of erotic display. His holidaymakers are not trying to impress one another, but to help one another. They do the right thing without thinking—'through habit'—and in fact it is precisely their lack of forethought which enables them to behave in a dignified and appropriate manner. If the 'cut-price crowd' in 'Here' is debased by its own acquisitiveness, then the holiday-makers in this poem are ennobled by their instinctive responses to the natural world, and the unselfish, time-honoured communalism of their behaviour. Their closeness to the natural world seems to have released them from the shoddy materialism of modern life, and realigned them with a more traditional, less self-centred form of existence.

Larkin's appreciation of communal tradition reappears in one of his most famous poems, 'The Whitsun Weddings',[22] which was written in 1958 and first appeared in the collection to which it gave its name. It describes Larkin journeying from Hull to London on the Saturday afternoon before Whit Sunday, and gradually realizing that his train is filling up with newly-married couples who are just embarking on their honeymoons. At the start of the journey, before the weddings catch his attention, he looks out of the window at a landscape which is being spoilt by the creeping shabbiness of modern Britain:

> Wide farms went by, short-shadowed cattle, and
> Canals with floatings of industrial froth;
> A hothouse flashed uniquely: hedges dipped
> And rose: and now and then a smell of grass
> Displaced the reek of buttoned carriage-cloth
> Until the next town, new and nondescript,
> Approached with acres of dismantled cars.

His disapproval is indicated by the phrase 'new and non-descript', and by the contrast between 'the smell of grass' and the 'acres of dismantled cars' which replace it.

When he begins to notice the wedding parties on the platforms, they seem at first to attract the same disapproval:

> The fathers with broad belts under their suits
> And seamy foreheads; mothers loud and fat;
> An uncle shouting smut; and then the perms,
> The nylon gloves and jewellery-substitutes...

This seems like a more detailed description of the 'cut-price crowd' mentioned in 'Here'. It is a crowd made up of two-dimensional caricatures, but it is appropriate to the poem in that these people, with their 'smut', 'perms', 'nylon gloves' and 'jewellery-substitutes' seem perfectly suited to the 'new and nondescript' landscape they inhabit. But as the narrator begins to take more and more interest in the weddings, he begins to see the crowds on the platforms in different terms too. He notes that the older women are all behaving as if they were at 'a happy funeral', while the young girls, 'gripping their handbags tighter', seem to respond to each wedding as if it were 'a religious wounding'. The effect of these phrases is still at least partly comical, but they also serve to suggest that the weddings are deeply-felt and serious events.

The most interesting aspect of the poem, however, is the way in which this newly-discovered depth of feeling is transferred from the crowd back into their shabby landscape, so that paradoxically, as the train approaches London and the

environment through which it moves becomes increasingly
urban ('Now fields were building-plots, and poplars cast/
Long shadows over major roads'), Larkin begins to describe
that environment in increasingly pastoral terms:

> I thought of London spread out in the sun,
> Its postal districts packed like squares of wheat

This pastoral image is picked up and developed in the last lines
of the poem:

>   We slowed again,
> And as the tightened brakes took hold, there
>   swelled
> A sense of falling, like an arrow-shower
> Sent out of sight, somewhere becoming rain.

The arrows are Cupid's arrows of love; but the shower is also
a shower of rain, which falls on London's 'squares of wheat'
and thus ensures their continued fertility.

Donald Davie discusses 'The Whitsun Weddings' in his
book *Thomas Hardy and British Poetry*,[23] where he argues
that Larkin is only able to sympathize with the other train-
passengers by virtue of the fact that he represses his aesthetic
responses to the natural world and the way in which it is being
ruined, as well as his historical awareness that the British landscape was once far more beautiful than it is now. In other
words, Larkin is making a special effort not to allow a sense of
outrage about the state of the countryside to destroy his
sympathy with the people who have been responsible for
spoiling it. But although it is true that Larkin is making a
special effort to sympathize with the 'common people' he sees
on the platforms and shares his journey with, it is not true to
say that there is no sense of history in the poem.

One of the points Larkin is making is that human actions
achieve a kind of dignity when they are unified and regulated
by a sense of tradition, which binds disparate groups of people
together and unites the present with the past. This kind of

tradition is the human equivalent of the seasonal impulses which regulate events in the natural world: it enables human beings to 'begin afresh' with some of the timeless readiness that Larkin discovers in 'The Trees'. In a sense, because they are acting 'through habit' like the holidaymakers in 'To the Sea', the marriage parties in 'The Whitsun Weddings' are free of that self-awareness from which Larkin seems to seek release and with which he habitually contrasts the serenity of the natural world. It is this unselfconscious compliance with tradition that enables the apparently ugly and absurd individuals who appear at the beginning of the poem to achieve a measure of communal dignity by the end. In the process, the shabby landscape they inhabit is temporarily transformed into a latter-day version of the pastoral ideal.

Of course, Larkin's love of tradition reminds us of his social and political conservatism; but it also directs our attention towards his version of the Fall-myth. The impression with which we are left by Davie's discussion of 'The Whitsun Weddings'—that Larkin achieves a clearheaded acceptance of present-day Britain by repressing his sense of historical perspective, which would otherwise remind him how a once-lovely landscape has been spoilt by the disease of modernity—is, as we shall see, very misleading. In fact Larkin's love of tradition is balanced by his ironic portrait of a modern world where tradition has been abandoned, and where individuals who would prefer not to admit their own mortal limitations allow themselves to be deluded by dreams of unattainable happiness. This is Larkin's vision of the fallen world: a world without traditions, without humility, where the chastening effects of Nature are unfelt, and people abandon themselves to their selfish illusions instead.

III

The two poems that deal most directly with Larkin's version of the Fall-myth are 'Going, Going' and 'MCMXIV'. The longer of the two, 'Going, Going',[24] was written in 1972 and first published in *High Windows*. Ostensibly, it is Larkin's only outspoken utterance on the subject of the environmental crisis. It begins as follows:

> I thought that it would last my time—
> The sense that, beyond the town,
> There would always be fields and farms,
> Where the village louts could climb
> Such trees as were not cut down.

Nowadays, Larkin goes on to say, he is starting to get a new sense that the countryside may not last his time after all:

> For the first time I feel somehow
> That it isn't going to last,
>
> That before I snuff it, the whole
> Boiling will be bricked in
> Except for the tourist parts.

His tone is one of helpless resignation ('Most things are never meant', he says towards the end of the poem; and the last line reads 'I just think it will happen, soon'), but all the same he is doing more than simply throw up his hands in horror at the changes taking place. He is also trying to show what forces lie behind these changes: namely, the expectations of profit and personal convenience on which our society is built.

> The crowd
> Is young in the M1 cafe;
> Their kids are screaming for more—
> More houses, more parking allowed,
> More caravan sites, more pay.
> On the Business Page, a score

Of spectacled grins approve
Some takeover bid that entails
Five per cent profit (and ten
Per cent more in the estuaries).

As Larkin says at the end of the poem, the process of change
now seems too well established to allow any reasonable expectation that it will stop before it is too late: 'greeds/And
garbage are too thick-strewn/To be swept up now'. In fact, he
suggests, our expectations of profit and personal convenience
are so entrenched that our luxuries have come to be seen as
essentials, and we will 'invent/Excuses that make them all
needs' rather than abandon them. We also fail or refuse to
make the connection between our way of life and the destruction of the English landscape: 'Most things are never meant'.
The combination of force of habit, greed, and inability to
perceive clearly the consequences of our own actions seems
unstoppable.

But the England Larkin wants to protect remains imprecise.
It is 'The sense that, beyond the town,/There would always
be fields and farms'; it is the 'old streets' and 'the unspoilt
dales'; and it is 'The shadows, the meadows, the lanes,/The
guildhalls, the carved choirs'. It is unclear what historical
period Larkin has in mind, but it certainly seems to predate
the Industrial Revolution; and one striking aspect of the
contrast which Larkin sets up between the old England and
the new is that although the older way of life is associated with
man-made objects ('lanes', 'guildhalls' and 'carved choirs') it
seems to be empty of people. The only exceptions are the
'village louts'—and Larkin seems to be suggesting that their
loutishness never becomes really harmful because they are
able to escape 'beyond the town' and let themselves go by
climbing trees.

But modern England, contrastingly, is overcrowded with
unpleasant characters. Larkin's description of what he dislikes
about the new England is in some ways more revealing than

his description of what he likes about the old. The material aspects, such as 'bleak high-risers' and 'concrete and tyres', are seen as outward manifestations of an all-pervasive moral viciousness. The younger generation seems to consist of 'kids... screaming for more', while the adults are depicted as businessmen with 'spectacled grins' and 'a cast of crooks and tarts'. Admittedly Larkin asks himself at one point whether these feelings are the result of 'age, merely', but his tone seems over-vehement nevertheless. Are demands for 'more houses' and 'more pay' always the results of greed rather than need? The poem makes it seem as if the destruction of the landscape has resulted from the descent into naked selfishness of a single generation.

The old England, then, was not preferable only because it was more beautiful, but because people were less greedy then. It is here that Larkin's lack of historical analysis becomes apparent. There is no sense in his poem that the seeds of destruction which are now coming to fruit may have been sown many generations ago. Indeed his concluding image emphasizes the lack of any organic connection between the present and the past: 'greeds/And garbage are too thick-strewn/To be swept up now...' The present seems to have been simply dumped on top of the past by an act of carelessness.

But Larkin does hint at one crucial difference between modern England and the England of the past, by setting up a dissonance between two phrases in the poem: 'that will be England gone', which sums up his feelings of loss about the past, and 'first slum of Europe', which epitomizes the disgust he feels when he contemplates our likely future. The beautiful past was English, but the ugliness of the coming era will be European. 'Going, Going' was written in 1972, shortly after Britain's entry into the EEC. Larkin seems to feel that the English are abandoning their traditions and their identity for the sake of a future as the uncared-for corner of a soulless super-state. The inhabitants of modern England have ceased to care about their communal and national identity; all they care about now are their needs as individuals. Thus the old England becomes a kind of Eden, characterized not only by aesthetic beauty but also by the corresponding moral worthiness of its inhabitants. The new England, on the other hand— 'first slum of Europe'—is the fallen world. The lack of organic connection between the present and the past expresses Larkin's feeling that we have tumbled from a state of grace into a state of degradation. This nationalistic version of the Eden-myth bears a surprisingly close resemblance to the sentiments which R. S. Thomas sometimes expresses about Wales and the Welsh.

'MCMXIV' also deals with the loss of an older and better England. The poem,[25] which was written in 1960 and first published in *The Whitsun Weddings*, is about the outbreak of the First World War, and how this event caused an irreversible change in the English way of life. As Larkin writes in the last stanza:

> Never such innocence,
> Never before or since,
> As changed itself to past
> Without a word.

He implies that one aspect of this change was the loss of a rural tradition which stretched back to Domesday. He describes the countryside in the last days before this tradition was broken:

> And the countryside not caring:
> The place-names all hazed over
> With flowering grasses, and fields
> Shadowing Domesday lines
> Under wheat's restless silence.

Larkin's double use of the word 'innocence' in the last stanza of the poem—'Never such innocence.../Never such innocence again'—alerts us to the fact that the significance of the event described is at least as much mythical as historical. Here, as in 'Going, Going', the lineaments of Larkin's Fall-myth lie partially buried, perhaps only partially recognized by the poet himself; and in both cases the myth is essentially the same—a traditional and rural way of life has been replaced by something less 'innocent'.

In both 'Going, Going' and 'MCMXIV', Larkin's feelings about the Edenic nature of old England, and the fallen state of the modern nation, are expressed through descriptions of English landscapes; and we have already seen how, in 'The Whitsun Weddings', he creates and exploits a link between the 'common people' and the landscape to which they belong, to convey his feelings about both. Likewise, in rather a crude way, 'Going, Going' uses a description of an urban environment as a means of highlighting the shortcomings of the 'cut-price crowd' which lives there. There are various other poems in which Larkin does the same thing rather more subtly and successfully. One example is 'Essential Beauty',[26] which was written in 1962 and first published in *The Whitsun Weddings*. It describes advertisement hoardings, and it plays on the disparity between the ideals of comfort and beauty they depict, and the drab realities of the urban environment in which they are placed.

The hoardings, Larkin tells us, 'block the ends of streets with giant loaves,/Screen graves with custard, cover slums with praise', but they

> Reflect none of the rained-on streets and squares
> They dominate outdoors. Rather, they rise
> Serenely to proclaim pure crust, pure foam,
> Pure coldness to our live imperfect eyes
> That stare beyond this world, where nothing's made
> As new or washed quite clean, seeking the home
> All such inhabit.

The hoardings express Man's longing for a perfection which he can never achieve. The disparity between the ideal way of life which the advertisements depict and the reality of 'rained-

on streets and squares' stands for the disparity between urban
Man's everyday life and his dreams. The advertisement hoardings 'dominate' the urban environment but 'reflect none of' it;
and the image of the blocked street suggests that in this way
they obstruct or divert people from the paths they might
otherwise have taken. They do this by tempting 'our live
imperfect eyes' to 'stare beyond this world', 'seeking the
home all such [all such visions of perfection] inhabit'.

Whereas the natural world chastens us and renews our
awareness of our own imperfections, the advertisement hoardings delude us into believing that perfection is within our
reach—but such a delusion can only prevent us from living as
we should. 'The home all such inhabit' is death, a point which
is made clear by the closing lines of the poem:

>   dying smokers sense
> Walking towards them through some dappled park
> As if on water that unfocused she
> No match lit up, nor drag ever brought near,
> Who now stands newly clear,
> Smiling, and recognising, and going dark.

Larkin is suggesting that a life haunted by expectations of
perfection cannot be lived properly at all: we do better to
accept our limitations and learn to live with them. Otherwise
we exist in a shallow dream, from which we are only awakened
by the shock of death. It is Larkin's belief as a rationalist that
the conditions of human life cannot be transcended. They
must be accepted, and not only accepted but always kept in
mind, if we are to number ourselves amongst the clear-sighted
'less deceived'.

Another poem on much the same theme is 'The Building',[27]
which was written in 1972 and first published in *High
Windows*. It describes a hospital and its surroundings, but the
building is never named as a hospital, and the poem is written
from the point of view of someone who doesn't understand
what hospitals are for:

> something has gone wrong.
> It must be error of a serious sort,
> For see how many floors it needs, how tall
> It's grown by now, and how much money goes
> In trying to correct it.

This stylistic device becomes rather strained at times ('Every few minutes comes *a kind of* nurse/To fetch someone away'— my italics) and towards the end of the poem it is abandoned altogether; but it serves the purpose of enacting the bewilderment and disbelief felt by modern Man when he is roused from his dreams of perfection and brought face-to-face with the inevitability of his own illness and death. Mortal frailty is seen as something that has 'gone wrong', an 'error of a serious sort' which 'money' is supposed to 'correct'.

The gap between the hospital, which has been built to correct the error of death, and the houses in which people live out their everyday lives, is just the same as the gap between the advertisement hoardings with their visions of perfection and the streets they 'block':

> Higher than the handsomest hotel
> The lucent comb shows up for miles, but see,
> All round it close-ribbed streets rise and fall
> Like a great sigh out of the last century.

The poem goes on to describe modern everyday life as

> unreal,
> A touching dream to which we all are lulled
> But wake from separately.

As in 'Essential Beauty', Larkin is suggesting that if human life is not chastened and guided by an awareness of its own limitations, it becomes a kind of dream from which we can only wake up when it is too late. The phrase 'we are all lulled' may seem to indicate that the dream is an inescapable part of our existence—that all human beings are doomed to delude themselves in this manner—yet the poem itself, like much of Larkin's work, represents an attempt to see things more clearly; and it encourages us, as his readers, to sharpen up our ideas in the same way. As usual, Larkin is implying that we cannot behave in a clear-headed and responsible manner unless we are prepared to face the unpleasant facts of our own mortality and frailty.

One point that emerges from Larkin's poems about the urban environment—'Ambulances' and 'The Large Cool Store'[28] are others written on similar lines—is that his descriptions of the man-made world express a different kind of awareness from his descriptions of Nature. He sees the man-made world in terms of what it tells us about ourselves, whereas he sees the non-human world in terms of its serene separateness. The description of the moon in 'Sad Steps', for example, is largely written in negative terms—the moon is not involved with us but 'separate', it stands above the coarse and lumpen earthly environment which the poem describes, it has not aged as has the speaker in the poem, and so forth. Larkin expresses his feelings about the moon by running through a number of stock poetic responses—such as 'Medallion of art' and 'Lozenge of love'—and discarding them as inadequate. 'No. One shivers slightly, looking up there...' He does not offer an alternative poeticism of his own, because his point about the moon is that it sails free of any such attempts to lay claim to it: it is beyond us. When he describes something man-made such as 'The Building', on the other hand, he finds a great deal to say about it. The man-made world is not mysterious and alien as the natural world is: it can be analysed, and the analysis exposes the ways in which Man builds his weaknesses and delusions into his urban environment.

Because Larkin describes the natural world in terms of its separateness from human problems, he seems disinclined to describe certain aspects of it at all. Despite the links between natural fertility and marriage suggested by 'Spring' and 'The Whitsun Weddings', Larkin's Nature is almost entirely sexless.

It is also devoid of conflict; and in order to achieve this sex-free and struggle-free vision, he generally ignores animals and birds in favour of plants, the sky and the sea. This is not to say, however, that he depicts the natural world as a completely static environment. His trees come into leaf, his seas heave and plunge, and he likes to fill his skies with strong cold winds and rapidly-moving clouds. But although this activity reminds us of the passing of time, the threat that accompanies such temporality is aimed at us rather than at the natural world itself.

Non-human things are not immune from time, but in Larkin's poems they seem to be immune from the fear of it. In 'The Trees', for example, the trees are no more immortal than their human observers—'No, they die too'—but they put those observers to shame by fearlessly discarding the past and beginning each new year 'afresh'. In 'At Grass'[29]—one of Larkin's rare animal-poems, written in 1950 and published in *The Less Deceived*—he asks himself about some retired race-horses: 'Do memories plague their ears like flies?'; and answers: 'They shake their heads'. The end of the poem confirms that the horses, far from regretting bygone glories,

> Have slipped their names, and stand at ease,
> Or gallop for what must be joy,
> And not a fieldglass sees them home,
> Or curious stop-watch prophecies:
> Only the groom, and the groom's boy
> With bridles in the evening come.

By slipping their names, they have freed themselves from the human world with its fears of mortality. The fact that their gallops are no longer measured by stop-watches makes the same point. The groom and the groom's boy coming with evening may strike us, the readers, as an omen of death; but the horses themselves have 'slipped' away from such human troubles into an unselfconscious world full of 'ease' and 'what must be joy'.

'Cut Grass',[30] written in 1971 and published in *High Windows*, deals with the theme of time more fully. The poem is only twelve lines long, like 'The Trees'; and like 'The Trees' it is a descriptive piece—but it would be difficult to say precisely what is being described. Larkin begins with cut grass, but quickly moves on to summertime and the English countryside in general:

> Cut grass lies frail:
> Brief is the breath
> Mown stalks exhale.
> Long, long the death
>
> It dies in the white hours
> Of young-leafed June.

He finishes with 'Lost lanes of Queen Anne's lace' and 'that high-builded cloud/Moving at summer's pace'. The real purpose of the poem is not to describe a specific scene, but to play off two different views of time against one another. The opening image of cut grass reminds us that 'all flesh is grass', and the use of the word 'frail' suggests mortality, so that 'Brief is the breath/Mown stalks exhale' serves as a reminder of the brevity of our own lives. Life is so brief that it amounts to no more than a fading scent of cut grass; and the span of a whole life can be summed up as a single 'breath'. On the other hand, the allusions to the grass's 'Long, long' death and to 'the white hours/Of young-leafed June' evoke the slowness with which time passes when we live it from the inside, moment by moment, without the sense of perspective which is offered by our usual awareness of the past and future. This way of living inside time is normal to the natural world itself; the phrase 'young-leafed June' suggests Nature's eternal willingness to begin 'afresh', unaware of the fact that in June the year is already half-finished.

But human beings are condemned to remember how much of their lives they have used up, and how little they have left.

The phrase 'summer's pace' can therefore be read in two ways—summer is either a 'long, long' progression of 'white hours', or it is as 'brief' as the 'breath' of the 'frail' grass. The poem is either celebrating the fearless glories of 'young-leafed June', or it is lamenting the fact that those glories die terribly rapidly, like the cut grass, and like ourselves. But the carefully-judged nostalgia of the line 'Lost lanes of Queen Anne's lace' is suggesting something else: that this rural scene, which seems to offer us a chance to live our lives at a slower pace, is now 'lost' and belongs to a past which we associate with Queen Anne. ('Queen Anne's lace' is a colloquial name for hedge-parsley.) The poem thus returns us to Larkin's version of the Fall-myth. It is unclear whether he is suggesting that in the past, when everybody lived out their lives amongst these rural scenes, it was possible for human beings to share Nature's fearlessness about time; but he is clearly suggesting that if we become separated from such rural scenes entirely, we will be condemned to see time only from the outside, from the perspectives of the present and the past, which seem to shrink the span of a single human life to a mere 'breath'. This suggestion—that contemplation of Nature offers an escape from the tyranny of time—is, as we shall see, one that is common to all of my five poets.

'Cut Grass' is one of Larkin's least rationalist poems, because it offers an evocation of how life would feel if we could achieve a transcendent union with the natural world and abandon our human awareness of time. Even here, though, he is careful to remind us that this unfallen world is 'lost', and the poem's ambiguity about time suggests that we can never free ourselves entirely from the sense that our own lives are 'brief'. Unlike the primitivists, Larkin never uses his poetry purely as a means of reconstructing an unfallen state of consciousness, and he refrains from suggesting that it would be possible to recapture such a state of consciousness if we were to change our lives in certain ways. Even in poems such as 'Absences' and 'Here', where Larkin describes an uninhabited natural world which offers release from the shortcomings of humanity, he insists on subtly and paradoxically reminding us that such a state of existence can only be guessed at, not shared, because our own presence would spoil it. 'The Whitsun Weddings', 'To the Sea' and 'Going, Going', on the other hand, all indicate his approval of more traditional, rural ways of life, where whole communities of people, by observing time-honoured customs, seem to attune themselves with natural cycles of death and rebirth, and thus escape from the squalid selfishness of modern life.

All of this points to a slight confusion in Larkin's mythological system. His poetry seems to refer to two different versions of the Fall-myth, and two different ideas of Eden. The first Eden is the natural world, described in terms of its separateness, simplicity, and freedom from human failings: the paradisal emptiness of 'High Windows' and 'Absences', the fearless self-renewal of 'The Trees', and the eternal self-sufficiency of 'Solar'. At some point Man separated himself—or was separated against his will—from the natural world, and this Fall from calm perfection into the toils of mortal existence is irreversible. Nevertheless, until recently men still lived in a relatively virtuous manner, leading rural lives governed by the dictates of tradition, and not allowing themselves to be consumed by individual greed or delusive dreams of unattainable perfection. This traditional and rural existence, which is associated with a nationalistic idea of the lost beauty of England, amounts to a second Eden, from which Man fell when he withdrew from the countryside, abandoned tradition, and gave himself over to an urban lifestyle dominated by the power of individual selfishness. The unselfconscious behaviour described in 'To the Sea' and 'The Whitsun Weddings' was thus replaced by the destructive rapacity of 'Going, Going' and the self-delusions depicted in 'Essential Beauty' and 'The Building'. The fact that in various poems Larkin seems to be recommending a return to a less self-centred, more traditional way of life seems to suggest that he does not believe the second Fall to be as irreversible as the first.

This element of confusion suggests that Larkin's mythology—like all mythologies—was formed unconsciously and organically rather than constructed in a rational manner; and we need not condemn him on this account, since the purpose of such a mythology is not to embody or illustrate a coherent philosophy, but to express certain deeply-felt attitudes which may not necessarily be very logical or coherent at all. What Larkin's mythology expresses, above all, is a deep suspicion of the solipsistic world-view which he associates with modern urban existence. He believes that in order to live well we must acknowledge the limitations of the self and commit ourselves to something other than mere personal fulfilment—hence his endorsements (occasionally prejudiced and unattractive) of tradition, nationalism and a generally conservative social philosophy. But beneath these social considerations there runs a suspicion of individual consciousness itself. Larkin longs to abandon self-awareness altogether, because of the problems it brings; but he also fears such an abandonment, firstly because it would lead to a delusive trance-state, and secondly because it could only be fully achieved by dying. The final paradox of his poetry, which underlies all his attitudes towards both the human and non-human worlds, is that the untroubled freedom he desires can only be achieved by accepting the thing he dreads most—death.

Larkin's recurrent fantasy—a fantasy with which he flirts in many of the poems I have examined in this chapter—is a dream of giving the difficulties of life the slip, by discarding his individuality and losing himself in the natural world. This fantasy of self-abandonment determines the kind of value that he places on Nature. Perhaps it can be seen at work most clearly in a late poem, 'The Winter Palace', which was written in 1978 and remained unpublished until the *Collected Poems* were issued after his death. In it, he complains about losing his memory—but then he suddenly decides that this will be no bad thing after all, if in the process he can manage to lose himself. And this notion of losing himself is expressed through an image of landscape, which immediately becomes symbolic of the natural world's perfect emptiness:

> It will be worth it, if in the end I manage
> To blank out whatever it is that is doing the damage.
>
> Then there will be nothing I know.
> My mind will fold into itself, like fields, like snow.[31]

NOTES

1. Rossen, *Philip Larkin: His Life's Work* (Harvester Wheatsheaf, 1989), p. 27ff.
2. Larkin, *Collected Poems* (Marvell/Faber, 1988), p. 163.
3. *Ibid.*, pp. 102–03.
4. *Ibid.*, p. 165.
5. *Ibid.*, pp. 181–82.
6. *Ibid.*, p. 284.
7. Larkin, *The North Ship* (Fortune Press, 1945; Faber, 1966), p. 9.
8. Larkin, *Collected Poems*, p. 293.
9. *Ibid.*, p. 292.
10. Larkin, *Required Writing* (Faber, 1983), p. 67.
11. Larkin, *Collected Poems*, p. 39.
12. Larkin, *Jill* (Fortune Press, 1946, Faber, 1964), p. 242.
13. Larkin, *A Girl in Winter* (Faber, 1947), p. 248.
14. Larkin, *Collected Poems*, p. 152.
15. *Ibid.*, p. 153.
16. *Ibid.*, p. 169.
17. *Ibid.*, p. 166.
18. *Ibid.*, p. 42.
19. *Ibid.*, p. 49.
20. *Ibid.*, pp. 136–37.
21. *Ibid.*, pp. 173–74.
22. *Ibid.*, pp. 114–16.
23. See Donald Davie, *Thomas Hardy and British Poetry* (Routledge & Kegan Paul, 1973).
24. Larkin, *Collected Poems*, pp. 189–90.
25. *Ibid.*, pp. 127–28.
26. *Ibid.*, pp. 144–45.

27. *Ibid.*, pp. 191–93.
28. *Ibid.*, pp. 132–33, 135.
29. *Ibid.*, pp. 29–30.
30. *Ibid.*, p. 183.
31. *Ibid.*, p. 211.

Chapter Three
R. S. Thomas: 'narrow but saved'

I

R. S. Thomas is a primitivist. He believes that modern Man has separated himself from the natural world by choosing to respond to his environment analytically rather than imaginatively. Modern culture, with its cities, its machines and its waste, reflects this state of separation. In Thomas's poetry, these ideas are often given a nationalistic slant, leaving us with the impression that the beauty and spiritual potential of ancient Wales has been ransacked and spoilt by an influx of English settlers, English tourists, English money and English modernity. But there is a religious dimension to his myth as well. He suggests that a close imaginative connection with the natural world is to be valued because through it we may sometimes achieve a close connection with God. By adopting a mechanistic, analytical view of Nature we effectively deny God's existence, and condemn ourselves to live in a spiritless cosmos. And this loss of spiritual awareness has taken place not only in Wales, but all over the world, wherever primitive ways of life have been uprooted and destroyed by the onset of modernity.

It must be admitted that to state the matter in these bald terms is to oversimplify the impact of Thomas's poetry. Primitivism is not a decoder that can be used to translate all of his work. Comparatively little criticism has been written about Thomas, but his two main commentators to date, W. Moelwyn Merchant and J. P. Ward, have both rightly emphasized the fact that his poems often contradict one another and sometimes seem to refuse to endorse any system

of values at all. Occasionally, Thomas has been moved to
declare that we have now lost Eden forever. On other occasions he has even seemed to deny the existence of God. But
these outbursts interrupt his customary religious and primitivist outlook without ever displacing it.

In 'Fugue for Anne Griffiths' (from *Welsh Airs*, 1987), the
religious and nationalistic dimensions of Thomas's myth are
both apparent simultaneously. Anne Griffiths (one gathers
from the poem) was an unlettered, nineteenth-century Welsh
country girl who became a mystic and a writer of hymns.
Thomas suggests that her vision of God was inspired by the
unspoilt countryside in which she grew up:

> a countryside
>   not fenced in
> by cables and pylons,
> but open to thought to blow in
>   from as near as may be
> to the truth.[1]

He ends by asking her:

> Does the one who called to you,
>
> when the tree was green, call us
> also, if with changed voice,
> now the leaves have fallen and the boughs
> are of plastic?[2]

He seems inclined to think that this question might be
answered in the negative; and it follows that in modern
Wales—a Wales which is 'fenced in' rather than 'open', and
decorated with 'plastic' rather than green trees—mystics such
as Anne Griffiths are unlikely to reappear.

Griffiths's modern counterpart, in fact, is Thomas himself:
a churchman who is often forced to confess in his poetry that
he has lost touch with God. Between the visionary country
girl and the troubled modern priest there has been a fall from

grace. The Welsh landscape has been spoilt by the English; but a similar degradation has taken place all over the world, and the changes in our environment seem to correspond with a deeper change in the hearts and minds of mankind. At times, Thomas traces the origins of this problem back as far as the ancient Greeks. Thus he writes in 'Pre-Cambrian' (from *Frequencies*, 1978):

> Plato, Aristotle,
> all those who furrowed the calmness
> of their foreheads are responsible
> for the bomb.[3]

The implication of these lines is that rational thought, far from solving our problems, merely spoils our serenity. It teaches us to rely on ourselves, instead of turning our attention outwards towards the natural world and thus (potentially at least) towards God. Again, 'Fugue for Anne Griffiths' sums up Thomas's feelings about these alternatives:

> If one asked you: 'Are you glad
> to have been born?' would you let
> the positivist reply for you
> by putting your car in gear, or watch
> the exuberance of nature in a lost
> village, that is life saying Amen
> to itself?[4]

Positivism, which Thomas frequently attacks, is a philosophical system originated by Auguste Comte, recognizing only non-metaphysical facts and observable phenomena. The 'car' and the primitive 'lost/village' are two of Thomas's favourite symbols. The car and the road on which it travels symbolize progress: the idea that life should involve a journey from an unsatisfactory state to a more satisfactory one. Since Thomas does not believe in progress, his roads and his cars never go anywhere in particular; but they stand for 'the positivist reply' to the question about whether human life is worth living. What this reply amounts to is that life is unbearable if we stay where we are put: it only becomes bearable if we begin to travel, in an attempt to outdistance our problems or to arrive at solutions for them. Spiritual considerations count for nothing: only material benefits and improvements should be taken into consideration. But the 'lost/village' represents the alternative answer, of staying still and learning to accept life as it is; and this answer is associated with a contemplation of the natural world ('watch/the exuberance of nature'), which shows us 'life saying Amen/to itself'. 'Amen', of course, means 'so be it'; so the natural world teaches us, by example, how to accept the conditions of life as we find them.

If we contemplate the natural world properly, we may even be able to share its 'exuberance'; because Thomas does not believe that our fallen state is irreversible. We have certainly made things more difficult for ourselves by allowing the poison of positivism into our thoughts, but all the same a condition of 'exuberance' does at least lie within the range of human possibilities. Thomas's description of Anne Griffiths's religious ecstasy indicates as much:

> Here for a few years
> the spirit sang on a bone bough
> at eternity's window, the flesh trembling
> at the splendour of a forgiveness
> too impossible to believe in, yet believing.[5]

Through faith, a human can believe what to the rational mind seems unbelievable. In her ecstasy, Anne Griffiths's spirit becomes like a bird perched on the 'bone bough' of her own mortal body. Thanks to God's 'forgiveness', she is able to respond to the 'splendour' of eternity as fully as if she were a part of the natural world. This is one of the points at which Thomas's primitivism diverges from the outlook of a rationalist writer such as Philip Larkin—because, as we have already seen, Larkin does not believe that it is possible for a human individual to transcend himself and mimic the inspired simplicity of the natural world in this way. No matter how dour Thomas's poetry may sometimes seem, and no matter how grim a picture he may paint of modern Man's fallen state, for him the possibility of redemption is still ever-present—which is appropriate, of course, for a man of the church.

II

Surprisingly enough, Thomas's first memories are of Liverpool, and he only began to teach himself Welsh in his late twenties. He was an only child, born in Cardiff in 1913. His father worked at sea, so the family moved from port to port for the first six years of his life, mostly in England. At the end of the First World War, when Thomas was nearly six, they moved to Holyhead in Anglesey so that his father could work on the Irish ferries, and he remained there until his grammar-school education was complete. It was here that his love of Welsh country life first arose, and Thomas was eventually to end his clerical career in the same area: Aberdaron, his last parish, is near the tip of the Lleyn (Llŷn) Peninsula.

The earlier an idea is formed, the more difficult it is to shake off: Thomas has never ceased to regard the north-west corner of Wales as 'the real Wales', the Welsh heartland, or to believe that the rest of Wales ought to conform to the pattern of life that he thought he glimpsed there as a boy. Brian Morris, in an excellent essay entitled 'The Topography of R. S. Thomas', has pointed out that when Thomas began to make a name for himself as a poet he was Rector of Manafon, yet the Wales he chose to describe bore little resemblance to the parish where he worked:

> The people of Manafon habitually speak English, not Welsh... And, contrary to what one might expect in reading Mr Thomas's first four published volumes of verse, Manafon is not an exposed hill-

> village... It lies very snugly in a small river valley, the
> fields are hedged, the pasture reasonably rich, and
> the hills which lie around it are no more than a few
> hundred feet high.
>
> The poems of this period find their origin not in
> Manafon, but in the hills and moorland of Cefn
> Coch above Adfa, more than ten miles to the west...[6]

In other words, Thomas literally went out of his way to seek
out the kind of primitive, Welsh-speaking communities he
wanted to describe; and this perhaps exemplifies his anxiety to
rediscover the Wales of his childhood.

At the start of his career in the Church, Thomas evidently
felt displaced from the Welsh heartlands he wanted to
describe. Of his first parish in Maelor, he later wrote that it
'might as well have been the English plain',[7] and went on to
add:

> I realised what I had done. My place was not here on
> this plain among these Welsh with English accents
> and attitudes. I set about learning Welsh, so as to get
> back to the real Wales of my imagination.[8]

The last phrase is both odd and revealing. How can a vision of
Wales be 'real' and yet imaginary at the same time? One
answer is that for Thomas the 'real' Wales is not the Wales the
English tourists or the materialistic hill-farmers see, but a
Wales lit up by the spark of imaginative response: the Wales of
the poets and of visionary individuals such as Anne Griffiths.
But another answer is that the 'real' Wales, which Thomas
castigates the English for spoiling and the Welsh for throwing
away, is not a 'real' place at all but a myth: and if this judgement seems harsh, we should ask ourselves whether the
pastoral England that Larkin imagines is a real place or a myth,
or whether the primitive Ireland to which (as we shall see)
Heaney's poetry refers is 'real' either.

Thomas's attitude towards the Welsh landscape has

remained essentially romantic and visionary, but his early
attraction towards the historical and mythological aspects of
Wales is replaced, as his poetry develops, by a rejection of
historic sites and tourist-traps in favour of obscure corners of
bleak wilderness. In 'The Paths Gone By', an essay about his
early life, he describes how, when he was a student of theology,
he used to take the train from Cardiff to Shrewsbury, and how
he would feel attracted to the Welsh hills to the west of the
railway-line. The terms in which he describes this attraction
make it obvious that at this stage he was fascinated by Welsh
history and mythology:

> In the west, the sky would be aflame, reminding one
> of ancient battles. Against that light, the hills rose
> dark and threatening as though full of armed men
> waiting for a chance to attack. There was in the west
> a land of romance and danger, a secret land.[9]

'Welsh Landscape' (from *Song at the Year's Turning*, 1955),
expresses the same kind of fascination:

> To live in Wales is to be conscious
> At dusk of the spilled blood
> That went to the making of the wild sky[10]

but the poem also shows Thomas's dissatisfaction with the
failure of the Welsh people to live up to their own past:

> There is no present in Wales,
> And no future;
> There is only the past,
> Brittle with relics,
> Wind-bitten towers and castles
> With sham ghosts;
> Mouldering quarries and mines;
> And an impotent people,
> Sick with inbreeding,
> Worrying the carcase of an old song.

In his later poems, Thomas displays an increasing aversion
to the parts of the Welsh landscape which are glamorized by
obvious historical associations. For one thing, those areas are
constantly overrun by tourists, particularly English tourists;
but for another, the process of selling Welsh history and Welsh
culture to strangers has turned the places concerned into
cheap and ghastly imitations of themselves. As Thomas writes
in 'Reservoirs' (from *Not That He Brought Flowers*, 1968):

> There are places in Wales I don't go:
> Reservoirs that are the subconscious
> Of a people...
> The serenity of their expression
> Revolts me, it is a pose
> For strangers, a watercolour's appeal
> To the mass, instead of the poem's
> Harsher conditions.[11]

He adds later:

> I have walked the shore
> For an hour and seen the English
> Scavenging among the remains
> Of our culture...

In his later poetry, Thomas seems to take the attitude that
'Historic Wales' has been too throughly infected by the
tourist disease, and too completely overrun by the scavenging
English, to be of any further value. Areas that he once thought
attractive, mysterious and exciting because of their historical
and mythological associations are later excised from his
mental chart of the Welsh heartlands; and the allusions to
Arthur, Glendower and others that are common in his early
poetry are absent from his later collections. His aesthetic
reactions to the landscape change too: he begins to prefer
harsher, more inaccessible regions where the Welsh are more
likely to be left to themselves. And as W. Moelwyn Merchant
notes, this rejection of 'Historic Wales' is balanced by an

increasing fascination with ignorant Welsh peasants who
neither know nor care about their past:

> If, in a position of bogus mythology, 'there is no
> present in Wales' (and hence, tragically, 'no future'),
> for the poet there *is* a present in his immediate envi-
> ronment, in the harshness of the soil's sustenance
> and the movement of the seasons. The peasant is no
> heir to the legends and impelled by no romanticism.
> His impulses are organic...[12]

Thomas's interest in the landscape becomes mythical rather
than mythological. The remaining corners of wilderness
to which he turns his attention are portrayed as bleak and
unwelcoming places, that will only reveal their secret splen-
dours to Welsh natives, never to tourists. 'The Chapel' (from
Laboratories of the Spirit, 1975) describes such a place; here is
the poem in full:

> A little aside from the main road,
> becalmed in a last-century greyness,
> there is the chapel, ugly, without the appeal
> to the tourist to stop his car
> and visit it. The traffic goes by,
> and the river goes by, and quick shadows
> of clouds, too, and the chapel settles
> a little deeper into the grass.
>
> But here once on an evening like this,
> in the darkness that was about
> his hearers, a preacher caught fire
> and burned steadily before them
> with a strange light, so that they saw
> the splendour of the barren mountains
> about them and sang their amens
> fiercely, narrow but saved
> in a way that men are not now.[13]

As in 'Fugue for Anne Griffiths', the 'main road' and the tourist's car represent modernity and the idea of progress, so the fact that the chapel is 'a little aside from the main road' indicates an escape from the disease of modernity—it is still 'becalmed in last-century greyness'.

It is also 'ugly' and 'without appeal/to the tourist'; and the phrase 'narrow but saved' signifies that it offers salvation only to insiders, and then only to those who are content to live a 'narrow' life undiluted by any communication with the modern world. On these conditions, Thomas is suggesting, certain remote, untamed, old-fashioned and apparently ugly corners of Wales may offer their inhabitants visions of the secret 'splendour of the barren mountains'—but the poem also suggests that such visions may always have been rare, and may now be a thing of the past. The moment of insight occurred only 'once'; it struck the congregation as 'strange'; and 'men are not now' capable of being 'narrow but saved' in the same way. As we have already seen from 'Fugue for Anne Griffiths', Thomas sometimes wonders whether the possibility of religious inspiration has disappeared altogether 'now the leaves have fallen and the boughs/are of plastic'.

Thomas is acutely aware that 'unspoilt' corners of Wales, where it is still possible to be 'narrow but saved' in the old-fashioned way, are now very few and far between; and he seems to feel that it will only take a little bit more poking and prying from the English to finish off old Wales entirely. Certainly his poetry provides plenty of evidence of his resentment of tourists. He feels that even the most remote corners of Wales are no longer safe from them. His own home in Aberdaron is just about the most inaccessible corner of Wales; and Thomas enjoys this remoteness in much the same way that Larkin used to enjoy being tucked away in Hull. Tourists come even here, though, as Thomas writes in *The Echoes Return Slow* (1988):

The end of a peninsula is a long way from anywhere,
but with the help of the motor they found it. All
that way to eat ice-cream; to raise the newspaper as
protection from the beauty of the sea.[14]

In 'Retirement' (from *Experimenting with an Amen*, 1986),
the mere presence of such intruders is enough to increase the
distance between Thomas and the natural world with which he
is seeking to make contact:

> I have crawled out at last
> far as I dare on to a bough
> of country that is suspended
> between sky and sea.
>
> Strangers
> advance, inching their way
> out, so that the branch bends
>
> further away from the scent
> of the cloud blossom.[15]

The image of the bending bough suggests that the peninsula
can only sustain a certain amount of human weight; and that if
the weight becomes too much, it may give way altogether. But
the lines also seem to suggest that only 'strangers' have this
detrimental effect. Either Welsh natives never come there, or
if they did they would not overburden the peninsula in the
same way.

It seems that outsiders are incapable of making the proper
imaginative response to the Welsh landscape. All they can do
is scavenge amongst the remains of the Welsh culture, thus
cheapening and dirtying it still more than is already the case,
or overburden the landscape so that the Welsh themselves can
no longer communicate with 'the splendour of the barren
mountains' or enjoy 'the scent/of the cloud blossom'. Only
the Welsh themselves can achieve the proper imaginative
response to their landscape; and in order to do so they need to

find a part of the country that has not been spoilt by
outsiders, and live in it in a 'narrow' way that is not compro-
mised by the luxuries of modern life.

Thomas's disapproval is not reserved purely for outsiders,
however. At times he takes his own countrymen to task as
well. In 'Those Others' (from *Tares*, 1961), he describes how
Wales has taught him to feel hate, 'Not for the brute
earth/That is strong here and clean', but

> for my own kind,
> For men of the Welsh race
> Who brood with dark face
> Over their thin navel
> To learn what to sell;
>
> Yet not for them all either,
> There are still those other
> Castaways on a sea
> Of grass, who call to me,
> Clinging to their doomed farms;
> Their hearts though rough are warm
> And firm[16]

Here Thomas divides the Welsh into two camps. On the one
hand, there are those who still cling to traditional Welsh
ways of life ('doomed farms') despite the fact that these ways
of life are rapidly becoming extinct. He describes these old-
fashioned 'castaways' in sympathetic—perhaps even sentimental—terms. On the other hand, he feels only 'hate' for
those who 'brood with dark face/Over their thin navel/To
learn what to sell'—Welshmen who have abandoned their
traditional ways of life, and who are now only obsessed with
their own Welshness because it represents a source of profit.

But Thomas is not always sympathetic towards the old-
fashioned farmers, either. In 'The Survivor', another poem
from *Tares*, he describes an eighty-five-year-old peasant as 'the
land's thug'. He sees this man's marriage as a

> theft
> Of health and comeliness from her
> Who lay caught in his strong arms

and his relationship with the land he farms is described in just
the same terms:

> My mind went back
> Sombrely to that rough parish,
> Lovely as the eye could wish
> In its green clothes, but beaten black
> And blue by the deeds of dour men
> Too like him.[17]

The old peasant and his kind treat their landscape in the same
way that they treat their wives: they take whatever they need
from it by cudgelling it into submission, and they spoil its
beauty in the process.

In poems such as this, Thomas will not accept a traditional
lifestyle as a guarantee of good-heartedness. Elsewhere, he
describes the dour existence of the hill-farmers in more
ambiguous terms, as in 'The Unvanquished' (from *Experimenting with an Amen*, 1986):

> Farmers I
> knew, born to the ills
> of their kind, scrubbed bare
> by the weather...
>
> Proudly
> they lived, watching the spirit,
> diamond-faceted, crumble
> to the small, hard, round, dry
> stone that humanity
> chokes on. When they died, it
> was bravely, close up under the rain-hammered
> rafters, never complaining.[18]

There is a note of admiration here, but not unqualified. The

farmers in this poem are certainly 'narrow', but there is little
suggestion that they are 'saved'. Their spirits, far from flourishing or being redeemed by some visionary connection with
the natural world, are worn down instead until they cease to
be 'diamond-faceted' and become merely 'the small, hard,
round, dry/stone that humanity/chokes on'. Perhaps they
contribute to this process themselves, by relying too much on
their own stubborn pride, which is exemplified by their refusal
to complain, even when they are dying.

Thomas recognizes their bravery, but he also seems to
suggest that their determination not to be bested may leave
them spiritually impoverished, clenched-up and unreceptive.
Yet, in another poem from the same collection, 'West Coast',
he depicts the same people in terms of their childlike open-
heartedness:

> Here are men
>   who live at the edges
> of vast space.
>   Light pours on them
> and they lift their faces
>   to be washed by it
> like children. And their minds
>   are the minds of children.[19]

These different attitudes recur throughout Thomas's work.
He never has any time for the English or for tourists in
general, nor for the Welshmen who have given up their traditional lifestyles and allowed themselves to become Anglicized
and modernized. But as regards the peasants and hill-farmers
who still live old-fashioned lives in the Welsh heartlands, his
attitudes towards them vary from one poem to the next. At
one moment he seems to despise their mean-spirited materialism; and at another, to think of them as innocent and open-
hearted children. This inconsistency of opinion—which also
characterizes his treatment of other themes such as religion
and science—is actually one of the more attractive aspects

of his work. It prevents his images from solidifying into an allegorical system in which everything has a fixed meaning and moral value; and it leaves us with the impression, instead, that his poems record and dramatize a genuine struggle between the ideal vision of Wales which he holds in his mind and the more problematic and unsatisfactory experiences that challenge his ideas from time to time.

The rural environment and the traditional way of life seem as likely to produce a mean-spirited dullness as they do to provoke an imaginative response to the natural world; and the 'Fugue for Anne Griffiths', which I have already quoted several times, shows how Thomas measures these two possible responses against each other. Anne Griffiths was brought up in rural Powys, and Thomas writes:

> I know
> Powys, the leafy backwaters
> it is easy for the spirit to forget
> its destiny in and put on soil
> for its crown. You walked solitary
> there and were not tempted,
> or took your temptation as calling
> to see Christ rising in April
> out of that same soil and clothing
> his nakedness like a tree.[20]

The 'soil' of the natural world is not itself to be worshipped or 'put on' as the spirit's 'crown'—to do so is to give in to 'temptation'. The natural world is the medium through which God expresses himself, and its voice should be interpreted 'as calling/to see Christ rising in April'. But this vision of Christ is always in danger of being displaced by the 'temptation' to become involved in the materialism of the 'soil' for its own sake.

One can easily imagine how Thomas's experiences as a priest might have forced him to admit that the inhabitants of his beloved Welsh countryside were not always inspired by its beauty as he would have liked them to be. On the contrary, it seems evident from his poetry that many of them ignored the beauty of the land altogether, and saw it merely in terms of what they could get out of it. Perhaps as a result of this, a sense emerges from his poetry that the countryside has two aspects—a spiritual aspect and a material aspect. When we become obsessed by the material aspect—the ploughed field, and the struggle to make a profit from the land which it represents—we are just as far from God, Thomas suggests, as we are if we abandon rural life altogether and go to live in the city. But rural life does at least always contain the possibility of spiritual enlightenment, whereas in modern, urban life any possibility of a spiritual response to the non-human universe is rapidly being destroyed by the scientific world-view and the ever-increasing dominance of the machine.

Thomas's advice about machines and the modernity which they represent is given most succinctly in 'Lore', from the 1961 collection *Tares*:

> What to do? Stay green.
> Never mind the machine,
> Whose fuel is human souls.[21]

It is because of his hatred of technological modernity that Thomas—even though he realizes that a rural lifestyle is no guarantee of spiritual enlightenment—sometimes describes pre-industrial Wales as a lost Eden, in which the Welsh people were themselves as beautiful and unspoilt as any other part of the environment. One example of this is 'The Bush' (from *New Poems*, 1983):

> And in this country
> of failure, the rain
> falling out of a black
> cloud in gold pieces there
> are none to gather,
> I have thought often

of the fountain of my people
that played beautifully here
once.[22]

The image of gold pieces falling from a black cloud typifies what Thomas looks for in the Welsh landscape: a sudden flash of beauty and inspiration in an apparently sombre and unpromising context. The context has to be dour, in order to discourage unwanted outsiders. As we have already seen, Thomas rejects 'a pose for strangers' and 'a watercolour's appeal/To the mass' in favour of 'the poem's/Harsher conditions'. But the dourness serves another purpose too: it helps to explain why the Welsh have lost faith. This is the 'failure' to which Thomas alludes. It is the reason why there are now 'none to gather' the beauty of the golden rain.

The fountain-image is meant to suggest what the Welsh people must have been like before their fall from grace. Evidently they were not stubborn or materialistic in those days: they were self-forgetful, expressive and spontaneous instead. Whether this image bears any resemblance to the picture of ancient Wales that might be drawn by a professional historian is perhaps beside the point. We are clearly in the realm of myth here, rather than the realm of historical analysis. The fountain-image is of interest, not because it tells us anything valuable about Welsh life in previous centuries, but because it shows us how Thomas thinks people would have behaved in a prelapsarian world. In this way, it sets his feelings about Wales in the context of his philosophical beliefs about human behaviour in general.

III

Thomas's primitivism does not end at the Welsh border. One proof of this is a poem called 'No, Señor' (from *Not That He Brought Flowers*, 1968) which is set in Spain. It reads as follows:

We were out in the hard country.
The railroads kept crossing our path,
Signed with important names,
Salamanca to Madrid,
Malaga to Barcelona.
Sometimes an express went by,
Tubular in the newest fashion;
The faces were a blurred frieze,
A hundred or so city people
Digesting their latest meal,
Over coffee, over a cigarette,
Discussing the news from Viet Nam,
Fondling the imaginary wounds
Of the last war, honouring themselves
In the country to which they belonged
By proxy. Their landscape slipped by
On a spool. We saw the asses
Hobbling upon the road
To the village, no Don Quixote
Upon their backs, but all the burden
Of a poor land, the weeds and grasses
Of the mesa. The men walked
Beside them; there was no sound
But the hoarse music of the bells.[23]

In this Spanish landscape, of course, Thomas himself is one of
the tourists. He seeks to overcome the problem by associating
himself with the peasants ('We were out in the hard country')
rather than with the 'city people/Digesting their latest meal'
in the comfort of the train. '*We* saw the asses', he tells us, but
to the train-travellers the landscape is devoid of such details:
'*Their* landscape slipped by/On a spool'. Thomas would
like us to believe that, because he is prepared to go 'out in
the hard country', to get close to the peasants with their
donkeys, and to experience for himself their living-conditions,
his relationship with the landscape is more genuine than that

of the train-passengers, who journey from city to city without ever setting foot in 'the mesa', and who only belong to the country 'By proxy'. We might be forgiven for wondering if he would be prepared to accept this claim himself, if it were voiced by an English tourist who was prepared to travel on foot through Wales in a similar fashion.

The train-passengers discuss 'news from Viet Nam' and 'imaginary wounds/Of the last war' because for them these events and places—read-about rather than experienced at first hand—seem as real as their own native land. Their modern way of life has detached them from hardship, but by doing so it has also detached them from reality. They could almost be the English, and the men outside on the mesa could almost be the Welsh hill-farmers.

Thomas evidently believes, in fact, that the contrast between town-dwellers and country-dwellers is universal, and fundamental to our understanding of the human condition. He demonstrates this by describing it, on occasion, in completely unspecific terms. One example is 'Fair Day' (from *Between Here and Now*, 1981), which begins as follows:

> They come in from the fields
> with the dew and buttercup dust
> on their boots. It was not they
> nor their ancestors crucified
> Christ. They look up at what
> the town has done to him.[24]

Here, Thomas is clearly concerned to write out his idea of the relationship between the country and the city in universal terms. 'The fields' in this poem could represent the rural part of any country, just as 'the town' could represent any modern conurbation. Thomas's argument is that *all* country-dwellers are guiltless of Christ's crucifixion, as are 'their ancestors'.

The town-dwellers, on the other hand, are responsible for

> hanging his body in stone on a stone
> cross, as though to commemorate
> the bringing of the divine beast
> to bay and disabling him.

Thomas sees Christ as a 'divine beast'—a part of the natural world, or perhaps a personification of Nature itself—hunted down and disabled by the town-dwellers and their machines. To remove Christ from the countryside to the city is to disable him or crucify him all over again, because it perpetuates Man's fall from the innocence of the natural world. The poem goes on:

> The town
> is malignant. It grows, and what
> it feeds on is what these men call
> their home. Is there praise
> here? There is the noise of those
> buying and selling and mortgaging
> their conscience...

The cultural imperialism of the English is now transformed into a universal vision of the growth and hunger of the town. The town feeds off the countryside as it grows, just as the English insist on spoiling the Welsh landscape and scavenging through the remains of Welsh culture as they spread outwards. But beyond this there lies another complaint: that in town-life the sound of 'praise' has been replaced by the 'noise' of 'buying and selling and mortgaging'. In other words, a spontaneous and self-forgetful response to the beauties of the natural world—like the playing of the fountain in 'The Bush'—has been replaced by a selfish obsession with personal gain. This is why townspeople spoil the countryside when they visit it: they are unable to respond to it selflessly; they have to consume it in order to enjoy or understand it; and for the same reason, the town 'feeds on' the homelands of the country-dwellers as 'It grows'.

In 'The Gap' (from *Laboratories of the Spirit*, 1975) the transition from unselfconscious self-expression to selfish rationality is explicitly related to Thomas's idea of how Man fell from his primal innocence. Here is the whole poem:

> The one thing they were not troubled
> by was perfection; it was theirs
> already. Their hand moved in the dark
> like a priest's, giving its blessing
> to the bare wall. Drawings appeared
> there like a violation of the privacy
> of the creatures. They withdrew with their work
> finished, leaving the interrogation of it
> to ourselves, who inherit everything
> but their genius.
>
>   This was before
> the fall. Somewhere between them and us
> the mind climbed up into the tree
> of knowledge, and saw the forbidden subjects
> of art, the emptiness of the interiors
> of the mirror that life holds up
> to itself, and began venting its frustration
> in spurious metals, in the cold acts of the machine.[25]

The suggestion in this poem is that prehistoric cave-painters expressed their appreciation of the natural world secretly and compulsively, without bothering about 'the interrogation' or analysis of their subjects, and without even displaying their paintings when they were finished. The act of creation took place 'in the dark', with no audience involved, and therefore with no suspicion that its purpose was to exalt the painter rather than his subject. Thomas sees this kind of response to Nature as religious as well as artistic—hence his use of the words 'priest' and 'blessing' to describe the activities of the cave-painters—and its keynotes are the self-forgetfulness of the artist and his non-analytical apprehension of his subjects.

His work is in a sense 'a violation of the privacy/of the creatures'; but in another sense he leaves their privacy intact by withdrawing when the paintings are finished and leaving them buried in the darkness. He leaves 'the interrogation'—both of the paintings and of the creatures they depict—'to ourselves'.

It is modern Man, whose mind has 'climbed up into the tree/of knowledge', who has taken light into the prehistoric caves to reveal 'the forbidden subjects/of art', which correspond in this particular version of the Eden-myth with Adam and Eve's forbidden fruit. To modern Man, all subjects are forbidden and likely to bring about the Fall, because unlike the cave-painters Man now responds to them analytically rather than imaginatively. Mankind therefore discovers not inspiration, but 'the emptiness of the interiors/of the mirror that life holds up/to itself'. The mind which interrogates Nature, instead of responding imaginatively and self-forgetfully, is the mind of an individual who wants to know the same thing about everything—what's in it for him. His apparent examination of the universe is therefore only another way of looking at himself in a mirror, and because he is empty himself the end result, as when two empty mirrors are held up to reflect one another, is a never-ending series of empty 'interiors'.

Primitive men did not examine the world in this way because they were not looking for 'perfection'—an escape from mortality, suffering, and human weakness—for such perfection was 'theirs/already', by virtue of their self-forgetfulness. As soon as men begin to search for perfection, they have lost it; they cannot find it in the natural world, because they are no longer able to respond to that world properly; and 'the cold acts of the machine' result from their 'frustration' with the apparent imperfections which they discover all around themselves.

The Fall-myth which underlies this poem is that Man fell when his 'mind climbed up into the tree/of knowledge', when he became self-obsessed, and when the created universe began to seem empty to him because he was asking it the wrong questions in the wrong way. Thomas blames the shortcomings of modern urban existence on the rational, analytical and individualistic way of thought which began (as he sees it) with Plato; and he advocates as an alternative either a vegetable-like mindlessness or an inspired communion with the natural world. In his early collections he often describes Welsh peasants as near-vegetables whose apparent imbecility betokens their closeness to the Nature. Even in later poems such as 'Strands' (from *Experimenting with an Amen*, 1986), Thomas is still referring to 'Eden, the mindless place';[26] but on the whole in his later poems he tends to admire a visionary and poetic response to the natural world rather than a mindless conformity with it.

His dislike of science and technology is unchanged, however. In *The Echoes Return Slow* (1988) he describes himself as 'In need of salvation, yet not wanting to be made safe by science',[27] and he tells (in the third person) of his sermons when he was still a vicar:

Because Coleridge had said that the opposite of poetry was not prose but science, that was what he preached from the pulpit at times... He defended himself with the fact that Jesus was a poet.[28]

These remarks about Coleridge resemble parts of Thomas's 1963 Introduction to *The Penguin Book of Religious Verse*:

What is the common ground between religion and poetry?... Perhaps Coleridge can help here. The nearest we approach to God, he appears to say, is as creative beings. The poet by echoing the primary imagination, recreates. Through his work he forces those who read him to do the same, thus bringing them nearer the primary imagination themselves, and so, in a way, nearer the actual being of God displayed in action. So Coleridge in the thirteenth

chapter of his *Biographia Literaria*. Now the power
of the imagination is a unifying power, hence the
force of metaphor... The world needs the unifying
power of the imagination. The two things which
give it best are poetry and religion. Science destroys
as it gives.[29]

Thomas's claim that 'Jesus was a poet' is also made in his
1966 essay 'A Frame for Poetry', in which he remarks that 'If
the message is the man, then Jesus was a poet... He is God's
metaphor, and speaks to us so.'[30] But the rationale by which
Thomas justifies his claim is really less significant than his
anxiety to bring poetry and religion into alignment, and set
them both up in opposition to science. On the one hand, his
argument runs, there is the 'unifying power' of the creative
imagination, whether that imagination belongs to God, to
Jesus, to the poet or to the reader of poetry; and on the other
hand there is science, which 'destroys as it gives'. Science—so
Thomas would have it—is based on a technique of separation
rather than a technique of unification. By analysing things it
separates them out from the continuum of the creative world
and then chops them up into smaller and smaller pieces in
order to find out how they work; and this process is begun by
separating the human observer from the world in which he
lives, turning him from a subjective participant into an objective analyst. (I am aware that the chopping-up approach has
recently been called into some question within the scientific
establishment by the proponents of holism and chaos theory,
but Thomas would have formulated his ideas about science
before these modern trends became widely talked-about.)
Creative thought, unlike science, unites the poet or artist with
the observed world through his imaginative response, and
reunites the different parts of the world with one another into
a newly-integrated whole—particularly, as Thomas would
have it, through the power of metaphor, which brings things
together by comparing them with each other.

None of these ideas is new. When Thomas cites Coleridge as an authority, he reminds us that the early Romantics often distinguished the scientific and poetic states of mind from each other too. Wordsworth's phrase 'We murder to dissect', and William Blake's attacks on such rationalists as Newton and Locke, are expressions of a revulsion against scientific analysis and the apparent tyranny of the rational mind: both poets, believing that the power of rational thought was being exalted and deified by their contemporaries to a dangerous degree, urged the counter-claims of a more imaginative response to the external world, and they both made it clear that they associated this response with both artistic and religious feelings.

Thomas is following in the same anti-rationalist tradition, but he also expresses a primitivist philosophy that has only been fully formulated in our own century. In his 1931 book *Apocalypse*, for example, D. H. Lawrence gives his own version of the Fall-myth as follows:

> Perhaps the greatest difference between us and the pagans lies in our different relation to the cosmos. With us, all is personal. Landscape and the sky, these are to us the delicious background of our personal life, and no more. Even the universe of the scientist is little more than an extension of our personality, to us. To the pagan, landscape and personal background were on the whole indifferent. But the cosmos was a very real thing. A man *lived* with the cosmos, and knew it greater than himself.
>
> ...We have lost the cosmos, by coming out of responsive connection with it, and this is our chief tragedy. What is our petty little love of nature— Nature!!—compared to the ancient magnificent living with the cosmos, and being honoured by the cosmos![31]

Apocalypse contains a number of attacks on Christianity with which Thomas would presumably take issue; but he would probably sympathize with Lawrence's condemnation of any system involving cut-and-dried classifications of good and evil, with matching rewards and punishments being doled out in a sanitized afterlife. And he would certainly agree with Lawrence's complaint that 'With us, all is personal'—that Man's fallen self-awareness has turned the non-human universe into a mere backdrop to the life of the individual—that the 'universe of the scientist' is an 'extension' of this way of seeing things—and that 'We have lost the cosmos, by coming out of responsive connection with it'.

Another twentieth-century writer to express a similar system of ideas is Robert Graves, whose famous and influential book *The White Goddess*, an investigation of poetic myths, first appeared in 1948 (it was revised in 1952 and 1961: my quotations are from the 1961 edition). Chapter Thirteen begins as follows:

> What interests me most in conducting this argument is the difference that is constantly appearing between the poetic and prosaic methods of thought. The prosaic method was invented by the Greeks of the Classical age as an insurance against the swamping of reason by mythographic fancy. It has now become the only legitimate means of transmitting useful knowledge.[32]

Graves goes on to argue that to modern Man 'money, though the root of all evil, is the sole practical means of expressing value', and 'that science is the only accurate means of describing phenomena'.[33] He concludes:

> No: there seems no escape from our difficulties until the industrial system breaks down for some reason or other, as it nearly did in Europe during the Second World War, and nature reasserts herself with grass and trees among the ruins.[34]

Graves closely identifies poetry with religion, and declares that both of them were originally expressions of Man's proper awareness of, and responsiveness to, Nature:

> The function of poetry is religious invocation of the Muse; its use is the experience of mixed exaltation and horror that her presence excites... This was once a warning to man that he must keep in harmony with the family of living creatures among which he was born...; it is now a reminder that he has disregarded the warning, turned the house upside down by capricious experiments in philosophy, science and industry, and brought ruin on himself and his family.[35]

These ideas may derive from Romantic originals, but the notion that the natural world, far from being benign, fills us with a 'mixed experience of exaltation and horror', is distinctly post-Romantic.

R. S. Thomas depicts the non-human universe from this same post-Romantic point of view; and so, as we shall see, does Ted Hughes, another primitivist. This representation of the non-human world, or of God, or of both, as neither good nor bad but above and beyond all moral categories, is doubtless very ancient, as all of these writers and poets would argue. But the advent of Darwinism has lent new force to the idea that Nature is not governed by either moral good or moral evil, but simply by laws of necessity; while the arguments of the anti-rationalists have gained a new tenor from modern psychology, with its suggestions that rational thought and 'civilized' behaviour correspond only with one small part of the human mind. Furthermore, since the Industrial Revolution, and especially since the beginning of the twentieth century, there has been a growing belief that science and analytical thought have given Man the power to alter his relationship with the natural environment—indeed, to alter the natural environment itself—fundamentally, permanently, and perhaps catastrophically. This has caused, in some quarters, a particularly severe reaction against the rational mind and all its works, and a particularly emphatic endorsement of the supposedly impulsive, intuitive and imaginative life of the natural world and primitive Man.

Graves traces the predominance of rational thought back to Socrates, who, he claims, 'was a confirmed townsman who never visited the countryside'.[36] Lawrence does the same: 'With the coming of Socrates and "the spirit", the cosmos died.'[37] And R. S. Thomas, although he does not despise the notion of 'spirit' as Lawrence does, also dates the degeneration of Man's state of mind from the days of classical Greece. A poem from *Frequencies* (1978), entitled 'Synopsis', exemplifies this; here it is in full:

> Plato offered us little
> the Aristotelians did not
> take back. Later Spinoza
> rationalised our approach;
> we were taught that love
> is an intellectual mode
> of our being. Yet Hume questioned
> the very existence of lover
> or loved. The self he left us
> with was what Kant
> failed to transcend or Hegel
> to dissolve: that grey subject
> of dread that Søren Kierkegaard
> depicted crossing its thousands
> of fathoms; the beast that rages
> through history; that presides smiling
> at the councils of the positivists.[38]

The words 'rationalised', 'intellectual' and 'questioned' are all used disapprovingly here. They signify attacks on 'the very existence of lover/or loved'.

Love, in Thomas's terminology, stands for the imaginative, intuitive and self-forgetful response to the external world which is symbolized by the cave-paintings in 'The Gap' and the fountain in 'The Bush'. When this love is broken down or discarded we are left with the modern 'self', a 'grey subject/of dread' that 'presides smiling/at the councils of the positivists'. The mention of positivism links this poem with the already-quoted question from 'Fugue for Anne Griffiths':

> If one asked you: 'Are you glad
> to have been born?' would you let
> the positivist reply for you
> by putting your car in gear...?

but 'Synopsis' takes Thomas's representation of positivism a little further, by characterizing the positivist self as 'the beast that rages/through history', and thus associating it with a certain conception of time.

In a sense it is the positivist belief in progress which *causes* history. Positivism insists that only tangible things matter, and it follows from this that if life is to be improved then it must be improved materially rather than spiritually. This way of seeing things gives rise in turn to the concept of progress— the idea that we should see life as a forward movement rather than as a constantly-returning cycle. In order to discard the positivist reliance on rationality and progress, we must also discard the positivist view of time. This is what Thomas is hinting at when he refers to 'the beast that rages/through history'; and the implication of this hint is that Thomas's Eden is a timeless place, or at least a place where time is cyclic rather than forward-moving.

IV

Thomas writes in 'Aside' (from *Pietà*, 1966):

> Turn aside, I said; do not turn back.
> There is no forward and no back
> In the fields, only the year's two
> Solstices, and patience between.[39]

We have already seen how he associates positivism with roads, cars and fast journeys. 'Aside' shows that he associates primitivism with the fields, with turning-aside, and with an abandonment of the ideas of 'forward' and 'back'. Rejection of progress involves rejection of the linear or directional view of time, and a return to 'the fields' involves acceptance of a state in which there are 'only the year's two/Solstices, and patience between', recurring in an eternal cycle.

This cycle is Thomas's idea of Eden. He makes the point explicit in 'Again' (from *Not That He Brought Flowers*, 1968):

> What to do? It's the old boredom
> Come again: indolent grass,
> Wind creasing the water
> Hardly at all; a bird floating
> Round and round. For one hour
> I have known Eden, the still place
> We hunger for. My hand lay
> Innocent; the mind was idle.
>
> Nothing has changed; the day goes on
> With its business, watching itself
> In a calm mirror. Yet I know now
> I am ready for the sly tone
> Of the serpent, ready to climb
> My branches after the same fruit.[40]

In the first half of the poem, the fallen narrator rediscovers Eden by virtue of achieving a temporary mindlessness—'the mind was idle'. Because of this mindlessness, his hand, which is usually the tool he uses to meddle with the external world, becomes 'innocent'. The 'old boredom' and 'Eden' are one and the same thing; but the use of the word 'boredom' suggests that the fallen mind cannot remain inactive for long without becoming restless; and we are thus prepared for the second half of the poem, in which 'the serpent' of intelligence climbs back into the 'branches' of the tree of knowledge. The imagery is reminiscent of 'The Gap':

> This was before
> the fall. Somewhere between them and us
> the mind climbed up into the tree
> of knowledge...

but in this poem ('Again') Thomas places more emphasis on the timelessness of the prelapsarian state. The grass is 'indolent'; the water is hardly disturbed by the breeze; a bird is 'floating/round and round'; the mind is 'idle'; and Eden itself is 'the still place'. Inactivity is the keynote. Even in the second half of the poem, where the Fall recurs, 'Nothing has changed'—the natural world, which is still unfallen, remains eternally 'calm'. Only the fallen mind goes back to its sinful, acquisitive ways.

Other poems carry the same message: that the rediscovery of Eden involves a turning-aside from the modern world and a return to Nature, which is associated with a sense of timelessness. In 'The Bright Field' (from *Laboratories of the Spirit*, 1975), Thomas writes:

> I have seen the sun break through
> to illuminate a small field
> for a while, and gone my way
> and forgotten it. But that was the pearl
> of great price...
>
> Life is not hurrying

> on to a receding future, nor hankering after
> an imagined past. It is the turning
> aside...[41]

and in 'Arrival' (from *New Poems*, 1983) he writes of

> the village in the Welsh hills
>   dust free
>   with no road out
> but the one you came in by.
>
>   A bird chimes
>   from a green tree
> the hour that is no hour
>   you know...[42]

In his 1976 essay 'Abercuawg', Thomas relates this idea of timelessness to his primitivism and his nationalism. Abercuawg, he explains, is an imaginary and ideal Welsh village that the present-day Welsh ought to be striving to recreate. He begins by telling us that

> whatever Abercuawg might be, it is a place of trees
> and fields and flowers and bright unpolluted
> streams, where the cuckoos continue to sing.[43]

and he goes on to argue that in looking for Abercuawg

> We are searching... within time, for something which
> is above time, and yet, which is ever on the verge of
> being.[44]

Like other aspects of his primitivism, this notion of time-lessness is not unique to Thomas. Lawrence writes in *Apocalypse* that

> Our idea of time as a continuity in an eternal
> straight line has crippled our consciousness cruelly.
> The pagan conception of time as moving in cycles is
> much freer...[45]

A similar argument emerges in John Berger's book *Pig Earth*. Berger is certainly not a primitivist in the same sense as Lawrence, Graves, Thomas or Ted Hughes—in fact his outlook is broadly Marxist—but he has spent a lot of time among peasants and has learnt to sympathize with their world-view. *Pig Earth* is primarily a collection of stories about the peasants of the French Alps; but Berger adds to the book a 'Historical Afterword', which is a discussion of the peasants' characteristic religious and philosophical outlook, and of their place in the modern world. He argues that

> the peasant has a cyclic view of time... Those who have a unilinear view of time cannot come to terms with the idea of cyclic time: it creates a moral vertigo since all their morality is based on cause and effect.[46]

He identifies peasant culture as a 'culture of survival'—to be contrasted with bourgeois culture, which is a 'culture of progress'—and he writes:

> Modern history begins—at different moments in different places—with the principle of progress as both the aim and the motor of history...
> Cultures of progress envisage future expansion. They are forward-looking because the future offers ever larger hopes... A culture of survival envisages the future as a sequence of repeated acts for survival. Each act pushes a thread through the eye of a needle and the thread is tradition. No overall increase is envisaged.[47]

Cultures of survival, says Berger, are characteristic of peasant life, which involves a constant struggle to force the natural world to yield up the basic necessities; whereas cultures of progress are characteristic of urban life, where citizens are offered 'comparative security, continuity, permanence'.[48]

Thus peasant existence involves a constant struggle to keep

things the same—to sustain long-established traditions—
whereas urban life involves a desire to overthrow or exploit
the existing state of affairs in order to change fundamentally
the circumstances of the individual:

> The peasant... cannot contemplate the disappearance
> of what gives meaning to everything he knows,
> which is, precisely, his will to survive. No worker is
> ever in that position, for what gives meaning to his
> life is either the revolutionary hope of transforming
> it, or money, which is received in exchange against
> his life as a wage earner, to be spent in his 'true life'
> as a consumer.[49]

Berger says that a belief in reincarnation (life repeating itself
over and over again) is characteristic of peasant societies,
whereas a belief in Paradise (life as an opportunity to earn
some great reward which is only payable in the future) is
characteristic of urban society. In this he differs from
Lawrence, who ascribes belief in progress and delayed rewards
to Judaeo-Christian philosophy rather than to any particular
set of socio-economic circumstances. But Lawrence, Berger
and Thomas all offer the cyclic view of time as an alternative
to the idea of progress, and this sense of alternative views of
time, as we shall see later, is also a feature of the poetry of Ted
Hughes, Charles Tomlinson and Seamus Heaney.

Where Berger really does differ from Lawrence, Thomas
and the other primitivists is in his refusal to dismiss or blithely
accept the material difficulties which are attendant on peasant
life:

> It must follow from what I have already said that
> nobody can reasonably argue for the preservation
> and maintenance of the traditional peasant way of
> life... As soon as one accepts that peasants are a class
> of survivors—in the sense in which I have defined
> the term—any idealisation of their way of life

becomes impossible. In a just world such a class would no longer exist.[50]

Berger's view of peasant life is untranscendent: he does not believe that it holds out the possibility of a spiritual fulfilment which would render its material hardships insignificant—a spiritual fulfilment of the sort that Thomas believes to have been experienced by Anne Griffiths, for example.

There is no Fall-myth in Berger's writing, and for this reason he never represents the peasant world as a kind of Eden. On the other hand, despite his attempt to dissociate himself from ideas of progress and millenial futures, the sentence 'In a just world such a class would no longer exist' undeniably betrays a millenial outlook. What is this 'just world', and how is it to be arrived at if not by a process of 'improvements' and 'progress'? On the one hand there are those who insist that we should be struggling to create a 'just world'; while on the other hand there are those who insist that we must go back to 'living with the cosmos' as the primitives do, and that the spiritual rewards of such a lifestyle will outweigh or transcend the inconvenience and suffering from which primitive cultures cannot free themselves. There is no need to arbitrate between the two sides of this dispute: only to point out that both world-views are equally mythical.

Berger's 'just world' is a mythical Paradise to exactly the same degree that the 'living, incarnate cosmos' of the primitivists is a mythical Eden. Our desire for escape from the difficulties that beset us in the present propels us towards either a millenial future or an Eden-like past; but to label these world-views as 'mythical' is not to dismiss them. Our fears about the present are well-founded, and our desire for escape in one direction or another will have consequences for our actions in the 'real world' of society, of politics and of economics. By drawing attention to the mythical aspects of these world-views I do not intend to belittle or attack them; only to point out that their content is not entirely rational, and that they

can only be fully understood by understanding the psychological truths which lie behind them. Primitivism cannot be
instantly disposed of by arguing that it is impractical, any
more than Marxists can be disposed of by arguing that the
Millenium will never come, or Christianity, by arguing that
Paradise is imaginary. Practicality and logic are not the only
considerations in these matters.

V

Lawrence's remark that 'The pagan concept of time as moving
in circles is much freer' than our own idea of 'a continuity in
an eternal straight line' actually relates, in *Apocalypse*, to his
discussion of the poetic style of the Revelation of St John (it
should be noted that Lawrence always refers to the Book of
Revelation by its alternative title of 'the Apocalypse'):

> To get at the Apocalypse we have to appreciate the
> mental working of the pagan thinker or poet—
> pagan thinkers were necessarily poets—who starts
> with an image, sets the image in motion, allows it to
> achieve a certain course or circuit of its own, and
> then takes up another image.[51]

The 'pagan conception of time' helps here, says Lawrence,
because

> it allows movement upwards and downwards, and
> allows for a complete change of the state of mind, at
> any moment. One cycle finished, we can drop or
> rise to another level, and be in a new world at once.[52]

To some extent these remarks help to illuminate R. S.
Thomas's poetic style, which tends to jump from one image to
another in rather the manner that Lawrence describes. This is
exemplified by the lines I have already quoted from 'The
Bush':

And in this country
of failure, the rain
falling out of a black
cloud in gold pieces there
are none to gather,
I have thought often
of the fountain of my people
that played beautifully here
once in the sun's light
like a tree undressing.[53]

The problem with these lines is that the images they contain
are difficult to relate to one another. Before Wales was a
'failure', did the 'fountain' of the Welsh people collect the
'gold pieces' that now go ungathered? If so, how? Are we
supposed to imagine a fountain with a basin full of gold coins,
or a spring being renewed by the rain? If the 'tree undressing'
is also an image for the Welsh people, how is this tree
supposed to collect a shower of 'gold pieces'? And if the
image of the fountain and the image of the 'tree undressing'
are supposed to be equivalents, how are we supposed to
imagine the fountain 'undressing'? Doesn't the image of the
fountain suggest vitality, whereas the image of a tree shedding
its leaves suggests a loss of vitality? The answer to all of
these questions is the same: that Thomas expects us to
consider his images one at a time rather than attempt to relate
them to one another in any strictly pictorial way. Each image
has its own little cycle of meaning, and they are all linked to
a central theme, which has to do with the Welsh response to
the natural environment. The experience of reading the poem
is like the experience of examining coloured beads on a necklace: the shape of the necklace as a whole is less important
than the central thread and the activity of going from one
bead to the next.

I have picked on 'The Bush' rather unfairly: many of
Thomas's poems are more conventionally pictorial. All the

same, the sensation of disjunction between one image and the next is one that will be familiar to readers of his poetry; and it tells us something about his way of deploying his images. For Thomas, each image is charged with meaning— not an allegorical meaning, but a symbolic one which may vary considerably from one poem to the next—and his use of images is therefore characterized by a concern with meaning rather than with pictorial design. Almost any poem will serve to illustrate this point: I shall refer to another one that I have already examined, namely 'Again':

> For one hour
> I have known Eden, the still place
> We hunger for. My hand lay
> Innocent; the mind was idle.
>
> Nothing has changed; the day goes on
> With its business, watching itself
> In a calm mirror. Yet I know now
> I am ready for the sly tone
> Of the serpent, ready to climb
> My branches after the same fruit.

The hand, the mind, the day, the mirror, the serpent, the branches and the fruit—all of these are primarily emblematic rather than descriptive details; they mean something, and what they mean is more important than how they look.

The hand represents human intelligence and skill, the means by which we seek to control and change our environment. The mirror represents self-awareness: but here it is the 'calm' self-awareness of the natural world, as opposed to the frustrated self-awareness of the analytical mind, which Thomas characterizes in 'The Gap' as a mirror full of empty interiors. The 'serpent', 'branches' and 'fruit', of course, all refer to the myth of Eden and the Fall; but the 'serpent' here is also rational thought, which climbs through the 'branches' of the individual's awareness in search of the 'fruit' of knowledge. There is a pictorial element here: we imagine the calmness of the day, and the corresponding inactivity of the poet; but the poem's primary function is not to build up a coherent picture. Nor, on the other hand, does it initially present us with a coherent argument. It offers us a sequence of images, and we can only come at the 'meaning' of the poem once we have interpreted these images and related their meanings to each other.

Thomas's descriptions always seem short of observed details and overburdened with symbolic significance, because he is always attempting to find his way beyond outward appearances to God. As he says in the 'Fugue for Anne Griffiths', the temptation that must be avoided is for

> the spirit to forget
> its destiny... and put on soil
> for its crown...

and the mental state which he hopes to achieve is the state of revelation in which he describes Anne Griffiths herself:

> Here for a few years
> the spirit sang on a bone bough
> at eternity's window...

The spirit sees through the appearances of this life to the eternal truth that lies beyond them. The various aspects of the natural world are beautiful because they express this eternal truth, rather than for their own sakes; and mortal life is a 'bone bough' on which we perch 'for a few years', and from which we ought to bear witness to the eternal.

In Thomas's descriptions, everything means something, and Thomas is so anxious to emphasize the meaning—to go beyond any particular set of appearances to the eternal truths that underlie them—that as his poetic style develops he gives less and less detail about the appearances of the things themselves. When Thomas mentions a tree, it might be any tree—oak, ash, sycamore, birch or horse-chestnut. It might be large or small; it might be a long way off or nearby, growing in a field or a hedgerow or a forest. By leaving all these matters unspecified, he makes it easier for himself to turn the tree into something symbolic—the tree of life, the tree of knowledge, or the tree on which Christ was crucified. At its best, his poetry gives us a kind of stripped-down, laconic, bleak, visionary grandeur; and the price he pays for the spare power of his better moments is a loss of almost all specific details. He delineates a world of symbols, and in the end this symbolic view of reality conflicts with both his Welsh Nationalism and his declared love of Nature. His often-declared allegiance to Wales and to the traditional lifestyle of the Welsh hill-farmers is undermined by the fact that his poetry works to disembody both the landscape and the people who live there. His descriptions of the natural world, likewise, are too devoid of detail to convey any real sense of aesthetic passion or rapt observation. In the work of a writer who so often insists on the importance of a proper response to Nature in general and to the Welsh landscape in particular, this sense of disembodied and undetailed symbolism must be considered a weakness.

NOTES

1. Thomas, *Collected Poems 1945–1990* (Dent, 1993), p. 470.
2. *Ibid.*, p. 474.
3. *Ibid.*, p. 339.
4. *Ibid.*, p. 474.
5. *Ibid.*, p. 474.
6. Brian Morris, 'The Topography of R. S. Thomas', reprinted in: Sandra Anstey (ed.), *Critical Writings on R. S. Thomas* (Bridgend: Poetry Wales Press, 1982), pp. 140, 142.
7. Thomas, 'The Paths Gone By', from *Selected Prose* (Bridgend: Poetry Wales Press, 1983), p. 138.
8. *Ibid.*, p. 138.
9. *Ibid.*, pp. 137–38.
10. Thomas, *Collected Poems 1945–1990*, p. 37.

11. *Ibid.*, p. 194.

12. W. Moelwyn Merchant, *R. S. Thomas* (Cardiff: University of Wales Press, 1979), p. 26.

13. Thomas, *Collected Poems 1945–1990*, p. 276.

14. Thomas, *The Echoes Return Slow* (Papermac, 1988), p. 80.

15. Thomas, *Collected Poems 1945–1990*, p. 503.

16. *Ibid.*, p. 111.

17. Thomas, *Selected Poems 1946–1968* (Newcastle upon Tyne: Bloodaxe, 1986), p. 74.

18. Thomas, *Collected Poems 1945–1990*, p. 451.

19. *Ibid.*, p. 463.

20. *Ibid.*, pp. 472–73.

21. *Ibid.*, p. 114.

22. *Ibid.*, p. 422.

23. Thomas, *Selected Poems 1946–1968*, p. 109.

24. Thomas, *Collected Poems 1945–1990*, p. 380.

25. *Ibid.*, p. 287.

26. *Ibid.*, p. 498.

27. Thomas, *The Echoes Return Slow*, p. 110.

28. *Ibid.*, p. 88.

29. Thomas, *Selected Prose*, p. 64.

30. *Ibid.*, p. 90.

31. D. H. Lawrence, *Apocalypse* (first published 1931; Penguin, 1980), p. 27.

32. Robert Graves, *The White Goddess* (1948, 1952; Faber, 1961), p. 223.

33. *Ibid.*, p. 476.

34. *Ibid.*, p. 482.

35. *Ibid.*, p. 14.

36. *Ibid.*, p. 11.

37. D. H. Lawrence, *Apocalypse*, p. 53.

38. Thomas, *Collected Poems 1945–1990*, p. 357.

39. *Ibid.*, p. 169.

40 Thomas, *Selected Poems 1946–1968*, p. 114.

41. Thomas, *Collected Poems 1945–1990*, p. 302.

42. *Ibid.*, p. 427.

43. Thomas, *Selected Prose*, p. 158.

44. *Ibid.*, p. 163.

45. D. H. Lawrence, *Apocalypse*, p. 54.

46. John Berger, *Pig Earth* (Chatto & Windus, 1985), p. 201.

47. *Ibid.*, pp. 203–04.

48. *Ibid.*, p. 206.

49. *Ibid.*, p. 205.

50. *Ibid.*, p. 211.

51. D. H. Lawrence, *Apocalypse*, p. 54.

52. *Ibid.*, p. 54.

53. Thomas, *Collected Poems 1945–1990*, p. 422.

Chapter Four
Charles Tomlinson:
'The Insistence of Things'

I

It would be true to say that Charles Tomlinson is less interested in the non-human world for its own sake than for what
it tells us about ourselves; but it would also be true to say that
for him human beings only come fully to life when they turn
to confront the non-human world that lies beyond them. His
favourite subject is neither Man nor Nature but the point at
which the two meet. The term 'Eden', as he uses it, signifies
the moment at which a human observer abandons or loses his
preconceptions, and experiences the non-human world afresh,
thus experiencing afresh his sense of self. By confronting the
non-human world in this way its observers sometimes achieve
a kind of rebirth, but they also discharge their moral responsibility to recognize their own littleness and the mystery of the
universe in which they find themselves. The fallen world, for
Tomlinson, is a world in which this responsibility has been
shirked. Yet the individual, in observing the outside world,
must never attempt to lose himself in it. Self-forgetfulness is
as morally reprehensible, to Tomlinson, as self-obsession. We
should be as fully aware of the non-human world as possible,
but we should always remain separate from it. It is this
insistence on separateness and responsibility that marks
Tomlinson as a rationalist rather than a primitivist.

One of the most striking aspects of Tomlinson's descriptive
style is the scrupulousness with which he holds himself in
check. He always tries to do full justice both to his own

limitations as a fallible observer, and to the ambiguity and inscrutability of whatever he is trying to describe. Unlike D. H. Lawrence, R. S. Thomas, Ted Hughes and the other primitivist writers, who recommend a subjective and imaginative response to the external world rather than a scientifically detached one, Tomlinson distrusts the distortions to which an indisciplined and individualistic view of things can give rise. He draws attention to this aspect of his aesthetic philosophy in 'The Poet as Painter', the essay with which he introduces *Eden*, a collection of poems and graphics published in 1985:

> I wrote a poem called 'Cézanne at Aix', a kind of manifesto poem where I wanted my poetry to take its ethic of perception from Cézanne, an ethic distrustful of the drama of personality of which Romantic art had made so much, an ethic where, by trusting to sensation, we enter being, and experience its primal fullness on terms other than those we dictate.[1]

Tomlinson sees Cézanne as an artist who was 'distrustful of the drama of personality of which Romantic art had made so much', and who was therefore prepared to experience the non-human world in terms of its otherness, 'terms other than those we dictate'. The 'manifesto poem' to which Tomlinson refers here, 'Cézanne at Aix', comes from the 1958 collection, and reads as follows:

> And the mountain: each day
> Immobile like fruit. Unlike, also
> —Because irreducible, because
> Neither a component of the delicious
> And therefore questionable,
> Nor distracted (as the sitter)
> By his own pose and, therefore,
> Doubly to be questioned: it is not
> Posed. It is. Untaught

Unalterable, a stone bridgehead
To that which is tangible
Because unfelt before. There
In its weathered weight
Its silence silences, a presence
Which does not present itself.[2]

The poem refers to the innumerable paintings of Mt Sainte
Victoire produced by Cézanne during his time at Aix (where
he died in 1906). Cézanne also painted numerous portraits
and still-lives with fruit, of course, but the mountain became a
particular obsession of his in his later years, and Tomlinson's
poem suggests that this was because it was more completely
non-human and mysterious than any of Cézanne's other
subjects. Fruit is 'questionable' because it is 'a component of
the delicious'—we can enjoy it, consume it, and thus meet it
on our own terms. Human sitters are 'doubly to be questioned', firstly because, like the fruit, they are easily met
and understood on our own terms, and secondly because the
sitter is aware that he is being observed, and thus becomes
'distracted.../By his own pose'. The mountain, on the other
hand, 'is not/Posed'—it is 'a presence/Which does not present
itself'—'It *is*'. What the artist must come to terms with is the
fact that the mountain is unconscious of him. It cannot be
consumed by him: its presence cannot be translated into the
human idiom. Instead, it offers the human observer a glimpse
of the mystery of the non-human world—it is 'a stone bridge-
head/To that which is tangible/Because unfelt before'. The
fact that this world is new, 'unfelt before', because it has not
been rendered-down into human terms, is what makes it
'tangible' and therefore valuable. By facing up to this mystery,
the human observer is able to experience the external world as
something other than an extension of himself.

Despite its title, 'Cézanne at Aix' tells us very little about
Cézanne himself. There is no attempt to portray him in the
sense of describing how he looks or behaves. He exists in

the poem only as an observer attempting to come to terms
with the mystery of the mountain. Yet by the same token, the
mountain exists in the poem only as the non-human object on
which Cézanne chooses to fasten his attention. Each of them
fixes the other in place, and the poem is about neither one nor
the other, but the moment of encounter between the two.

Cézanne's role in this poem—as an anonymous observer,
only brought to our attention by virtue of his relationship to
the thing observed—is the equivalent of the poetic voice or
narrative persona which Tomlinson himself often adopts elsewhere. His descriptions generally have an air of fascinated
detachment: he holds his ego in check to the point where it
becomes invisible. 'In March', a poem from his 1974 collection *The Way In*, exemplifies this point:

> These dry, bright winter days,
>   When the crow's colour takes to itself
> Such gloss, the shadows from the hedge
>   Ink-stain half way across
> The road to where a jagged blade
>   Of light eats into them: light's guarded frontier
> Is glittering everywhere, everywhere held
>   Back by naked branchwork, dark
> Fissurings along the creviced walls,
>   Shade side of barn and house, of half-cut stack
> Strawing the ground, in its own despite
>   With flecks of pallid gold, allies to light:
> And over it all, a chord of glowing black
>   A shining, flying shadow, the crow is climbing.[3]

Tomlinson makes no attempt to take us beyond the surface
appearances of this scene to show us its inner life or inner
meaning, as a primitivist poet might. We remain detached
from the non-human world, and the non-human world
remains detached from us; but this sense of detachment is
not dramatized either, as Larkin dramatizes it when he refers
to himself as an 'indigestible sterility',[4] or when he draws

attention to the emptiness of the natural world by exclaiming 'Such attics cleared of me! Such absences!'[5]

Tomlinson's comparative unwillingness to lay hold of the external appearances he describes and make them his own—by offering a personal interpretation of them or by adopting a dramatized stance towards them—is exemplified by the fact that the whole poem is one long 'sentence' without a main verb. The opening phrase, 'These dry, bright winter days', seems to promise an opinionated conclusion—that these are the most beautiful days of the year, or that they always remind the poet of his youth, or something of the sort. Tomlinson seems to be setting out to say something definite about them, but he never actually does so. He interprets what he describes, of course, and he shapes and patterns his observations. He describes the whole scene in terms of a conflict between light and dark, using military terms throughout—'light's guarded frontier', 'held/Back' and 'allies to light'—until at the end of the poem he resolves and transcends the conflict (as well as bringing the poem full circle) by reintroducing the crow, whose 'gloss' unites light and dark in 'a chord of glowing black/A shining, flying shadow'.

This sequence of images is an artistic device which enables Tomlinson to pull his various observations together into a pattern, and thus to shape them into a poem: but it does not amount to a full-blooded interpretation of what is being described. We cannot decode it into an abstract 'message' or 'meaning'. This is not to say that the poem is an unmeditated record of raw sensations: Tomlinson leaves us in no doubt that he has carefully reordered his observations into a pattern, and in this sense he makes no attempt to conceal his presence, or the intelligence and skill with which he has worked on his materials. But although he makes a pattern out of them, he does not 'make sense' of them for us. He tries to allow them their otherness. As in the poem about Cézanne, the mystery of the non-human world and the searching, pattern-making intelligence of the artist are poised against one another, and the poem is an attempt to capture the drama of their encounter.

Perhaps this un-Romantic attitude towards the non-human world is more responsible than any other factor for Tomlinson's comparative neglect by British critics and the British poetry-reading public. He is still a much less popular and well-known poet than he seems to deserve in terms of the technical excellence and general intelligibility of his poems; but his way of describing the non-human world, which has always been one of his most important subjects, involves an austerity, a detachment and an intellectual rigour that may strike readers as dry and chilly compared with the unabashed imaginative sympathy and outright symbolism of a primitivist poet such as Ted Hughes, or the irony and pathos of a more romantic rationalist such as Philip Larkin. But Tomlinson's comparative restraint in these respects—his preference for aesthetic reactions to the non-human world, rather than emotional and personal ones—is, as we shall see, fundamental to many aspects of his poetic style.

II

When he was a student of English literature at Cambridge University, one of Tomlinson's supervisors was the poet and critic Donald Davie, who was later to become a firm friend and a great champion of Tomlinson's verse. As Blake Morrison has pointed out in his book *The Movement*, both Davie and Tomlinson seem to have been influenced at about this time by *I and Thou*, a short work by the German–Jewish religious philosopher Martin Buber.[6] In fact, Buber's aesthetic philosophy, as expressed in *I and Thou*, resembles Tomlinson's in several respects. He describes the act of creation, for example, as follows:

> This is the eternal source of art: a man is faced by a
> form which desires to be made through him into a
> work. This form is no offspring of his soul, but is an
> appearance which steps up to it and demands of it
> the effective power. The man is concerned with an
> act of his being. If he carries it through, if he speaks
> the primary word out of his being to the form which
> appears, then the effective power streams out, and
> the work arises.[7]

According to Buber, a work of art represents an artist's
attempt to recognize a 'form' or aspect of the external world,
whilst also recognizing that this 'form' is 'no offspring of his
soul'.

Artists must confront the external world (Buber is not
necessarily talking about the non-human world) in all its
otherness; and the way they do this is to speak 'the primary
word', which is 'Thou'. If they fail, they will speak the other
word, which is 'It': they will reduce the 'form' which
confronts them to a thing they can manipulate, or an idea they
can fit into a system of ideas, or a symbol they can use to
denote something else. In this way they will have failed to
achieve a proper relationship with what lies beyond them; and
instead of reaching outwards, they will have turned back on
themselves. The artist's work, therefore, is to achieve a proper
relationship with the external world—and Buber goes on to
argue that this is also the task of any human being who wishes
to achieve spiritual enlightenment. 'In the beginning is relation', he claims.[8] He also insists that such 'relation' cannot be
achieved by dissolving the self:

> The primal condition of salvation is undivided
> confrontation of the undivided mystery.[9]

And later on, Buber says:

> All doctrine of absorption is based on the colossal
> illusion of the human spirit that is bent back on

itself, that spirit exists in man. Actually spirit exists
with man as starting-point—between man and that
which is not man.[10]

Tomlinson's insistence that the self must achieve a poised
relationship with the not-self closely resembles these arguments of Buber's; as does his insistence that the self must not
be dissolved or 'violated'. As he writes in his 1981 book *Some
Americans*:

My own basic theme [is] that one does not need to
go beyond sense experience to some mythic union,
that the 'I' can only be responsible in relationship
and not by dissolving itself away into ecstasy or the
Oversoul.[11]

These arguments would be almost indistinguishable from
Buber's, were it not that Tomlinson introduces a moral
concern of his own, exemplified by his assertion in the lines
above that 'the "I" can only be responsible in relationship'.
For Tomlinson, the preservation of the self is desirable not
only for the sake of achieving spiritual enlightenment, but also
because abandonment of self is an abandonment of moral
responsibility. He sees the achievement of a proper relationship with the external world as a moral task with consequences for society at large as well as for the individual. In
this, he differs from Buber, who insists that the 'I–Thou' relationship is purely spiritual, and cannot be transferred into the
workaday world: 'It does not help to sustain you in life, it only
helps you to glimpse eternity.'[12] So whereas Buber is unwilling
to see his 'I–Thou' relationship as the basis of a social order or
a way of life, Tomlinson believes that the struggle to achieve a
proper relationship with the external world has social implications; and as a result he has written a number of poems which
describe various ways of life in terms of whether or not they
achieve this relationship successfully.

In his early poetry, as Michael Edwards has noted,

Tomlinson's moral and social concerns express themselves in the form of several 'poems on great houses'.[13] *Seeing is Believing* (1958) includes poems entitled 'The Mausoleum', 'At Holwell Farm' and 'On the Hall at Stowey'; and *A Peopled Landscape* (1963) includes 'Return to Hinton', 'The Farmer's Wife: at Foston's Ash', 'Harvest Festival: at Ozleworth' and 'The Chestnut Avenue: at Alton House'. These are not all poems about stately homes, but they all use ancient buildings as emblems of traditional ways of life, in which the human and non-human worlds are properly balanced. Such ways of life are now being threatened or abandoned by the modern world, which regards Nature as a mere thing to be exploited.

'On the Hall at Stowey' is typical: it describes a deserted farmhouse, the architecture of which expresses the productive relationship that once existed between the farmers and their lands:

> Five centuries—here were (at the least) five—
> In linked love, eager excrescence
> Where the door, arched, crowned with acanthus,
> Aimed at a civil elegance, but hit
> This sturdier compromise, neither Greek, Gothic
> Nor Strawberry, clumped from the arching-point
> And swathing down, like a fist of wheat,
> The unconscious emblem of the house's worth.[14]

The terms 'linked love' and 'compromise' both suggest that the house and the way of life it represents have been shaped by the developing relationship between the inhabitants and their non-human environment, rather than by mere human greed or willpower. The architecture of the house aims at 'civil elegance'—an elegance which is purely human, detached from an awareness of the natural world—but achieves instead a 'sturdier compromise', epitomized by the carvings around the door, 'like a fist of wheat/The unconscious emblem of the house's worth'. Tomlinson evidently does not value a 'civil elegance' which expresses dissociation from Nature; but nor, he goes on to make it clear, does he value a natural world emptied of any human influence:

> Five centuries. And we? What we had not
>   Made ugly, we had laid waste—
> Left (I should say) the office to nature
>   Whose blind battery, best fitted to perform it
> Outdoes us...

The natural world, unleavened by any human presence, amounts to a 'blind battery' that produces a mere 'waste'. Nature must be balanced and ordered by humanity if it is to be of value. This idea parallels the view of art which Tomlinson expresses elsewhere. In another poem from *Seeing is Believing* entitled 'A Meditation on John Constable', for example, he writes that 'Art/Is complete when it is human'.[15] Just as painters such as Constable and Cézanne complete the natural world, bring it to life and make it valuable in human terms by painting it, so the inhabitants of the hall at Stowey completed their estate and brought it to life by farming it.

Tomlinson's descriptions of this desirable 'compromise' between Man and Nature are not confined to poems about big houses, however. In 'Arizona Desert', from *American Scenes and Other Poems* (1966), he finds the same 'compromise' being lived out among the mud huts of the Hopi Indians:

> Villages
> from mud and stone
> parch back
> to the dust they humanize
> and mean
> marriage, a loving lease
> on sand, sun, rock...[16]

The 'loving lease' here is the same as the 'linked love' Tomlinson discovered at Stowey. The Hopi villagers 'humanize' the dust of the desert they inhabit; they build huts from it, and in the course of time it claims the huts back.

The word 'dust', by evoking the phrase 'dust to dust', reminds us that eventually the villagers will themselves be reclaimed by the desert in the same way as their huts: and the word 'lease' is another gentle reminder of human impermanence. Tomlinson is suggesting that the Hopi's 'loving lease' expresses not only their love of the land but also their awareness of the fact that it will outlast them.

The same theme is developed by the next poem in the collection, 'A Death in the Desert', also about the Hopi:

> There are no crosses
> on the Hopi graves. They lie
> shallowly
> under a scattering
> of small boulders. The sky
> over the desert
> with its sand-grain stars
> and the immense equality
> between
> desert and desert sky,
> seem
> a scope and ritual
> enough to stem
> death and be its equal.[17]

The fact that the Hopi do not put crosses on their graves expresses their acceptance of mortality. Sooner than lie beneath a monument which declares his hope of eternal life, and which is itself a vain attempt to preserve his individuality, the Hopi villager is content to be reclaimed by the landscape. It is in the landscape itself that his hope of permanence lies; the desert is big enough 'to stem/death and be its equal', and as long as the Hopi continue to inhabit the desert, they share in its permanence.

Tomlinson has written a number of poems about the native peoples, the Indians, of both North and South America. Two of his literary antecedents in this area are D. H. Lawrence and

William Carlos Williams, who both also showed great interest in the Indians; and the free-verse of his poems on these subjects indicates that he is consciously following the modernist tradition to which Lawrence and Williams both belonged—whereas the more formal verse of 'On the Hall at Stowey' and similar poems shows an awareness of the British 'great house' tradition stretching from the Elizabethans down to W. B. Yeats. But despite these stylistic obeisances, Tomlinson's view of the Indians is finally quite different from the views of Lawrence and Williams, because he does not share their primitivism. Williams, for example, in his book *In the American Grain*, writes of the South American Indians in the following terms:

> It was in these chapels that the religious practices took place which so shocked the Christians. Here it was that the tribe's deep feeling for a reality that stems back into the permanence of remote origins had its firm hold. It was the earthward thrust of their logic; blood and earth; the realization of their primal and continuous identity with the ground itself, where everything is fixed in darkness... The earth is black and it is there... The figures of the idols themselves were of extra-human size and composed, significantly, of a paste of seeds and leguminous plants, commonly used for food, ground and mixed together and kneaded with human blood, the whole when completed being consecrated with a bath of blood from the heart of a living victim.[18]

Williams is claiming here that ancient Indian culture expressed a closeness with the non-human world that the European invaders had lost, and that this was the reason why the 'religious practices' of the Indians 'so shocked the Christians'. He implies that the Christians were wrong to be horrified—or that their horror was symptomatic of the modern narrowness of their outlook.

Because the Indians identified with 'the ground itself', they did not think of themselves as individuals in the Western sense, and the shocking rituals and human sacrifices which they performed on one another were not shocking from their own point of view. Williams is striving to define a state of collective consciousness in which the sufferings of the individual cease to matter, because each individual sees himself as an expendable expression of a universal life-force, which is here referred to as 'the ground itself'. The crucial word in the passage is 'identity', when Williams speaks of the Indians' 'primal and continuous identity with the ground itself'. In order to assume such an 'identity' with the earth, the tribesmen must abandon at least some of their awareness of themselves as human individuals. For this reason, Tomlinson would never use the word 'identity' in such a way and in such a context. For him, the self must always be fully self-aware. It must never assume 'identity' with the not-self; it must always be poised against it, going out to meet it but never surrendering to it. This sense of poised relationship is what he expresses in his poems about the Hopi and other Indians. The dignity of the Hopi in 'A Death in the Desert' arises from the fact that they are able to accept the inevitability of death without either promising themselves an afterlife (as the Christians do with their cross-marked graves) or abandoning their sense of themselves as individuals and seeking safety in 'darkness'. They are rational, self-aware people, calmly living in the light of day and accepting the realities of the situation in which they find themselves.

As Donald Davie said in his review of *Seeing is Believing*, for Tomlinson 'the irreducible Otherness of the non-human world, its Presence in the sense of being present, its being bodied against the senses' is 'the irreplaceable first principle of all sanity and morality'.[19] From this first principle arises a chastening sense of our limitations, including our mortality. Tomlinson values this sense of limitation as much as Larkin does, and in some ways he goes further. He links the desire to escape our human limitations, and to deny or transcend the empirical realities of sense-experience, with political extremism.

'Prometheus', a long poem from *The Way of a World* (1969), exemplifies this link between sensory transcendence and political irresponsibility. The poem describes a radio-broadcast of the composer Scriabin's tone-poem, also called 'Prometheus'. While the piece is being broadcast, a thunderstorm is taking place outside, and the destructive violence of the storm symbolizes the destructive violence of the music:

> Summer thunder darkens, and its climbing
> Cumulae, disowning our scale in the zenith,
> Electrify this music: the evening is falling apart.
> Castles-in-air; on earth: green, livid fire.[20]

The phrases 'disowning our scale' and 'castles-in-air' are both indications that Scriabin's music is an attempt to defy or transcend everyday reality: and a third phrase, 'the evening is falling apart', makes clear Tomlinson's feeling that to attempt such transcendence is to unleash the forces of destruction. He goes on to link Scriabin's music with such events as the Russian Revolution:

> I cannot hear such music for its consequence:
> Each sense was to have been reborn
> Out of a storm of perfumes and light
> To a white world, an in-the-beginning.
>
> In the beginning, the strong man reigns...

Partly, of course, Tomlinson is simply arguing that if we abandon all established social forms for the sake of 'a white world, an in-the-beginning', we will create a state of chaos in which 'the strong man reigns'. But there is more to his argument than simple conservatism: he is also objecting to the idea that 'Each sense was to have been reborn'—that the world as we discover it through our senses is somehow not enough, and must therefore be transcended or swept away.

The thunderstorm, that symbolizes both Scriabin's music and the revolutionary violence with which Tomlinson associates it, is also the means by which he contains and controls them. Since a thunderstorm belongs to the world of everyday perceptions, we are confident that its violence, however frightening it may be, is not apocalyptic. Accordingly, when the thunderstorm ends, the poem itself concludes by reasserting the presence of the unapocalyptic world, which imposes itself again on the senses of the individual:

> Hard edges of the houses press
>> On the after-music senses, and refuse to burn,
> Where an ice-cream van circulates the estate
>> Playing Greensleeves, and at the city's
> Stale new frontier even ugliness
>> Rules with the cruel mercy of solidities.

Tomlinson is fully aware that the everyday world has its drawbacks, as the oxymorons 'stale new' and 'cruel mercy' indicate. The ice-cream van playing 'Greensleeves' suggests both the loss of a rural environment and the commercialized vapidity of what remains of our rural traditions. All the same, he is grateful that the houses 'refuse to burn'.

His acceptance of a cut-price suburban present in some ways resembles Larkin's acceptance of the same thing in 'The Whitsun Weddings'; but the difference is that Larkin makes his present-day suburbia acceptable by transforming it into an image of timeless pastoral fertility ('postal districts packed like squares of wheat'), whereas Tomlinson's reconciliation with the contemporary British landscape arises from his awareness of international history. He accepts the ugly solidity of 'the city's/Stale new frontier' because it bespeaks a culture which has resisted the revolutionary dramas of Eastern Europe. This sense of international history and its lessons is one example of the strong rational element in Tomlinson's poetry, which is in turn an aspect of his poised, self-aware stance with respect to the external world. He is not a poet who abandons himself to his sensations: he feels them vividly, but he also thinks about them. He deduces things from them and sets them in a rational context. Not only does he experience 'The hard edges of the houses' in terms of the impression they make on his senses; he also experiences them in terms of their historical significance. His ability to do so arises from his belief that 'the "I" can only be responsible in relationship and not by dissolving itself away'. It must therefore be self-aware; and full self-awareness means rational thought.

Another indication of Tomlinson's approval of rational thought is the fact that he does not share the dislike of science and analytical logic which is expressed by primitivist poets such as R. S. Thomas and Ted Hughes. In his Introduction to the critical anthology on Marianne Moore which he edited in 1969, Tomlinson praises Moore as 'the kind of poet for whom there is no war between science and poetry, and for whom fact has its proper plenitude'.[21] For Tomlinson, science and analytical thought are simply extensions of the rational self-awareness which individuals must maintain if they are to achieve a proper relationship with the external world. The evils of modern life and the ugliness of urban existence do not, according to Tomlinson, arise from the triumph of analytical thought and technology, but from Man's misuse of those tools. Instead of exploring and responding to Nature we are inclined to ignore and subdue her. Science and technology have thus become a means of imposing our will on her, of reducing her to the narrow shapes of our preconceptions and desires; and the ugliness of most modern urban environments is the result. Technology and science themselves, Tomlinson would argue, are not to blame for this ugliness. The true culprit is not Man's capacity for rational thought but his inclination towards mental laziness and self-conceit.

III

Tomlinson has often expressed or demonstrated his sympathy with the Modernist movement and his taste for Modernist experimentation, but his rationalism limits the extent to which he is able to indulge these feelings. His observations of the non-human world, vivid as they are, are almost always presented to us in an ordered and intelligible manner. They are set within a continuum of rational thought, and this continuum itself is rendered orderly and accessible through his adherence to the conventions of normal grammar and syntax. This adherence is not automatic: 'In March', which I examined above, is a single 'sentence' with no main verb, and this departure from the syntactical norm expresses a decision not to offer a rational interpretation of the experiences described, but to order them into an aesthetic pattern instead. But 'In March' remains grammatically orderly in all other respects; the details of the description are not jumbled together in an attempt to enact the way in which they flash upon the senses; they are presented to us in a carefully-structured manner, and the framework of this structure is the syntax of the poem.

Other verses by Tomlinson are more freely written, but the vast majority adhere to the norms of rational syntax. In this respect, Tomlinson may have been influenced by the ideas of his old tutor Donald Davie. In his book, *Purity of Diction in English Verse*, Davie declares:

> it is impossible not to trace a connection between the laws of syntax and the laws of society, between bodies of usage in speech and in social life, between tearing a word from its context and choosing a leader out of the ruck. One could almost say... that to dislocate syntax in poetry is to threaten the rule of law in the civilised community.[22]

Davie argues in his book that there is a connection between

Ezra Pound's abandonment of conventional syntax and his eventual support for Mussolini and Fascism. His argument, in fact, parallels what Tomlinson has to say about Scriabin in 'Prometheus'. Davie, like Tomlinson, has expressed his admiration for Modernism elsewhere; but both writers are obviously concerned that experimentation should not become a means of dismissing or attacking ordinary, orderly, familiar experiences; and for both of them, this concern is fundamentally a moral one. In their view, we owe it to ourselves and our world to face everyday life responsibly, instead of trying to transcend or destroy it. Modernism is valuable when it makes things fresh for us by representing them in new ways; but not when the appetite for newness inspires—or feeds—an impatience with the limitations of mundane sensory experience.

Tomlinson has written 'experimental' verse himself, but it mostly follows innovations first made by other writers, and his *oeuvre* as a whole does not leave one with the impression that he is primarily an 'experimental' writer. On the whole he is scrupulous rather than adventurous. His characteristic style of writing is certainly far less abrupt and exclamatory, his diction far less colloquial, his descriptions more obviously-wrought and craftsmanlike, than is the case with primitivists such as D. H. Lawrence and Ted Hughes, or even with the Modernists he admires, such as William Carlos Williams and Ezra Pound. But his thoughtful, self-restrained manner has strengths of its own. It seems particularly well-suited to the task of examining contradictions and ironies—for example, when assessing the implications of Man's impact on his environment. 'Above Carrara', from *The Flood* (1981) illustrates this point:

> Climbing to Colonnata past ravines
>   Squared by the quarryman, geometric gulfs
> Stepping the steep, the wire and gear
>   Men use to pare a mountain: climbing

With the eye the absences where green should be,
    The annihilating scree, the dirty snow
Of marble, at last we gained a level
    In the barren flat of a piazza, leaned
And drank from the fountain there a jet
    As cold as tunneled rock. The place—
Plane above plane and block on block—
    Invited us to climb once more
And, cooled now, so we did
    Deep between church- and house-wall,
Up by a shadowed stairway to emerge
    Where the village ended. As we looked back then
The whole place seemed a quarry for living in,
    And between the acts of quarrying and building
To set a frontier a nominal petty thing,
    While, far below, water that cooled our thirst
Dyed to a meal now, a sawdust flow,
    Poured down to slake those blades
Slicing inching the luminous mass away
    Above Carrara...[23]

The process by which we destroy the natural landscape,
observes Tomlinson, is often also the process by which we
build and preserve a way of life. The climbers' first reaction to
the activities of the quarrymen is one of disgust at the damage
they are doing to the mountain: 'the absences where green
should be,/The annihilating scree, the dirty snow/Of marble'.
But when they reach the village above the quarries they drink
from a fountain in the piazza, and the fact that the refreshing
water is 'As cold as tunneled rock' reminds them that foun-
tains and villages would not exist without Man's determination to change his environment to suit himself.

The destructive act of quarrying and the creative act of
building both arise from this same human characteristic.
Having realized this, they arrive at a new impression of the
mountainside:

> As we looked back then
> The whole place seemed a quarry for living in,
> And between the acts of quarrying and building
> To set a frontier, a nominal petty thing...

Yet the water that cooled their thirst is the same water that cools the blades at work in the quarry. The final note of the poem is ominous:

> those blades
> Slicing inching the luminous mass away
> Above Carrara...

'Luminous mass' reminds us of the beauty of the mountain, encouraging us to regret its destruction. 'Slicing inching' evokes the gradualness of the destructive process—the stone is pared away so slowly that there always seems to be plenty of mountain left—but one day, nevertheless, it will all be gone. The poem does not arrive at a conclusion. Tomlinson cannot help reacting against the destruction of the mountain; yet neither can he wish that the village and the fountain had never been built. He is able to give both of these reactions their full weight because his perceptions of the landscape at Carrara are set within a continuum of contemplation and rational thought. But 'Above Carrara' also illustrates another characteristic feature of Tomlinson's style: his *penchant* for including various apparently contradictory viewpoints in his poems and playing them off against one another. In this way he forces the reader to look beyond the poem in order to find his own answers to the dilemmas it poses; and he thus brings the poem's status as an artefact to the reader's attention, along with the limitations which that status implies.

Michael Kirkham, in his essay 'An Agnostic's Grace',[24] has drawn attention to Tomlinson's use of 'fragmentation', as he calls it. So far as I am aware, however, no critic has yet connected Tomlinson's interest in this kind of fragmentation with his interest in Modernist painting. In his book *Poetry and*

Metamorphosis, for example, Tomlinson cites Braque's preference for a metamorphic—rather than metaphorical—descriptive technique. Instead of substituting a single image for the real object he was portraying, Tomlinson argues, Braque fragmented the image to suggest not one coherent response but many possible ones, throwing more emphasis onto the medium of portrayal and the process of metamorphosis by which the object finds its way into that medium. 'In both visual and literary art, the notions of fragmentation and metamorphosis travel together', writes Tomlinson, adding that:

> by realistically imitating the appearance of an object, by letting your imitation stand in place of that object, you are denying the creative mind its full plastic power. By metamorphosis, as distinct from metaphor in Braque's sense, the mind could transform that object into a less predictable, more variously faceted image... By the twentieth century metamorphosis has become a primary component of style itself.[25]

The unreconciled viewpoints which sometimes feature in Tomlinson's poetic descriptions represent his attempt to find a poetic equivalent to the fragmentation which appears in Modernist paintings from Cézanne to Cubism.

Tomlinson wants to avoid presenting the reader with a fixed interpretation of a perceptual experience, an interpretation which can be accepted as a substitute for the experience itself. As a result (as Michael Kirkham points out in the essay mentioned above) his poetry has taken more and more delight in uncertainty as it has developed: uncertainties of interpretation, and uncertainties of perception too. In some of his later verses, illusions are just as important as reality. One example of this is 'Mushrooms' from *The Shaft* (1978). The poem is about mushroom-picking; but it is also about the way in which the human eye, straining to identify mushrooms, will pick out and be fooled by all sorts of other things that are only slightly mushroom-like in appearance:

> Eyeing the grass for mushrooms, you will find
> A stone or stain, a dandelion puff
> Deceive your eyes—their colour is enough
> To plump the image out to mushroom size...[26]

Rather than being irritated by these illusions, says Tomlinson, we ought to value them, because they challenge our idea that there is a single 'true' interpretation of our perceptions. They take us beyond the illusion of certainty, and thus refresh our awareness of the mystery and otherness of the non-human world:

>   a resemblance, too,
> Is real and all its likes and links stay true
> To the weft of seeing. You, to begin with,
> May be taken in, taken beyond, that is,
> This place of chiaroscuro that seemed clear,
> For realer than a myth of clarities
> Are the meanings that you read and are not there...

Despite the strong elements of rationality and interpretation in Tomlinson's poetry, he is aware of the dangers of abstract thought. There is a point at which such thought ceases to respond to the promptings of new sensory perceptions and begins to impose itself upon them instead. An interpretation moves from the realm of speculation to the realm of certainty, becomes fixed rather than fluid, and makes itself too important to be discarded or reconsidered in the light of new evidence. At that point, the individual begins to construct a 'myth of clarities' which alters his perceptions of the external world, turning it from a 'place of chiaroscuro' into one that seems 'clear'. He is no longer seeing the external world itself: he is seeing his own interpretation of it, which is more settled and therefore more comfortable. When this happens, the external world seems to lose its power to threaten him, but it also loses its power to refresh him. He is like the painter who, 'by realistically imitating the appearance of an object, by letting [his] imitation stand in place of that object', is 'denying the creative mind its full plastic power'.

Tomlinson values resemblances and deceptions because they call our attention to those parts of 'the weft of seeing' that we usually prefer to ignore. They remind us that the world is a 'place of chiaroscuro' which will not yield up a single pattern of settled meanings. Objectively viewed, it yields instead 'the meanings that you read and are not there'—interpretations which can never become cast-iron certainties. This does not mean that in Tomlinson's view we should shrink from the task of interpretation altogether: to do so would be to place ourselves at the mercy of our sensory perceptions, which would constitute a retreat from proper self-awareness. It is our moral responsibility to interpret what we observe; but it is also our moral responsibility to realize the limitations of our own thought-processes, to constantly re-examine the external world, and to constantly re-evaluate our interpretations in the light of new experiences.

The natural world is particularly worthy of our attention because, like Cézanne's mountain, it is 'not/Posed'. It will not strike an attitude in accordance with our ideas about how it ought to look. Instead, it insists on being itself, always changing, always surprising, and always bigger than our attempts to make sense of it. As Tomlinson says in his prose-poem 'The Insistence of Things', from his 1974 collection *The Way In*:

> At the edges of conversations, uncompleting all acts
> of thought, looms the insistence of things which,
> waiting on our recognition, face us with our own
> death, for they are so completely what we are not.
> And thus we go on trying to read them, as if they
> were signs, or the embodied messages of oracles.[27]

The man-made world is less valuable than Nature in artistic

terms because it is less 'completely what we are not'. It is at its best when—like the Hall at Stowey or the huts of the Hopi Indians—it seems to express what Martin Buber would term an 'I–Thou' relationship with the non-human world: a relationship in which human limitations are accepted, and the mystery of the non-human world is recognized. But it is at its worst when it seems to express what Buber would term an 'I–It' relationship with Nature, dominating and exploiting her without making any attempt to recognize or come to terms with her mystery.

Increasingly, the modern, man-made environment expresses an 'I–It' relationship with the non-human world; and this means, according to Tomlinson, that it discourages us from questioning our preconceptions, from seeing the external world afresh and thus renewing our self-awareness. He expresses his sense of the mental staleness engendered by the urban environment by invoking his own interpretation of the Fall-myth: in his essay 'The Poet as Painter' he speaks of 'the tragic fall from plenitude in our own urban universe'.[28] He believes that Man should continually seek to test and refresh himself by confronting those things which 'face us with our own death, for they are so completely what we are not'. The moments when this confrontation is successfully achieved are what Tomlinson calls Eden—but the state in which such a confrontation goes unattempted, and the self seeks protection from the not-self by turning away or by reinterpreting it on its own terms, is Tomlinson's idea of the fallen world.

IV

Tomlinson often displays a more detailed knowledge of history than either Philip Larkin or R. S. Thomas. 'Prometheus' is one example of this historical awareness: but he has also written poems about the assassinations of Marat and

Trotsky, about the industrial history of the Midlands, and about the politics of modern Italy. Yet a feeling of timelessness is equally important to his poetry, and his attempts to represent the Eden-state, the moment of 'undivided confrontation of undivided mystery', suggest an escape from the usual human sense of time. When individuals confront the non-human world as it should be confronted, they cease to mourn the loss of the past or to plan their way into the future. Instead, their whole consciousness is filled with awareness of the present. As Buber puts it,

> The real, filled present, exists only in so far as actual presentness, meeting, and relation exist. The present arises only in virtue of the fact that *Thou* becomes present... The world of *Thou* obliges us to live in this present and thus sets us free from the past and the future... In so far as man rests satsified with the things that he experiences and uses, he lives in the past, and his moment has no present content. He has nothing but objects... True beings are lived in the present, the life of objects is in the past.[29]

In Tomlinson's poetry, these ideas manifest themselves as a feeling that we should pay proper attention to the here-and-now, instead of trampling across the present as quickly as possible in an attempt to catch up with some desired goal in the future. One poem on this theme is 'The Barometer', from the 1963 collection *A Peopled Landscape*:

> It runs ahead. And now
> Like all who anticipate
> Must wait. Rain was what
> Peremptorily it said and
> Rain there is none. The air
> As still as it, has dimmed
> But not with drops, nor with
> That sudden progress—when

All that is not black is green—
From intensity to purity. Rain
The repetitive, unmoving finger
Still insists, the name
With numerical corroboration under
Its arrow index. The storm
Hides in the stormhead still
That, heaping-over, spreads
And smokes through the zenith, then
Yields to a sordid-white
Identical image of itself
That climbs, collapsing as before.
The glass door reveals
The figured face, the one
Certainty in all these shifts
Of misty imponderables, pale
Seeping pervasions of each tone,
And the baleful finger
Balances, does not record them.[30]

The barometer stands for the simplification of events that
occurs when we are interested only in outcomes and not in
processes. Once we have fixed our minds on an outcome, as
the barometer fixes its needle on 'rain', everything that inter-
venes and delays its arrival is relegated to the status of a
nuisance and a distraction.

It runs ahead. And now
Like all who anticipate
Must wait.

To run ahead like the barometer is to condemn yourself to
wait. The barometer 'does not record' all the 'misty imponderables' that precede the rain's arrival, because it deals only in
'certainty'.

As is often the case in Tomlinson's poetry, we are presented
with the idea that fresh perception equates with uncertainty or

danger, whereas certainty equates with mental stasis. The natural world, which is always changing and always inviting us to look at it afresh, frees Man from the tyranny of his own ideas; but it can also free him from the tyranny of time. Time seen as a series of objectives with waiting-spaces in between seems short; but time seen as a continuous present, in which the natural world is constantly renewing itself and thus constantly renewing our sense of life, seems huge. So despite the fact that one function of the natural world in Tomlinson's poetry—as in Larkin's—is to remind us of our human limitations, including our mortality, it also offers a compensation for the certainty of death, by expanding our lives into a seemingly endless sequence of present moments crammed with new sensations and thus with value.

A sense of complete immersion in the present moment is one aspect of the state of mind that Tomlinson refers to as Eden. This is complemented by a sense that the external world is being seen afresh, without preconceptions, as if for the first time. But the gift of fresh perception cannot be conjured up at will. To quote Martin Buber again:

> The world which appears to you in this way is unreliable... you cannot hold it to its word... it comes even when it is not summoned, and vanishes even when it is tightly held.[31]

Tomlinson's Eden is similarly elusive. This is only to be expected: since it often results from sudden disruptions, encounters with the unforeseen, and the overturning of preconceptions, it would be a contradiction if it could be achieved by a predetermined course of action.

The poem 'Eden' from *The Way of a World* (1969) associates the Fall with an urban environment ('This insurrection of sorry roofs') but also makes it clear that an escape from the urban environment does not amount to a reversal of the Fall. Eden is not to be come by so easily:

Eden
Is given one, and the clairvoyant gift
Withdrawn. 'Tell us', we say
'The way to Eden', but lost in the meagre
Streets of our dispossession, where
Shall we turn, when shall we put down
This insurrection of sorry roofs? Despair
Of Eden is given, too: we earn
Neither its loss nor having...[32]

The poem is fragmented between personal and social view-points. On the one hand, it suggests that Man in general has barred himself from Eden by surrounding himself with 'meagre/Streets' and 'sorry roofs'. This seems to imply that we could rediscover Eden by removing ourselves from the urban environment; but on the other hand, on an individual level, the poem suggests that 'the clairvoyant gift' comes and goes without reference to any particular set of circumstances, or any attempt we might make to capture it: 'we earn/Neither its loss nor having'. Tomlinson refuses to be prescriptive. The urban environment may be one in which Eden is hard to come by, but there is more to Eden than a trip to the countryside.

In another poem—'In Arden' from *The Shaft* (1978)—Tomlinson suggests that even in a rural environment the 'clairvoyant gift' comes and goes according to the changing mental attitudes of the human observer:

Arden is not Eden, but Eden's rhyme:
Time spent in Arden is time at risk
And place, also: for Arden lies under threat:
Ownership will get what it can for Arden's trees:
No acreage of green-belt complacencies
Can keep Macadam out: Eden lies guarded:
Pardonable Adam, denied its gate,
Walks the grass in a less-than-Eden light
And whiteness that shines from a stone burns with
his fate.[33]

The closeness of the names Adam and Macadam hints that Macadam is Man's *alter ego*, the destructive side of 'pardonable Adam'. Eden is beyond threat, and therefore must be beyond the reach of Adam, because Adam *is* the threat. He goes to Arden, a wood in the fallen world, seeking to escape from himself, but because he is unable to 'keep Macadam out' there is always a danger that he will begin to see the wood in terms of ownership, which wants to 'get what it can for Arden's trees'; therefore 'Time spent in Arden is time at risk'.

Adam is unable to escape from his own rapacious and manipulative inclinations; but he is also unable to escape his sense of his own mortality. In the 'less-than-Eden light' of the fallen world he inhabits, 'whiteness that shines from a stone burns with his fate'. The stone reminds us of a gravestone; but it is also one of those 'things which... face us with our own death, for they are so completely what we are not'. It reminds Adam that he is an exile in a non-human world. Yet the non-human world, if he can resist the temptation to see it in Macadam's terms, may be less implacable and threatening than it seems: it offers the possibility of redemption, by reminding us of Eden. It is 'Eden's rhyme'. Thus at the end of the poem we are told

> Adam in Arden tastes its replenishings:
>> Through its dense heats the depths of Arden's
>>> springs
> Convey echoic waters—voices
>> Of the place that rises through this place
> Overflowing, as it brims its surfaces
>> In runes and hidden rhymes, in chords and keys
> Where Adam, Eden, Arden run together
>> And time itself must beat to the cadence of
>>> this river.

The 'place that rises through this place' is Eden, which resurfaces through a proper perception of Arden; Eden comes welling up through the fallen world like a river in springtime.

There is a pun here on 'springs', meaning the time of year as well as the sources of a river; and the river-image leads on to the idea of Arden's 'replenishings', which are Nature's self-renewals, the power of natural life. Adam is able to 'taste' this power when he is in Arden, and by doing so he puts himself beyond the control of time: 'time itself must beat to the cadence of this river'.

Tomlinson's poetry suggests that it is easier to discover Eden in a natural landscape than in a man-made one, but this is because he takes most man-made landscapes—certainly most modern ones—to represent 'Macadam' rather than 'pardonable Adam': in other words, to represent the world of 'I–It' rather than of 'I–Thou'. Where the man-made landscape embodies a response to the natural world instead of a failure to respond to it, it can help to guide us to Eden. This is the message of 'Revolution (Piazza di Spagna)' from *The Return* (1987). The poem describes the Spanish Steps in Rome, and the way in which they follow the shape of the hill on which they are built:

> unfolding by degrees
> what was once a hill,
> each step a lip
> of stone and what they say
> to the sauntering eye
> is clear as the day
> they were made
> to measure out and treasure
> each rising inch
> that nature had mislaid:
> for only art
> can return us to an Eden where
> each plane and part
> is bonded, fluid, fitting and
> fits like this stair.[34]

The difference between the human impact on the landscape

here and Madacam's intrusion into Arden is that Macadam represents an 'ownership' that 'will get what it can for Arden's trees', whereas the Spanish Steps 'measure out and treasure/ each rising inch' of the hill. Macadam pretends that he owns Nature in order to exploit her, whereas the makers of the Spanish Steps were attempting to find an adequate response to the landscape on which they were building. As in 'On the Hall at Stowey', Tomlinson's message here is that the natural world only becomes valuable in human terms when it is brought to life by human appreciation—hence his claim that 'nature had mislaid' the rising inches of the hillside, and that 'only art/can return us to ... Eden'. Again, as so often in Tomlinson's work, the emphasis is on achieving a proper relationship. Eden cannot be found either in the human world by itself or in the natural world by itself, but only in the relationship between the two.

In his essay 'The Poet as Painter', Tomlinson describes how as a boy he used to go fishing in the countryside around Stoke-on-Trent, and how this experience helped to awaken his artistic temperament:

> The fisherman, if he is to be more than a random dabbler, must acquire an intuitive knowledge of the ways of fish and water, and within his stillness, at the centre of his capacity to wait and contemplate, there is a sense that is ready to strike at the exact moment, that even knows, perhaps, how to lure into its own mental orbit creatures that he cannot even see under that surface on which his whole attention is concentrated. Piscator is an artist, as Walton knew. His discipline, looking out of himself but with his inner faculties deeply roused, might make a poet or painter of him if he had the latent powers within.[35]

The fisherman, as described here, symbolizes Tomlinson's own ideal stance as an artist, 'looking out of himself but with his inner faculties deeply roused'. He is still, contemplative and receptive, concentrating patiently on what is in front of him: and this parallels the detached-but-attentive stance which Tomlinson adopts as a descriptive poet.

Characteristically, he concerns himself far more with the particularities of specific scenes, observed at specific times of the day and specific seasons of the year, than do either Philip Larkin or R. S. Thomas. We are often given the impression that he has stood or sat in front of a particular scene and noted down the details, almost as a landscape painter would do. Objects are placed in relation to one another in a manner which conveys a sense of three-dimensional depth. Different types of trees, flowers and rocks are distinguished from one another instead of being lumped together and spoken of in general terms. Yet at the same time there is a concern with the possibilities of misapprehension or misrepresentation; a fascination with ambiguities of perception; and an acute awareness of the artist's moral responsibility not to pretend to know more about his subject than is really the case.

All of this may at times seem rather over-scrupulous and superfine. Tomlinson's poems certainly tend to deal with the world's aesthetic effect on the individual rather than its grosser physical impact. His protagonists are rarely freezing cold or soaked to the skin or covered in mud. He appears in his own descriptions as a man who flies, drives or walks across the landscape, or who stands contemplating it, without his awareness of it often being tempered by a sense of the physical effort or difficulty with which it confronts him. The diction and scansion of his poems project a sense of fascinated detachment—like the detachment of the fisherman—rather than the sense of physical involvement which might be conveyed by a more colloquial, onomatopoeic choice of words and more urgent, broken, heavily-stressed rhythms. Yet these aspects of his work must be seen as consequences of his insistence on the importance of achieving a proper relationship with non-human things: a relationship which refreshes our perceptions and thoughts, without overwhelming us or releasing us from our sense of self.

And after all, Tomlinson's detached stance makes him our representative. Most of us, his readers, are aware of the non-human world as something to be contemplated from a distance rather than as something to be struggled with and suffered. We may hanker after a poetry that will enable us vicariously to abandon our detachment and live out fantasies of extreme sensation; and Tomlinson's verse may not be as popular as it should be, simply because it does not satisfy this hankering; but in the end perhaps it tells us more about ourselves than more extreme poetry can, and gives us a better idea of how our modern lifestyles can yield a morally responsible attitude towards the world on the other side of our double-glazing.

NOTES

1. Tomlinson, *Eden* (Bristol: Redcliffe Press, undated but probably 1985), p. 14. All of the poems appearing in *Eden* are taken from Tomlinson's other collections.

2. Tomlinson, *Collected Poems* (Oxford University Press, 1985), p. 37.

3. *Ibid.*, pp. 255–56.

4. Larkin, 'Spring', from *Collected Poems*, p. 39.

5. *Ibid.*, 'Absences', p. 49.

6. See Blake Morrison, *The Movement*, pp. 268–69.

7. Martin Buber, *I and Thou* (New York: Charles Scribner's Sons, 1958; first published in Germany as *Ich und Du*, 1923), pp. 9–10.

8. *Ibid.*, p. 18.

9. *Ibid.*, p. 91.

10. *Ibid.*, p. 93.

11. Tomlinson, *Some Americans* (Berkeley and Los Angeles: University of California Press, 1981), p. 9.

12. Buber, *I and Thou*, p. 33.

13. Michael Edwards, 'The Poetry of Charles Tomlinson', in Kathleen O'Gorman (ed.), *Charles Tomlinson, Man and Artist* (Columbia, Missouri: University of Missouri Press, 1988), p. 140.

14. Tomlinson, *Collected Poems*, pp. 40–42.

15. *Ibid.*, p. 34.
16. *Ibid.*, pp. 121–22.
17. *Ibid.*, pp. 122–23.
18. William Carlos Williams, *In the American Grain* (first published 1925; New York: New Directions, 1956), pp. 33–34.
19. Donald Davie, 'See, and Believe' (review of *Seeing is Believing* by Charles Tomlinson), *Essays in Criticism*, IX:2 (April 1959).
20. Tomlinson, *Collected Poems*, pp. 156–57.
21. Tomlinson (ed.), *Marianne Moore: A Collection of Critical Essays* (New Jersey: Prentice-Hall, 1969), p. 3.
22. Donald Davie, *Purity of Diction in English Verse* (Chatto & Windus, 1952; Routledge & Kegan Paul, 1967), p. 99.
23. Tomlinson, *Collected Poems*, pp. 337–38.
24. Michael Kirkham, 'An Agnostic's Grace', in Kathleen O'Gorman (ed.), *Charles Tomlinson, Man and Artist*, pp. 153ff.
25. Tomlinson, *Poetry and Metamorphosis* (Cambridge University Press, 1983), p. 24.
26. Tomlinson, *Collected Poems*, pp. 293–94.
27. *Ibid.*, p. 260.
28. Tomlinson, *Eden*, p. 15.
29. Buber, *I and Thou*, pp. 12–13.
30. Tomlinson, *Collected Poems*, p. 98.
31. Buber, *I and Thou*, p. 32.
32. Tomlinson, *Collected Poems*, p. 159.
33. *Ibid.*, pp. 305–06.
34. Tomlinson, *The Return* (Oxford University Press, 1987), p. 2.
35. Tomlinson, *Eden*, p. 10.

Chapter Five
Ted Hughes: 'depraved with life'

I

According to Ted Hughes, the whole cosmos is shaped and driven by the workings of a universal life-force, which is constantly being defeated by death, only to re-emerge in a new shape, somewhere else, at the very moment of destruction. One theme of his writing is a celebration of this life-force; but another theme is the lamentable state of Western civilization, a civilization which, he would have us believe, has buried the life-force, turned away from it, and even attempted to deny its existence. Because of these preoccupations, Hughes's poetry is more concerned with the inner life of things than it is with their outward appearances, and his guiding principle is always imaginative sympathy rather than scrupulous observation. His descriptions, in fact, are deliberately and boldly subjective. Of course, the danger of this method is obvious: if the poet's descriptions of the external world are shaped by his imagination, rather than disciplined by a strict fidelity to external appearances and physical sensations, then there is nothing to stop him from projecting his inner life into the things he is describing, to such an extent that he ceases to recognize them as embodiments of a separate reality, and begins to treat them instead as extensions of his own mind. But in some ways this is exactly the effect for which Hughes is striving; and to understand why, we must first understand his version of the Fall-myth, and his theories about the power of the imagination.

Hughes has given slightly different accounts of his ideas at different times, but the broad outlines are clear enough. They

follow the arguments published by Robert Graves in his book
The White Goddess, which we have already examined briefly in
relation to R. S. Thomas. In a 1976 article entitled 'Myth and
Education', for example, Hughes follows Graves closely in
dating Man's reliance on objective thought from the time of
the later Greek philosophers:

> Plato is human and familiar; he invented that
> careful, logical step-by-step style of investigation, in
> which all his great dialogues are conducted, and
> which almost all later philosphers developed, until it
> evolved finally into the scientific method itself. But
> his predecessors stand in a different world. By
> comparison they seem like mythical figures, living in
> myth, dreaming mythical dreams.[1]

He claims that Greece was a point of convergence for people
'from Africa via Egypt, from Asia via Persia and the Middle
East, from Europe and from all the shores of the Mediterra-
nean... Greece had become the battle-ground of the religious
and mythological inspirations of much of the archaic world'.[2]
In seeking to reconcile all these conflicting cultures and ideas,
the pre-Socratic philosophers, according to Hughes, achieved
'a bright, manifold perception of universal and human truths'.[3]
    But Plato, for the sake of greater precision and certainty,
began the process of replacing this 'bright, manifold perception' with his 'careful, logical step-by-step style of investigation'. As a result of this new style of thought, argues
Hughes, we have lost contact with our inner selves: 'It dawns
on us that in order to look at the inner world "objectively" we
have had to separate ourselves from what is an exclusively
"subjective" world, and it has vanished.'[4] Because we find it
difficult to understand the inner world—to think in any
way other than objectively—we tend to ignore that world
completely. As a result 'we are disconnected. The exclusive-
ness of our objective eye, the very strength and brilliance of
our objective intelligence, suddenly turns into stupidity—of

the most rigid and suicidal kind'.[5] This state of affairs has been exacerbated by 'the rising prestige of scientific objectivity and the lowering prestige of religious awareness' during 'the last three hundred years, and especially ... the last fifty'.[6]

Hughes goes on to say that 'If we do manage to catch a glimpse of our inner self, by some contraption of mirrors, we recognize it with horror—it is an animal crawling and decomposing in a hell. We refuse to own it.'[7] This last image, of the inner self as a crawling animal, hints at the way in which Hughes habitually associates the inner self with the natural world; and it also suggests the style in which, during the 1970s, he used images of anthropomorphized animals and birds to represent states of consciousness. The words serve, in fact, as an excellent introduction to one of the poems from *Crow* (1972): 'Crow's Elephant Totem Song' was one of the seven new poems which Hughes added to the second edition of the book in 1974. It recasts Hughes's Fall-myth in the form of a mock-Kiplingesque story, telling how the Elephant came to be the size and shape he is now:

> Once upon a time
> God made this Elephant...[8]

The Elephant attracts the attention of the tormented Hyenas, who admire his serenity and beauty and want him to release them from their sufferings:

> The Hyenas sang in the scrub: You are beautiful—
> They showed their scorched heads and grinning
>   expressions
> Like the half-rotted stumps of amputations—
> We envy your grace...
>
> Lift us from the furnaces
> And furies of our blackened faces
> Within these hells we writhe...

The description of the Hyenas' 'scorched heads and grinning

expressions' brings the appearance of a hyena's face to mind
with uncanny accuracy; but clearly what interests Hughes
most here is what the Hyenas represent in symbolic terms,
rather than what they actually look like. Their 'scorched
heads' betoken the fact that they are inhabitants of hell, and
the phrases 'the half-rotted stumps of amputations' and
'Within these hells we writhe' bear more than a coincidental
resemblance to the description I quoted earlier, of the inner
self, as 'an animal crawling and decomposing in a hell'. The
Hyenas, in other words, are representatives of the inner
world, and the Elephant re-enacts Hughes's notion of the Fall
by refusing to have anything to do with them:

> he was not God no it was not his
> To correct the damned
> In rage in madness then they lit their mouths
> They tore out his entrails
> They divided him among their several hells
> To cry...

If an individual will not voluntarily open negotiations with the
inner world, it will transform itself into a pack of demons and
tear him to pieces.

On one level, the smug self-contentment of the Elephant
represents the egocentricity of the child, and the trial he
undergoes when the Hyenas tear out his entrails is a particularly violent version of the process by which every child must
learn that he is no more immune to death and suffering than
anybody else. On another level, the Elephant represents Man
(or Man's conscious mind), choosing physical contentment at
the expense of psychological insight. Whichever way we interpret the poem, the most difficult aspect to understand—for a
reader unacquainted with Hughes's ideas—is that the moment
at which the Elephant is torn apart is supposed to represent
his chance to redeem himself. The Hyenas give him an opportunity 'to cry', and in Hughes's mythological poems crying
represents an openness to the reality of suffering, and thus a

willingness to face up to the full range of experience. Furthermore, Hughes believes that the fallen self can only achieve rebirth once it has been shattered or torn to pieces. All of his mythological narratives describe the protagonist's death or dismemberment followed by his spiritual regeneration. So the Elephant is being given a chance of rebirth; but he repeats Man's error by choosing invulnerability rather than understanding:

> At the Resurrection
> The Elephant got himself together with correction
> Deadfall feet and toothproof body and bulldozing
> bones...

The poem ends by showing the separation between the Elephant and the Hyenas as a state of affairs that now seems irreversible:

> The Elephant goes his own way, a walking sixth
> sense,
> And opposite and parallel
> The sleepless Hyenas go...

Both these versions of the Fall-myth—the one put forward in 'Myth and Education' and the one suggested by 'Crow's Elephant Totem Song'—emphasize how Man has fallen from grace by losing contact with his inner self, rather than by losing contact with the natural world. But for Hughes the two themes are always closely interconnected. He believes that the natural world is a world of repressed demons, just as the inner world is; and in both cases these demons are repressed because they represent truths about suffering and death that Man has chosen to hide from himself for the sake of bolstering his own egocentricity and physical comfort.

Hughes believes that to reconnect ourselves with our unconscious minds involves reconnecting ourselves with the natural world, and vice versa. We cannot see the natural world properly through the medium of rational thought, but only through the medium of the imagination; and if we open our minds to the truths that have been locked away in the unconscious then we are bound to discover that the same truths also dwell in the natural world, beneath the orderly rational surface that we have sought to impose on it. It follows that Hughes's descriptions of the natural world will be subjective and imaginative rather than objective and rational; and that his concern in any such descriptions will be to pierce the rational surface of the external world and release the demons trapped within.

One illustration of the way in which Hughes equates the natural world with the human unconscious is provided by the manner in which he describes and interprets the activity of fishing. Like Charles Tomlinson, he sees the fisherman as a symbol for the poet. He has written numerous poems about fishing, and in his book *Poetry in the Making* (which started life as a series of radio broadcasts, mainly for children, in the period 1961–67) he uses fishing as an example of the kind of mental concentration that the would-be writer must learn:

> Your whole being rests lightly on your float, but not drowsily: very alert, so that the least twitch of the float arrives like an electric shock. And you are not only watching the float. You are aware, in a horizonless and slightly mesmerized way, like listening to the double bass in orchestral music, of the fish below there in the dark. At every moment your imagination is alarming itself with the size of the thing slowly leaving the weeds and approaching your bait. Or with the world of beauties down there, suspended in total ignorance of you. And the whole purpose of this concentrated excitement, in this arena of apprehension and unforeseeable events, is to bring up some lovely and solid thing like living metal from a world where nothing exists but those inevitable facts which raise life out of nothing and return it to nothing.

So you see, fishing with a float is a sort of mental exercise in concentration on a small point, while at the same time letting your imagination work freely to collect everything that might concern that still point...⁹

In some ways this passage is strikingly similar to Tomlinson's piece on the same subject, with which I ended my previous chapter. Both men suggest that the fisherman is somehow luring the fish into his 'mental orbit'. As Tomlinson puts it:

The fisherman, if he is to be more than a random dabbler, must acquire an intuitive knowledge of the ways of fish and water, and within his stillness, at the centre of his capacity to wait and contemplate, there is a sense... that even knows, perhaps, how to lure into its own mental orbit creatures that he cannot even see under that surface on which his whole attention is concentrated.

But there are important differences. Tomlinson's fisherman is armed with 'stillness' and 'capacity to wait and contemplate'. His attention is concentrated on the 'surface' of the water, beneath which lies the unknown. He is alert, receptive and contemplative, waiting for the moment of contact. Even though the right kind of concentration seems to bring this moment closer, the fish remain 'creatures that he cannot even see'—they are inhabitants of a mysterious world, and he must keep an open mind about them until they choose to reveal themselves.

But Hughes's fisherman already knows about his fish before it takes the bait: 'At every moment your imagination is alarming itself with the size of the thing slowly leaving the weeds and approaching your bait.' By imagining it, he makes it happen: 'the whole purpose of this concentrated excitement... is to bring up some lovely solid thing like living metal'. Hughes blurs the distinction between internal and external worlds: the fish inhabits 'a world where nothing exists but those inevitable facts which raise life out of nothing and return it to nothing'—words which describe Hughes's idea of the unconscious mind as much as his idea of the natural world. In fact, so far as he is concerned, the two worlds are one and the same. The imagination does not simply allow us to see the truth about the natural world; it allows us to enter that world and influence it. Hughes's vision of Nature is more than subjective—it is magical. He believes that what we imagine about Nature becomes the truth. Likewise, when we enter into imaginative sympathy with objects or creatures from the natural world, they come into our minds and gain power over us.

'Learning to Think', from which the above remarks about fishing were taken, was first broadcast in 1963. Its precursor is a poem called 'Pike', from the 1960 collection *Lupercal*. The final stanzas, which describe Hughes fishing for enormous pike in a deep pool at the site of a vanished monastery, read as follows:

> past nightfall I dared not cast
>
> But silently cast and fished
> With the hair frozen on my head
> For what might move, for what eye might move.
> The still splashes on the dark pond,
>
> Owls hushing the floating woods
> Frail on my ear against the dream
> Darkness beneath night's darkness had freed,
> That rose slowly towards me, watching.[10]

Whereas in the passage from *Poetry in the Making* the fish succumbs to the power of the fisherman's imagination, here the fisherman succumbs to the power of the fish. He is being forced to continue fishing against his conscious will: 'I dared not cast/But silently cast'. The pike exists in his mind as much as in the external world: he describes it as a 'dream'.

The 'Darkness beneath night's darkness' is the darkness of his own unconscious mind as well as the darkness of the pond, and the pun on 'I' in 'for what eye might move' indicates that the pike is a manifestation of his inner self.

Certain aspects of Hughes's later landscape poetry are anticipated in this piece. He leads up to the passage given above by telling us that the pond is 'as deep as England'; yet he also states that its 'lilies and muscular tench/Had outlasted every visible stone/Of the monastery that planted them'. The pond, in other words, has outlived its original relationship to a historical building, a building of the kind we might normally associate with a sense of English history, and thus with ideas of Englishness. On one level, Hughes seems to be suggesting that the England in which he is interested is a place of deeply-lying demonic forces, which go deeper than the mere vicissitudes of history, and which are therefore immune to historical change. The lilies and the tench have turned out to be stronger than the monastery that planted them: proof that the natural world is capable of outlasting any man-made edifice.

But on another level, Hughes is noting the loss of a culture (represented by the monastery) in which Man was more receptive to the demonic forces which are now confined to the depths of the pond. In a 1971 interview with Ekbert Faas, Hughes claimed that the English confirmed their rejection of the natural world and their own inner selves when they rejected Catholicism in favour of Protestantism:

> The presence of the great goddess of the primaeval world, which Catholic countries have managed to retain in the figure of Mary, is precisely what England seems to have lacked, since the Civil War... where negotiations were finally broken off.[11]

The monastic remnants in 'Pike' therefore remind us of an England in which 'negotiations' with 'the great goddess' had not yet been 'broken off'—and the fact that the monastery has been abandoned and reduced to rubble explains why the depths of the pool (and, by implication, the depths of the unconscious mind) have become unexplored and 'legendary'.

II

One of Hughes's earliest landscape poems is 'Pennines in April', from *Lupercal*.[12] Even at this early stage of his development, he has already broken away from the discipline and detachment of objective observation. He wants to render the landscape to us, not as it might present itself to an observing eye, but as it strikes his own powerfully subjective imagination. The poem therefore opens with an immediate movement away from realistic description and into the realm of metaphor—'If this county were a sea.../...these hills heaving/ Out of the east.../Must burst upwards and topple into Lancashire.' And we are encouraged to accept this metaphor, not merely as a descriptive equivalent, but as a discovered truth about the landscape. The hills really *are* moving like a sea, Hughes insists:

> Your eye takes the strain: through
>
> Landscapes gliding blue as water
> Those barrellings of strength are heaving slowly
>   and heave
> To your feet...

Furthermore, we are invited to imagine ourselves into the scene, standing looking at the hills, and feeling the force of their movement as if we had originated the sea-metaphor ourselves: '*Your* eye takes the strain.../Those barrellings of strength... heave/To *your* feet...'

The central conceit of the poem, that the landscape is not stationary but in motion, is used as a challenge to the reader, who finds himself asked to 'take the strain' of the titanic movement Hughes is trying to evoke. The effect is both exciting and deterring, because the opening stanza has already made the point that if the hills really are in motion, then no human boundary-lines will be able to contain them: 'If this county were a sea.../...these hills.../Must burst upwards and topple into Lancashire.' At the end of the poem, Hughes tells us that 'the larks' and 'the imagination'—representatives of the natural world and the inner world respectively—are both carried upwards by the energy-spray of the landscape-wave he has been describing; whereas it would seem that secular human structures, such as the boundary-lines between counties, are simply shattered and overwhelmed by it. In other words, Hughes is employing his landscape description to suggest the inadequacy of our attempts to control or cope rationally with the elemental forces which animate the earth. This is a theme which is to recur years later in *Remains of Elmet* (1979), where the dour attempts of Yorkshire people to make a living in and from the rugged landscape around the Calder Valley are constantly being thrown into frail relief against a background of unpredictable elemental forces.

In 1964, Hughes gave a radio broadcast entitled 'Writing about Landscape', which later became Chapter Five of his book *Poetry in the Making*. In this broadcast he argued that 'what makes landscape valuable to us' is 'not simply the presence of the elements, but the encounter between the elemental things and the living, preferably the human.'[13] Certainly an 'encounter' of this kind seems to characterize 'Pennines in April', where it serves to suggest the frailty of the man-made world. This is one of Hughes's most persistent themes, especially in his landscape poetry—that the structures of everyday human life, and particularly life in the industrialized West, turn out to be so much junk when they are placed in a perspective of elemental forces.

Another characteristic feature of 'Pennines in April' is its lack of detailed visual information. Hughes concentrates on describing what the hills seem to be doing rather than on what they look like: the poem is full of words suggestive of powerful movement, such as 'heaving', 'burst', 'topple', 'gliding' and 'barrellings'. This unconcern with pictorial representation is rationalized by some comments of Hughes's, recorded in A. C. H. Smith's book *Orghast at Persepolis*:

> The deeper into language one goes, the less visual/ conceptual its imagery, and the more audial/visual/ muscular its system of tensions. This accords with the biological fact that the visual nerves connect with the modern human brain, while the audial nerves connect with the cerebellum, the primal animal brain and nervous system, direct... Visualization in language is at odds with immediately expressive dramatic action in that it is the conceptual substitute for physical action.[14]

It is certainly fair to say that many of Hughes's landscape poems are hardly descriptive at all, in the visual sense. The notable exception to this rule, as we shall see, is the main narrative of *Gaudete*, which was originally conceived as a shooting-script for a film.

Elsewhere, Hughes's technique is to strip a scene down to its most basic elements, to transform those elements by means of a metaphor or a conceit, and then to develop the conceit hyperbolically, until we are left with an audacious reinterpretation of the original material, anchored to reality by its reference to those few elements of sensory information on which he has seized. A late example of this technique is the poem 'Telegraph Wires' from the 1989 collection *Wolfwatching*. In this poem Hughes turns a set of telegraph wires into a symbol of Man's desire to hide away from the elemental powers that rule the natural world, and his ultimate inability to do so.

> Take telegraph wires, a lonely moor,
> And fit them together. The thing comes alive in
>   your ear.

Towns whisper to towns over the heather.
But the wires cannot hide from the weather...

In the revolving ballroom of space,
Bowed over the moor, a bright face

Draws out of telegraph wires the tones
That empty human bones.[15]

The sun-god becomes 'a bright face' bowing over the wires as a violinist would bow over his instrument, and the sound of the wind in the wires becomes the tune he plays (Hughes characteristically showing as much interest in the sound a place makes as in its visual details); space becomes a 'revolving ballroom' dancing to the sound of the tune; and Man's invention, intended to protect him from 'the weather', is thus turned against him as a reminder that human beings can never escape the jurisdiction of elemental forces: 'Bowed over the moor, a bright face/Draws out of telegraph wires the tones/That empty human bones.' The 'encounter between the elemental things and... the human' is restaged in a new form, and the drama of this confrontation is refreshed by Hughes's attention to the details of a particular landscape—the lonely moor, the bright sky, and the sound of the wind in the wires. It is his ability to strip the landscape to its essentials, and then to reimagine it until it begins to express his personal world-view, that gives the poem its air of imaginative authority and its characteristic visionary self-confidence.

There are occasions, however, when Hughes's lack of concern with visual detail and his relentlessly subjective approach to external phenomena lead him to overload his descriptions with significance, to such an extent that the things being described become flat and lifeless beneath the weight of meaning which has been piled onto them. One example is 'Pibroch' from *Wodwo* (1967), which begins:

The sea cries with its meaningless voice
Treating alike its dead and its living,

Probably bored with the appearance of heaven
After so many millions of nights without sleep,
Without purpose, without self-deception.[16]

The rhythmic terseness and irregularity of these lines, and the
ironic offhandedness of the writing, both help to make the
poem work. But the thing being described here is not really at
the centre of the poem at all: what matters more is the *way* in
which it is being described. Hughes is deliberately flouting a
whole set of conventional Romantic assumptions about the
natural world. His sea is 'meaningless', 'bored' and 'without
purpose'—a grotesque reversal of the meaningful, purposeful,
divinely-interfused Nature evoked for us by the poets of
previous centuries. But the only directly descriptive phrase
here is 'the sea cries'. 'Probably bored' and 'millions of years
without sleep' obliquely suggest the restlessness of the sea's
movements, but their primary function is to evoke states of
mind—boredom or sleeplessness—which might explain why
the sea behaves as it does.

The language of the poem is intended to unsettle us rather
than to inform us about the details of a particular scene.
Hughes's description seems to start from a desire to make
certain assertions about the universe in which we find
ourselves, rather than from a fresh examination of any specific
places or things. We are left with the impression that the
things mentioned—the sea in this stanza, or a tree and a
pebble later on—are not real individual things which Hughes
has seen and made up his mind to write about, but imaginary
representatives of the natural world, chosen or conjured up in
order to evoke a certain feeling. The poem is always striving to
push beyond specifics, into the realm of mythic universality; a
point which becomes self-evident in the last few lines:

And this is neither a bad variant nor a tryout.
This is where the staring angels go through.
This is where all the stars bow down.

'Pibroch' is certainly capable of imparting a *frisson* to its
readers, but perhaps the *frisson* is a little too close for comfort
to the one which we receive from Blake's famous poem 'The
Tyger':

> When the stars threw down their spears
> And watered Heaven with their tears,
> Did he smile his work to see?
> Did he who made the Lamb make thee?

In both cases the imagery of stars and angels (Blake
compresses the two into one) is used to suggest a breakdown
in the rational and serene heavenly order of things; and in
both poems, images drawn from the natural world (the tiger
and the lamb for Blake; the sea, the pebble and the tree for
Hughes) are converted into symbols and enlarged to mythic
proportions, in order to carry a threatening yet thrillingly
subversive message about the dynamic disorder of our
universe.

The underlying movement is away from observations and
descriptions of the external world, and towards symbolic or
mythological systems organized and sustained by the imagination and philosophy of the individual artist. This was certainly
the case with Blake; and at the time when he wrote 'Pibroch',
it was the case with Hughes too, because he was moving
towards the mythic poem-cycles of the 1970s, which have so
fascinated the majority of his critics: *Crow, Prometheus on his
Crag, Adam and the Sacred Nine* and *Cave Birds* (I list them
in order of composition rather than of publication). There is
some excellent poetry in these collections, but there is a price
to be paid for the mythologizing tendency when it comes to
writing, without the backup of a symbolic system, about
objects drawn from the external world. The following poem
from the end of *Gaudete* (1977) shows what that price is:

> The sea grieves all night long.
> The wall is past groaning.

The field has given up—
It can't care any more.

Even the tree
Waits like an old man
Who has seen his whole family murdered.

Horrible world

Where I let in again—
As if for the first time—
The untouched joy.[17]

The state of despair which is ascribed to the sea, the wall, the field and the tree in the opening lines of this poem is foisted upon them in such an arbitrary manner that the reversal of perspective at the end functions only as a rhetorical device. We are not surprised by the sudden arrival of 'untouched joy', because we were never persuaded that the landsape ought to represent despair in the first place. The meaning of the poem, in other words, does not seem to be growing organically from any fresh observation of the external world. Instead, it is fastened arbitrarily onto a series of flattened images called up in the poet's imagination without any sensual richness or particularity. And this problem haunts all the poems at the end of *Gaudete*—poems which are not underpinned by enough of a symbolic or mythological system to compensate for their obvious detachment from specific sensory experiences.

Yet the main narrative of *Gaudete* gives quite a different impression. It is full of visual descriptions of great energy and resourcefulness:

The parkland unrolls, lush with the full ripeness of the last week in May, under the wet midmorning light. The newly plumped grass shivers and flees. Giant wheels of light ride into the chestnuts, and the poplars lift and pour like the tails of horses. Distance blues beyond distance.[18]

Gaudete is the story of an Anglican vicar, the Reverend Lumb, who is forced to confront the repressed aspects of his own personality when he is kidnapped by representatives of the underworld. His place in the overworld is taken by a change- ling fashioned from an oak tree. This changeling represents Lumb's own repressed physicality shorn of any rational or spiritual counterforces and set free in human form. Inter- preting the role of vicar according to his own nature, the changeling proceeds to have sex with every woman in the village. The main narrative of *Gaudete* describes this change- ling's last day on earth, during which the village husbands find out what he has been up to. The narrative ends with his death at their hands. In an Epilogue to the book, Lumb reappears in Ireland, evidently no longer divided against himself. He summons an otter from a lake, to indicate that he has re-estab- lished contact with the natural world (and the unconscious world with which it equates), and he leaves behind a collection of untitled poems, with which the book ends. The poem we examined earlier is one of these.

The narrative of *Gaudete* is thus highly symbolic; but although a critical examination of the book reveals more and more of this symbolism, and this is the aspect on which Hughes's critics tend to concentrate, the impression produced by a first reading is of a somewhat frenzied and melodramatic storyline, decorated with intensely vivid descriptions, espe- cially descriptions of landscape.

In fact, these landscape descriptions are vital to the thematic and symbolic development of the story. It is a land- scape bursting with life, and it seems to be trying to force itself onto the attention of the villagers. The season is an exag- gerated and concentrated version of springtime: everything seems to be coming into flower at once. This is an appropriate setting for the changeling–Lumb's frenzied fertility-rites, of course; but the seething and burgeoning life of the landscape also represents, like the changeling–Lumb himself, the life- force and the inner world of passions and irrational urges that the villagers have chosen to repress. For this reason they are unable to respond constructively either to the changeling–Lumb or to the beauties of the landscape. The village women are first possessed by a sexual frenzy, then driven to suicide or thoughts of suicide; while the men are at first revolted, and then find release in an orgy of destruction culminating in the death of the changeling–Lumb.

Thus Pauline Hagen, who has just been making love with Lumb and can no longer bear the thought of her rational, empty everyday life, wants to surrender her individuality and become part of the soil:

> She is gouging the leaf-mould,
> She is anointing her face with it.
> She wants to rub her whole body with it.
> She is wringing the bunched stems of squeaking
>   spermy bluebells...
>
> She wants to press her face into the soil, into the
>   moist mould,
> And scream straight downward, into earth-stone
>   darkness.
> She cannot get far enough down, or near enough.[19]

On the other hand Dr Westlake, a soured man of the world, feels the presence of the 'bulging green landscape' as an oppressive weight, and thinks of the burgeoning life all around him as a form of corruption:

> He stares at the piled hairy flowers, hedgerow beyond draped hedgerow. Hushed and claustrophobic. He imagines the still Sargasso of it, rising and falling, right across England. Funereal. Unearthly. Some bulky hard-cornered unpleasantness leans on him. He ignores it steadily. He searches for his car-keys, preoccupied, watching the mobs of

> young starlings struggling and squealing filthily in
> the clotted may-blossom, like giant blow-flies.[20]

Hughes is here describing the natural world in an unpleasant
and disturbing manner in order to indicate that it is being seen
in the wrong way. One of his techniques is to use terms that
remind us of sexual taboos, in order to suggest that the same
sorts of taboos explain our inability to face up to the realities
of Nature. The 'spermy bluebells' in the previous passage
correspond with 'hairy flowers' here, and one of the suggestions of 'young starlings... squealing filthily' is that they are
behaving in a disgustingly immodest manner. Likewise the
image of 'giant blow-flies' deliberatly violates the taboos
surrounding corruption and death. Whereas a poet such as
Philip Larkin describes the natural world in terms of its
simplicity, strength and purity, and thus preserves an essentially Romantic image of Nature, Hughes is always anxious to
emphasize those aspects of the natural world that the
Romantics found hardest to accept—suffering, death, corruption and sexuality.

Descriptions of the landscape thus play an important
thematic and symbolic role in *Gaudete*. So far as Hughes's
descriptive technique is concerned, however, the most
remarkable thing about the book is its wealth of specific
details, especially visual details. Apparently *Gaudete* started
life as a shooting-script for a film, and many of the descriptive
passages control the reader's point of view so firmly that we
almost feel as if we were watching camera shots:

> Clouds slide off the sun. The trees stretch, stirring
> their tops. A thrush hones and brandishes its echoes
> down the long aisles, in the emerald light, as if it
> sang in an empty cathedral. Shrews storm through
> the undergrowth. Hoverflies move to centre, angle
> their whines, dazzle across the sunshafts. The
> humus lifts and sweats.
>   Garten's eyes are quiet...[21]

In this passage Hughes guides the reader's imaginary field of sight from clouds to treetops to the 'long aisles' between the trees, then down to the sunshafts and undergrowth, and finally to the humus below, where we discover Garten, the poacher, who is lying stretched out on his front. The phrase 'Hoverflies move to centre' implies the centre of a field of vision, or even the centre of a screen. Admittedly Hughes's preference for non-visual descriptions is suggested by the details of the thrush's song, the hoverfly's whine and the shrew's storming movements. There is also an implied contrast between the elegant and apparently tranquil appearance of the sky and the treetops, and the ferociously urgent life going on at ground level—a contrast crystallized in the transition from the thrush singing 'as if in an empty cathedral' to the storming movements of the shrews in the undergrowth. But to anyone who has read Hughes's poetry *en masse*, the dominance of visual information in this passage, and many others like it, is what marks out *Gaudete* from all his other work.

It would be wrong to suggest that—either in *Gaudete* or in his later collections—Hughes has abandoned symbolic and mythical imagery in favour of objective delineations of the external world. But *Gaudete* marks a change of direction in his work nevertheless—or rather, it confirms the change suggested by *Season Songs*, which was first published a year earlier (1976) as a book for children—a renewal of interest in observation and description, and a lessening of his involvement with psychodramas, mythical icons and symbolic fables. His gaze seems to be turning outwards rather than inwards for the first time in some years, and it is this change of emphasis which prepares the ground for *Remains of Elmet* and *River*, the two collections most concerned with landscape.

III

Remains of Elmet and *River* have now been issued in one volume together with *Cave Birds*, under the collective title of *Three Books*. All three have been shorn of their illustrations. *Remains of Elmet* was originally published with black-and-white photographs by Fay Godwin, *Cave Birds* with pen-and-ink drawings by Leonard Baskin, and *River* with colour photographs by Peter Keen. The text of *Cave Birds* does not seem to have been changed at all, however, whereas both *Remains of Elmet* and *River* have been substantially altered. Some old poems have been taken out, various new ones have been added, the sequence of poems in both collections has been rearranged, and several of the pieces have been rewritten. At the risk of being obscure, I shall refer (unless I specifically say otherwise) to the original editions of both books. This is partly because that is the form in which I first got to know them, but also because I find the original versions superior to the later ones. The photographs add something, especially the black-and-white ones by Fay Godwin. Hughes's collaborations with visual artists of one type and another have not been given as much attention as they deserve, and to my mind *Remains of Elmet* is the collection in which the combination of words and pictures works to greatest advantage. But it is not only the loss of the illustrations which has weakened the books. Hughes's detailed revisions of individual poems are generally all to the good, but the same cannot be said of his tinkering with the thematic architecture of the books. *River* has suffered most. Its celebratory tone has been damaged by the introduction of new poems and, because the order of its contents has been changed, it no longer follows the pattern of the seasons from winter to summer and back to winter again.

Remains of Elmet (1979), in its original form, communicates a much stronger sense of place than does the revised version. The removal of Fay Godwin's photographs has something to do with this, of course: magnificently moody black-and-white images of buildings, streets, landscapes and landscape details, taken in and around the Calder Valley near Halifax. But the loss of the photographs also affects our reading of the poems. In a sense, the pictures allowed Hughes to write about the Calder district—where he was brought up—without having to describe it. His verses often referred to, or drew their inspiration from, the pictures opposite which they appeared, but they never attempted anything so mundane as a transcription into words of the scenes depicted. One example of his oblique approach is the poem 'Tree', which appears opposite a photograph of a flat horizon with a single tree growing from it, possibly an oak, silhouetted against a dirty sky.

Hughes's verses describe a priest who sets his face against the natural world:

> A priest from another land
> Fulminated
> Against heather, stones and wild water[22]

until he catches an inadvertent glimpse of the reality he has been trying to repress, and is magically transformed into a tree:

> he ran out of breath—

> In that teetering moment
> Of lungs empty...

> Transformed, bowed—
> The lightning conductor
> Of a maiming glimpse—the new prophet

> Gasped a cry

The transformation is not made explicit, but once having read the poem the reader notices that the tree in the photograph has a slightly teetering, upflung look, like somebody struck motionless in the middle of an exclamation. We find ourselves jumping to the conclusion that the priest has been turned into the tree—a change which appropriately symbolizes his spiritual alteration from a fulminating preacher into 'a new prophet'.

The later version of 'Tree' adds several extra lines, both to make the priest's transformation more apparent, and to emphasize the idea that it was his manipulation of words which previously shielded him from the power of the natural world, so that as soon as he is overwhelmed by that power, it strikes him dumb:

—the new prophet—

Under unending interrogation by wind
Tortured by huge scalding of light
Tried to confess all but could not
Bleed a word

Stripped to his root-letter, cruciform
Contorted
Tried to tell all

Through crooking of elbows
Twitching of finger-ends...

This is a perfectly decent bit of writing, but wordier than the earlier version (which is ironic, considering the message); and a reader who has never seen the photograph in the original book still may not realize that the preacher is supposed to be turning into a tree. He may be left wondering why the poem is called 'Tree' at all. And what we get from the original version which we do not get here is a full sense of Hughes's imaginative audacity. We need to see the photograph and the poem alongside one another in order to appreciate how freely he has interpreted the image which was his starting-point. He seems to have broken away from it almost completely—but not quite. The poem *does* describe the picture, and affects the way in which we look at it. In the end we are left wondering how on earth Hughes could have got such a strange flight of fancy from a photograph of a tree. In fact what he is doing is reversing the narrative of *Gaudete*, which tells of a tree becoming a preacher. But even when we recognize this, Hughes's way of interpreting Fay Godwin's image is still startling enough to excite our admiration—an effect which is lost in the later version.

Throughout the original version of *Remains of Elmet*, in fact, Hughes, instead of referring directly to Fay Godwin's pictures, presents us with an interpretive commentary on them; and one of the main themes of this commentary is an apocalyptic account of the industrial decay which was depopulating the Calder district at the time when the book was written. Again, this theme does not come through so strongly from the new version of the book. In 1979, when *Remains of Elmet* first appeared, monetarist policies seemed to be bringing economic extinction to the north of England. Hughes's poems described a region where industry and agriculture were both in a state of collapse; and he took this economic decline as a symptom of Man's inability to sustain his dominance over Nature. Many of the poems were written in terms suggesting that the long struggle to control the landscape in and around the Calder Valley had now ended in defeat.

'Hill Walls', for example, describes the drystone walls of the region as if they were the rigging of a ship, in which the local population set out on a 'great adventure', only to end in shipwreck:

> The stone rigging was strong.
> Exhilarated men
> Cupped hands and shouted to each other
> And grew stronger riding the first winters.
>
> The great adventure had begun...

The poem ends:

No survivors.
Here is the hulk, every rib shattered.

A few crazed sheep
Pulling its weeds
On a shore of cloud.[23]

Various other pieces express the same vision: 'When Men Got to the Summit', 'Willow-Herb', 'The Long Tunnel Ceiling', 'Heptonstall', 'Top Withens' and 'Heptonstall Old Church'.[24]

All of these pieces depict civilization as a failed experiment, the remains of which are now being shrugged off or swallowed by the natural world as the relentless push for survival goes on:

Now it is all over.

The wind swings withered scalps of souls
In the trees that stood for men

And the swift glooms of purple
Are swabbing the human shape from the freed
    stones.[25]

That is from 'Top Withens'. Hughes makes some attempt to outline a historical justification for his portrayal of the region in his untitled prose-preface to the book. The Calder Valley, he points out, was 'the cradle for the Industrial Revolution in textiles' during the 1800s. Since that period it has suffered a terrible economic decline:

Throughout my lifetime, since 1930, I have watched the mills of the region and their attendant chapels die. Within the last fifteen years the end has come. They are now virtually dead, and the population of the valley and the hillsides, so rooted for so long, is changing rapidly.[26]

Hughes may seem rather overanxious to strike a note of grim finality ('the end has come') and to sweep the landscape clean

of the last traces of human civilization; but these ideas should
be seen in the context of his generally apocalyptic view of
Western civilization. There is, for example, his 1970 review[27]
of Max Nicholson's book *The Environmental Revolution* in
which he declares that Western civilization is 'an evolutionary
dead-end' which is suffering 'the last nightmare of mental
disintegration and spiritual emptiness', whereas he describes
the natural world as 'the draughty radiant Paradise of the
animals which is the actual earth, in the actual Universe', and
insists that 'This is what will survive, if anything can.'

This apocalyptic theme recurs throughout his work. It is
the social counterpart of the individual trials of destruction
and suffering that feature in all of his mythological poem-
cycles. The protagonists of the poem-cycles must be torn to
pieces or burnt to cinders before they can achieve reunifica-
tion with the natural world and their own repressed inner
selves. Likewise, human civilization must be reduced to rubble
if it is ever to be reborn in a better form. One example of this
kind of imagery is 'Notes for a Little Play' from *Crow*, where
Hughes describes a world destroyed by a solar holocaust:

> First—the sun coming closer, growing by the
>   minute.
> Next—clothes torn off.
> Without a goodbye
> Faces and eyes evaporate[28]

and then imagines how new life, in the form of 'Mutations—at
home in the nuclear glare', might arise from the ashes:

> They have begun to dance a strange dance.

> And this is the marriage of these simple creatures—
> Celebrated here, in the darkness of the sun.

Remains of Elmet presents the same myth of destruction
and rebirth in a less extreme form. The use of the word 'remains'
in the book's title confirms that these are descriptions of a

civilization in ruins: the last crumbling remnants, as Hughes
sees it, of the chapel-based, industrialized society which once
dominated the region. But the title can be read in another way
too. 'Elmet', as Hughes tells us in his prose-preface, was 'the
last British Celtic kingdom to fall to the Angles'.[29] Here and
there throughout the book there are hints that Hughes is
searching the modern Calder Valley for the remains of an
ancient civilization which was more responsive to the natural
world than is our own. This is another theme of the book.
Certain aspects of the region hold the same significance for
Hughes as the monastery did in 'Pike'. He suggests that the
locals once had a closer relationship with Nature, but that it
was destroyed and buried by the Industrial Revolution and the
chapel-based religion that came with it—'the mills of the
region and their attendant chapels', as he puts it in his prose-
preface to the book, implying that the low-church religion is
merely a spinoff from the rational, profiteering, severely-prac-
tical world-view on which the Industrial Revolution was built.

'The Ancient Briton Lay Under his Rock', one of the
poems which is not reproduced in *Three Books*, tells of a great
slab of rock under which an Ancient Briton is supposed to be
buried—symbolizing the manner in which modern Man has
buried the reality of his inner life. The present-day valley-
dwellers attempt to gain control of this buried secret by
digging it up, but the slab of rock stubbornly—and even magically—resists their efforts. Their literal-minded Protestantism
prevents them from making contact with the buried powers of
the past:

> As we dug it waddled and squirmed deeper.
> As we dug, slowly, a good half ton,
> It escaped us, taking its treasure down.
>
> And lay beyond us, looking up at us
>
> Labouring in the prison
> Of our eyes, our sun, our Sunday bells.[30]

In another poem, 'Crown Point Pensioners', Hughes finds evidence of 'old roots' and 'Indigenous memories' amongst the pensioners of the area—particularly in the sounds of their voices:

> Singers of a lost kingdom.
>
> Wild melody, wilful improvisations.
> Stirred to hear still the authentic tones
> The reverberations their fathers
> Drew from these hill-liftings and hill-hollows
> Furthered in the throats.[31]

The suggestion in these lines is that 'the authentic tones' of the local dialect arose as a direct response to the local environment. The actual shapes of the landscape—'hill-liftings and hill-hollows'—are somehow 'furthered' or echoed in the sounds of the language.

Seamus Heaney, in his early poetry, makes the same connection between the Irish landscape and the Gaelic language; and like Hughes, he insists that the ancient relationship between the landscape and its inhabitants has been disrupted by more recent events. Furthermore, both poets blame the loss of this intimate relationship between the landscape and its human inhabitants on the hard-headed, mechanistic world-view which they associate with Protestant culture; but for Heaney, this culture was introduced into Ireland by English invaders, whereas for Hughes it arose first with the Civil War and then with the Industrial Revolution.

For Hughes, however, these ideas about language and place are parts of a wider thematic pattern, the overall purpose of which is to contrast the eternal newness or timelessness of the natural world with the self-destructive patterns of human history. Hughes's belief is that human life is only valuable at those times when it aligns itself with the natural world and the inner life of the spirit. Since most of human history has involved a movement away from the natural world and this inner life rather than towards them, he sees most of human history as a self-destructive error. His references to the historical background of the Calder Valley—particularly to its comparatively recent past, exemplified by the Industrial Revolution, the First World War, and his own boyhood memories of the area—are couched in these terms. The natural world, on the other hand, is offered as a timeless alternative: timeless because, unlike the man-made world with its inbuilt tendency to self-destruct, the natural world is always renewing itself. As Hughes writes in his review of Max Nicholson's book, quoted earlier, 'Even when it is poisoned to the point of death, its efforts to be itself are new in every second.'[32]

The contrast between the ever-new natural world and the time-dominated world of human history is an important aspect of Hughes's apocalyptic world-view. As in all his landscape poetry, he is attempting in *Remains of Elmet* to stage 'an encounter between the elemental things and the living, preferably the human'. The purpose of this encounter is to dramatize the fact that all living things—even humans, despite their attempts to protect themselves—must ultimately yield to the power of elemental forces. Hughes believes that unless we acknowledge this fact we will find ourselves in conflict with the life-force that dwells within us and manifests itself in the natural world all around us. He dramatizes this view in *Remains of Elmet* by showing a man-made civilization in a state of collapse, while the natural world lives on among the ruins, unconscious of Man's abortive attempts to tame or destroy it.

One poem on this theme is 'Lumb Chimneys'. Opposite the text is a photograph of a disused brick chimney festooned with young undergrowth, alongside which stands the sawn-off stump of a young sycamore.

> Days are chucked out at night.
> The huge labour of leaf is simply thrown away.
> Great yesterdays are left lying.

Nose upwind, the slogging world
Cannot look aside or backward.

Brave dreams and their mortgaged walls are let rot
    in the rain.
The dear flesh is finally too much.
Heirloom bones are dumped into wet holes.
And spirit does what it can to save itself alone.

Nothing really cares. But soil deepens.

And the nettle venoms into place
Like a cynical old woman in a food-queue.
The bramble grabs for the air
Like a baby burrowing into the breast.
And the sycamore, cut through at the neck,
Grows five or six heads, depraved with life.

Before these chimneys can flower again,
They must fall into the only future, into earth.[33]

Our attachments to 'Brave dreams', 'mortgaged walls' and
even 'dear flesh' are all misplaced, Hughes is suggesting—the
'spirit', if it is to 'save itself', must do so 'alone' and without
any of these things. By 'spirit' Hughes means 'life force', the
force which he believes to animate all aspects of the universe,
making it more than the collection of dead matter which is all
the rational mind can perceive. It is this spirit which drives the
'slogging world' relentlessly onwards, and which makes the
'soil' or 'earth'—the fundamental stuff of the natural world—
into the 'only future'. It has no time for sentimentality or
memories—it 'cannot look aside or backward'—and thus it is
completely uncaring about the past. And it animates human
beings as well as everything else, which is why a nettle is like a
cynical old woman and a bramble is like a baby. The slight
incongruity of the second image is intended to challenge the
sentimentality with which we commonly view babies, and to
remind us that a baby burrowing into the breast, just like a

bramble grabbing for air, is driven by an unthinking will to live.

The poem will stand on its own, but it benefits from the relationship with its photograph. The reference to 'these chimneys' at the end reminds us of the industrial collapse taking place in the Calder region, of which the disused, overgrown chimney shown in Fay Godwin's picture is a symbol. The mention of the 'sycamore, cut through at the neck' also draws our attention to the photograph: if we look at it closely, we will see that the sycamores and ferns that surround the old chimney are all showing youngish leaves. The season is evidently springtime, so the sense of 'depraved' life that pervades the poem is appropriate to the picture. The generalized life-view which the poem puts forward springs from a response to a particular glimpse of a particular place, and the closing lines—

> Before these chimneys can flower again
> They must fall into the only future, into earth.

—are enriched by a sense of the industrial history and economic decline of the Calder Valley. As usual, the timelessness of Nature is being offered as an alternative to the historical developments of the man-made world; but this sense of alternatives is made particularly vivid and effective in *Remains of Elmet* because it emerges from Hughes's close attention to (and personal memories of) a particular area and culture. In the new version of the book, from which Fay Godwin's photographs are missing, the philosophical content of the poems comes across more clearly, but to a large extent the sense of place is lost.

IV

In *River* (1983), as in *Remains of Elmet*, Hughes's poems are
accompanied by a sequence of photographs—in this case
colour photographs by Peter Keen. In general, however, the
relationship between words and images in *River* is much
looser than in *Remains of Elmet*. One element common
to both poems and pictures, as the title of the book indicates, is their focus on rivers and their surroundings; but
whereas Peter Keen's studies are all of rivers on the mainland
of Britain and Ireland, Hughes's poems refer to rivers in
Canada and Alaska—'That Morning' and 'Gulkana'[34]—as well
as Skye—'Milesian Encounter on the Sligachan'.[35] Another
common element is the way that poems and photographs are
both arranged in a cycle lasting just over one year—starting
with 'The Morning Before Christmas',[36] going through all the
seasons of the year back to winter, and ending with a moment
of rebirth in January with 'Salmon Eggs'.[37]

The portrayal of this yearly cycle is the collection's main
principle of organization: it controls the arrangement of the
poems and promotes a sense of their unity. It allows Hughes
to fit his dramas of suffering and rebirth into a framework
that anchors the poems firmly in empirical reality: in this way,
the yearly cycle of *River* serves much the same purpose as the
local history and references to specific places in *Remains of
Elmet*. Further elements of particularity are supplied by
constant references to the life-cycles of various plants and
fishes (especially salmon, which feature in a number of the
poems); and by Hughes's descriptions of himself as a fisherman, which are sometimes surprisingly humorous, as in 'A
Cormorant':

> My bag
> Sags with lures and hunter's medicine enough
>
> For a year in the Pleistocene.
> My hat, of use only

If this May relapses into March,
Embarrasses me, and my net, long as myself,

Optimistic, awkward, infatuated
With every twig-snag and fence-barb

Will slowly ruin the day...[38]

Thomas West, one of the few critics of Hughes's poetry who has paid much attention to *River*, presents the book as a portrait of an unfallen world:

> Hughes just turns his back on the old problem of the brain god... The poet simply surrenders to sensations: as the inner drama recedes, the importance of poetry as description grows, but a description where ideal interference is so reduced as to let Nature become radiant before it becomes symbolic. The threat of the brain god Logos of old is simply overwhelmed by the evidence of the surface of things...[39]

West seems to believe that the poetry of *River* is mainly descriptive rather than interpretive: myth and symbol have all but disappeared, for the reason that these poems are portraits of a 'radiant' Nature which has not been detached from us by the spectre of 'the brain god'. This is an unfallen vision of Nature, according to West, and because there is no Fall there is no need for myth or symbolism as a means of explaining what is the matter. In an unfallen world, 'the evidence of the surface of things' is enough.

In fact, as we shall see, there is plenty of myth and symbolism in *River*, the emphasis of the poetry is still on interpretation at least as much as description, and the Fall is very much a continuing concern. What probably leads West to suppose that *River* does not concern itself with the 'threat of the brain god' is that the collection presents us with a vision of the natural world where the influence of Man is merely peripheral. *River* has its dark moments—moments when the power of the natural world seems threatening or even diseased. 'Last Night' is the most striking example:

> Something evil about the sunken river
> In its sick-bed darkness. I stood in a grave
> And felt the evil of fish. The strange evil
> Of unknown fish-minds. Deep fish listening to me
> In the dying river.[40]

But the tone of the collection as a whole is celebratory, and even the sense of evil evoked in 'Last Night' is related to the yearly life-cycle of the river, which in this instance is passing through a stage of drought and apparent sickness. The arrangement of the poems, by following the progression of the year from one season to the next, places both the evils of disease and death and the ecstasies of rebirth within the cyclic context of Nature's annual self-renewals. What the collection as a whole amounts to is a portrayal and celebration of a world where darkness alternates with light, suffering alternates with creative joy, and death is constantly changing places with life. Man hardly appears at all, except as a marvelling observer dabbling on the edge of the flow: often in the form of Hughes himself, the poet and fisherman, awkwardly wading and fumbling his way towards moments of transcendental vision. But this is not to say, as we shall see, that the question of Man's fallen state is never dealt with.

In the revised version of *River*, which appears in *Three Books*, much of the celebratory tone has been lost. The poems are no longer arranged into a yearly cycle, and one new addition in particular—'1984 on "The Tarka Trail"'—strikes a discordant note which brings the influence of Man right into the foreground:

> The river's glutted—a boom of plenty for the algae.
> A festering olla podrida, poured slowly.
> Surfactants, ammonia, phosphates—the whole
>   banquet

Flushed in by sporadic thunderbursts...

> The tale of a dying river
> Does not end where you stand with the visitors
> At a sickbed, feeling the usual
> Nothing more than mangled helplessness.
> You cannot leave this hospital...[41]

It is a two-part poem which goes on for four pages, and it alters the feel of the whole collection. Of course, Hughes may well have decided, coming back to *River* after a lapse of ten years, that he could not reprint it without acknowledging in some way the damage being done to our waterways by pollution. Of the five poets I have chosen to examine in this book, he is the one who is most famed as a 'nature poet', and he is also the one who has made the most noise about environmental issues. But his environmentalist poems are not often his best work: they lack the imaginative audacity which characterizes his writing at its most arresting.

'1984 on "The Tarka Trail"' fails thoroughly to digest or transform its materials: its tone is one of angry reportage, expressed in a free verse which never quite becomes poetry. Another new poem, 'If', does rather better:

> If the sea drinks the river
> And the earth drinks the sea
>
> It is one quenching and one termination
>
> If your blood is trying to clean itself
> In the filter of your corrupted flesh
> And the sores run—that is the rivers
>
> The five rivers of Paradise[42]

But whatever the merits or demerits of these individual pieces, the real problem is that the environmentalist theme is not picked up by the rest of the collection. As with *Remains of*

Elmet, the general impression given by *River* is that the activities of Man are merely paltry or futile when set alongside the elemental power of Nature; and the insertion of new poems which directly confront environmental issues has the effect of making the reader feel that he is being jerked violently from one point of view to another. At one moment Man's influence seems peripheral, at the next moment it jumps dramatically into the foreground, and then it disappears again. The unity of the collection as a whole is badly damaged by these sudden changes of emphasis.

But to return to the original version of *River*: here we are introduced into a world dominated by the operations of the life-force, where the 'brain god Logos' has been pushed to one side and subdued into the role of an observer for the time being. But although Man and his fallen outlook do not dominate here as they do in *Crow* or *Cave Birds*, in *Gaudete* or even in *Remains of Elmet*, their presence is still important: Hughes wants to give us occasional glimpses of the fussy awkwardness of humanity to remind us of our fallen state, and he also wants to show that certain activities, such as fishing, can put us back into contact with Nature and thus help us to recover Eden, at least for a short while. His portraits of himself as a sweating fisherman lumbered with too much unwieldy gear touch on both these themes. The lures, the hat and the net in the passage quoted earlier are supposed to provide the fisherman with control of his environment and protection from it, but all they really do is embarrass him and ruin his day. Man has lost the art of stripping himself naked and becoming part of the natural world; he now feels that he can only deal with Nature with the help of ever-more-sophisticated tools and equipment; but the tools and equipment actually impede his return to the unfallen state.

Yet the fisherman contains two selves: the sweating, clumsy, awkward self who insists on equipping himself with hats, lures and nets before he confronts Nature; and the inner self which emerges at the opportune moment to merge with the natural world and rediscover the unfallen state. 'Go Fishing' describes the fisherman's transition from one self to the other and back again:

Go Fishing

Join water, wade in underbeing
Let brain mist into moist earth...

Lose words
Cease
Be assumed into the womb of lymph
As if creation were a wound
As if this flow were all plasma healing...[43]

The poem describes, in a new form, one of those experiences of destruction and rebirth that are so central to Hughes's work. The self allows itself to be swept away, pulled to pieces and supplanted by the natural world, in order to achieve spiritual rebirth.

As in 'Crow's Elephant Totem Song', the language of the poem emphasizes that the individual can only receive enlightenment once the conscious mind has been overwhelmed and broken apart—'Be supplanted... Be cleft... Displaced... Dissolved... Dismembered... Become translucent...' urges Hughes—but because this is now a voluntary experience the overall effect is less violent and disturbing than in the mythic poem-cycles. All the same the experience is essentially the same, and what the self achieves is the ability to see suffering and birth as part of a single creative process—a 'womb of lymph' which is also 'a wound' soothed by 'this flow' of 'healing'. The fisherman's experience of the natural world is associated with an abandonment of rational thought, especially of words and the sense of time. At the beginning of the poem he lets go of his 'brain' and his 'words', and at the end he comes back, reborn, into the secular world:

Crawl out over roots, new and nameless...

Let the world come back, like a white hospital
Busy with urgency words

Try to speak and nearly succeed
Heal into time and other people

The experience of fishing allows him to temporarily abandon
his rational, social self, his name, his involvement with words
and his sense of time, and thus to 'wade in underbeing'; and as
usual, Hughes is suggesting that contact with the natural
world and contact with the inner self are one and the same
thing, so that it is possible for the fisherman to 'wade in
underbeing' by means of wading in the river.

The Fall-myth has not been discarded or temporarily
shelved, then, but in *River* the natural world is often being
seen from a new angle, and with a new clarity: from the
unfallen state rather than from the fallen one. Nor is it true to
say that the mythic and symbolic content of the poems has
now been purged or washed away by sheer description, what
West calls 'the evidence of the surface of things'. 'River', the
title-poem of the collection, shows this clearly enough:

River

Fallen from heaven, lies across
The lap of his mother, broken by world.

But water will go on
Issuing from heaven

In dumbness uttering spirit brightness
Through its broken mouth.

Scattered in a million pieces and buried
Its dry tombs will split, at a sign in the sky,

At a rending of veils.
It will rise, in a time after times,

After swallowing death and the pit
It will return stainless

For the delivery of this world.
So the river is a god

Knee-deep among reeds, watching men,
Or hung by the heels down the door of a dam

It is a god, and inviolable.
Immortal. And will wash itself of all deaths.[44]

This is one of the few poems in the book which does seem to refer directly to the photograph with which it is paired. The photograph in question shows rough meadows, darkening at evening, with a twist of river flowing towards us in the middle. The river catches the last light of day and turns to silver, the only bright thing in the picture; but its path is littered with dark boulders, so that it really does seem 'Fallen from heaven' but 'broken by world'.

Despite this visual reference, the poem functions on an interpretive level as much as a descriptive one. The first two lines—

Fallen from heaven, lies across
The lap of his mother, broken by world.

—show the river in the form of a Pietà: the newly-crucified Jesus ('broken by world') lying across the knees of Mary his mother. Throughout the collection, the river is often characterized by Hughes as the offspring of God, God being identified with the sun from which (as Hughes sees it) the river derives its brilliancy and power. The river has 'fallen from heaven' in the form of rain, it lies across the lap of the earth, and it is 'broken by world' in the sense that its flow is broken or interrupted by rocks. All these details can be interpreted in a realistic way. But Hughes is also suggesting that the river has a mythological significance, that its father is the sun and its mother is the earth, and that it comes down from heaven with a gift of life and sacrifices itself in order that we may live. In this way he is setting up a comparison between Jesus and the river which is continued throughout the poem. The river is apparently dead and buried but 'Its dry tombs will split', as the tomb of Jesus split at the Resurrection, 'At a rending of veils', as the veil of the Temple at Jerusalem was rent when Jesus died; and 'After swallowing death and the pit' as Jesus did, spending three days in the underworld before he rose again, the river will 'return stainless/For the delivery of this world', just as Jesus did. Of course, these details all refer to physical events in the life of the river too—the 'rending of veils', for example, is the breakup of clouds as they release their burden of rain, renewing the river and thus bringing it back from the dead. But the controlling idea of the poem is the comparison with Jesus, leading to the assertion that 'the river is a god'.

Having set up the river as an equivalent to Christ, however, the poem finishes by defining the difference between them: the river 'will wash itself of all deaths'. Christ's mission on earth, according to orthodox Christian teaching, was to save the individual from personal extinction; but the river's mission is to shrug off any number of personal extinctions, and always to press forward towards new life. This was the theme of 'Lumb Chimneys', and it is a theme which is stated explicitly in the last poem of *River*, 'Salmon Eggs':

> *Only birth matters*
> Say the river's whorls.[45]

It is the quintessence of Hughes's philosophy: a relentless, merciless optimism in which individuals can redeem themselves only by attuning themselves to a survival process which involves their personal extinction.

In *River*, the barrier that separates Man from Nature and

from the inner life seems to have thinned or become permeable. This is one aspect of the collection that marks it out as the product of Hughes's later, more relaxed style. In the earlier collections the individual, like the Elephant in 'Crow's Elephant Totem Song', must be torn to pieces before he can achieve redemption. Such a shattering of the self can usually only come about involuntarily, through the agency of some terrible external force. But in the later poetry, Hughes's emphasis on the redemptive power of personal suffering begins to wane. Firstly, in *Remains of Elmet*, he broadens his focus from the individual to industrial society as a whole. Later, in *River*, he suggests that individuals can achieve a transcendent (albeit temporary) union with the natural world and the world of 'underbeing' simply by going fishing. The conscious mind must still be supplanted and broken apart, but this process now seems a much less anguished one than before. And although *River* still emphasizes the idea that the individual must be prepared to accept the inevitability of his own suffering and death, there is now a much stronger sense of the positive aspects of this world-view. The almost obsessive concentration on anguish and destruction that characterizes Hughes's middle-period collections—and dictates the terms in which most critics think of his work—is replaced in *River* by a celebration of the power and variety of the natural world.

But contrary to what Thomas West seems to think, Hughes's language is never the language of a man who is 'simply overwhelmed by the surface of things'. In *River* as much as anywhere else, his poems decode the landscape and invest it with meanings as much as they describe it. Often his descriptions depend on a type of knowledge that could not be garnered from mere sensory information. His depiction of the river as the offspring of the sun, for example, derives from the idea that the sun's atomic power constitutes the fountainhead of all life on earth. The scientific undertones of this idea are evident from another poem, 'Flesh of Light', which begins:

From a core-flash, from a thunder-silence
Inside the sun, the smelting
Crawls and glimmers among heather-topped stones.

The mill of the galaxy, the generator
Making the atoms dance
With its reverberations, brims out lowly

For cattle to wade...[46]

The phrases 'core-flash', 'smelting' and 'generator' all suggest some knowledge of nuclear physics and the fission–fusion process which we are told is at work in the sun, as does the idea that the sun's power has the effect of 'Making the atoms dance/With its reverberations'.

It could be argued that it is ironic to hear an anti-scientific poet describing the universe in such scientific terms; or it could be argued that Hughes's poetry remakes these scientific ideas so that they become part of a more vital, imaginative interpretation of the universe. The real point is that Hughes always prefers to describe things in dynamic terms—in terms of the life within, rather than in terms of mere surfaces. He is always on the lookout for inner demons or myths by means of which the external appearances of a thing or a place can be explained and characterized; and his references to nuclear physics in the lines above do not indicate an abrupt surrender to the scientific world-view, so much as a liking for any imagery, scientific or otherwise, that promises to expose the inner dynamism of the universe rather than remaining enslaved to stolid surface appearances.

Hughes is never content merely to describe what he sees. The foundation of his descriptive writing is imaginative sympathy with the subject, and there is never any sense of the imaginative self being held in check for fear that it might impose its own vision on what is being described, and thus violate or simply obscure the otherness and strangeness of the external world. The characteristic strengths of his poetry all derive from its emphasis on this kind of imaginative sympathy, but so does its characteristic weakness, which is this: that he always seems to know the inner truth of whatever he happens to be describing. There is never any attempt to convey hesitation, misinterpretation or plain ignorance. Hughes never seems to be plagued by uncertainties about his own beliefs and intuitions. His descriptive style is therefore limited by the fact that he appears to lack a certain type of honesty—a fidelity to what it actually feels like to inhabit a world which we only partly understand. We are much more likely to find this type of honesty in the works of rationalist writers such as Charles Tomlinson; but perhaps we should be cautious of rushing to the conclusion that for this reason rationalist descriptions are necessarily superior to primitivist ones. Hughes would argue that the poet's job is not to confirm the limitations of the rational mind but to carry us beyond them; and that it is our enslavement to the 'strength and brilliance of our objective intelligence'—and to 'the scientific method' which has evolved from it—which has led not only to our spiritual impoverishment, but to the environmental catastrophes which are now becoming apparent all around us.

For Hughes, the 'inner self' of Man and the soul of Nature are always magically connected. If we have repressed and ravaged our inner selves, then our brutality towards the natural world is only to be expected. And these ideas, strange as they may seem to some readers, have a well-respected literary ancestry. William Blake and D. H. Lawrence, to name but two, would doubtless concur with most of what Hughes has to say. Both Hughes's descriptive style, with its characteristic strengths and weaknesses, and his pronouncements on environmental questions, must be seen in the context of his primitivist philosophy, and of the literary traditions from which that philosophy is derived, if they are to be evaluated properly.

NOTES

1. Hughes, 'Myth and Education', from Geoff Fox et al (eds), *Writers, Critics and Children* (London: Heinemann, 1976), reprinted in Hughes, *Winter Pollen* (Faber, 1994), p. 137.
2. *Ibid.*, p. 138.
3. *Ibid.*, p. 138.
4. *Ibid.*, p. 144.
5. *Ibid.*, p. 146.
6. *Ibid.*, p. 146.
7. *Ibid.*, p. 149.
8. Hughes, *Crow* (Faber, 1972), pp. 57–58.
9. Hughes, *Poetry in the Making* (Faber, 1967), pp. 60–61.
10. Hughes, *Lupercal* (Faber, 1960), pp. 56–57.
11. 'Ted Hughes and *Crow*: An Interview with Ekbert Faas', originally printed in *London Magazine*, January 1971; reprinted in Ekbert Faas, *Ted Hughes: The Unaccommodated Universe* (Santa Barbara, California: Black Sparrow Press, 1980), pp. 197–208.
12. Hughes, *Lupercal*, p. 25.
13. Hughes, *Poetry in the Making*, p. 78.
14. *Orghast* is the name of a play, written by Hughes, which was staged in 1971 in Iran by Peter Brook and his company. Hughes wrote the play in a language of his own invention, also called 'Orghast'. Smith's book describes the whole theatrical experiment, and my quotation comes from some written notes which Hughes supplied to Smith outlining his theory of language. See A. C. H. Smith, *Orghast at Persepolis* (Eyre Methuen, 1972), p. 45.
15. Hughes, *Wolfwatching* (Faber, 1989), p. 16.
16. Hughes, *Wodwo* (Faber, 1967), p. 177.
17. Hughes, *Gaudete* (Faber, 1977), p. 194.
18. *Ibid.*, p. 23.
19. *Ibid.*, p. 32.
20. *Ibid.*, p. 71.
21. *Ibid.*, p. 30.
22. Ted Hughes (poems) and Fay Godwin (photographs), *Remains of Elmet* (Faber, 1979), p. 47; Hughes, *Three Books* (Faber, 1993), pp. 50–51.
23. Hughes, *Remains of Elmet*, p. 30.
24. *Ibid.*, pp. 56, 73, 76, 92, 103, 118.
25. *Ibid.*, p. 103.
26. *Ibid.*, p. 8.
27. Hughes, review of Max Nicholson, *The Environmental Revolution*, in *Your Environment*, vol. 1, no. 3; reprinted in Hughes, *Winter Pollen*, pp. 128–35.
28. Hughes, *Crow*, p. 86.
29. Hughes, *Remains of Elmet*, p. 8.
30. *Ibid.*, p. 84.
31. *Ibid.*, p. 89.

32. Hughes, *Crow*, p. 86.
33. Hughes, *Remains of Elmet*, p. 14.
34. Ted Hughes (poems) and Peter Keen (photographs), *River* (Faber, 1983), pp. 72, 78–84.
35. *Ibid.*, pp. 44–50.
36. *Ibid.*, pp. 8–12.
37. *Ibid.*, pp. 120–24.
38. *Ibid.*, p. 38.
39. Thomas West, *Ted Hughes* (Methuen, 1985), pp. 115–16.
40. Hughes, *River*, p. 76.
41. Hughes, *Three Books*, pp. 118–21.
42. *Ibid.*, p. 137.
43. Hughes, *River*, p. 42.
44. *Ibid.*, p. 74.
45. *Ibid.*, p. 120.
46. *Ibid.*, p. 16.

Chapter Six
Seamus Heaney:
From 'the older dispensation'
to 'the country of the shades'

I

At the heart of Heaney's early poetry about the Irish landscape is the myth of an Irish Eden: an undisturbed primitive
state in which the Irish people and the Irish land were united
by what he describes as 'a feeling, assenting, equable marriage
between the geographical country and the country of the
mind'. These words are taken from his 1977 lecture 'The Sense
of Place', where he asserts that this 'equable marriage ...
constitutes the sense of place in its richest possible manifestation', and goes on to relate this idea to a sense of personal
nostalgia:

> Only thirty years ago, and thirty miles from Belfast,
> I think I experienced this kind of world vestigially
> and as a result may have retained some vestigial
> sense of place as it was experienced in the older
> dispensation.[1]

But this is nostalgia tinged with nationalism. The 'older
dispensation' to which he refers here is the dispensation of a
predominantly Catholic culture; for Heaney believes that the
ancient, intimate pagan relationship between Man and Nature
was preserved in Ireland in the guise of Marian Catholicism
until the Protestants disturbed the tradition.

A few paragraphs later in the same lecture, he describes the
country customs of his childhood in the following terms:

> Then on May Eve, the buttercups and ladysmock
> appeared on the windowsills in obedience to some
> rite, and during the month of May the pagan
> goddess became the Virgin Mary and May flowers
> had to be gathered for her altar on the chest-of-
> drawers in the bedroom...[2]

Like Ted Hughes, Heaney associates Protestantism with a
rational, materialistic and exploitative attitude towards the
natural world, whereas Marian Catholicism is seen as a more
irrational and instinctive tradition, expressing more fully the
urges of the unconscious mind. Most critics who have written
about Heaney have acknowledged that Ted Hughes was an
important stylistic influence on his first book, *Death of a
Naturalist*; but none appears to have noticed that Hughes and
Heaney also share certain important beliefs about paganism
and primitivism, including the belief that Catholicism is more
responsive than Protestantism to the natural world and the
'inner life'. In Heaney's case, of course, this attitude towards
Catholicism carries a nationalistic implication, because he
associates Catholicism with the native Irish people, whereas
he associates Protestantism with English and Scottish
intruders. His nostalgia for an 'older dispensation' therefore
implies a lament for the time when Northern Ireland was still
part of a predominantly Catholic country, before partition cut
it off from the South and cast the Catholic Northern Irish
adrift in a predominantly Protestant United Kingdom.

   Under these circumstances, the surprising thing is that
Heaney is far less dismissive of the Protestant, rational
tradition and far less straightforwardly committed to the
Marian, pagan, irrational alternative than is Hughes: but his
refusal to be simplistic about these matters is only one
example of the characteristic subtlety of his thought. In an
interview with Seamus Deane which also dates from 1977 (the
same year as 'The Sense of Place'), Heaney, urged by Deane to
declare that the 'rationalist humanism' that he associates with

Protestantism is a 'dangerous feature' of Western civilization, seems at first to agree, but then sounds a note of caution:

> Yes, absolutely ... But I think there is a dialogue. I think the obstinate voice of rationalist humanism is important. If we lose that we lose everything too, don't we?[3]

It is this refusal to oversimplify, this determination to see both sides of every question, this almost obsessive insistence that every question must have two sides, which prevents Heaney from ever entirely committing himself to a reductive Fall-myth, or from ever finally embracing the primitivist world-view.

In Heaney's early poetry, we find him defining two types of human behaviour: firstly the rational, materialistic, assertive and exploitative behaviour which he associates with the English and with other conquering, 'sky-worshipping' cultures; and secondly the irrational, self-sacrificing, conservative and submissive behaviour which he associates with the Irish and other rural 'mould-huggers' (as he calls them elsewhere). Having made this division, he seems to express a preference for quiescent, earth-worshipping cultures rather than exploitative, sky-worshipping ones, and to construct a Fall-myth in which the earth-worshipping way of life represents a state of innocence and grace, while the sky-worshippers are seen as the serpent, the outside power whose arrival in Paradise precipitates the Fall. But although these ideas and patterns of symbolism certainly play an important part in his early poetry, he never gives himself over to primitivism as wholeheartedly as R. S. Thomas or Ted Hughes.

'Digging', the first poem of Heaney's first collection (*Death of a Naturalist*, 1966), dramatizes his determination to define two antagonistic modes of behaviour and to decide which, as a poet, he should choose for himself. The poem begins:

Between my finger and my thumb
The squat pen rests; snug as a gun.

And it ends:

Between my finger and my thumb
The squat pen rests.
I'll dig with it.[4]

Heaney himself has called 'Digging' a 'big coarse-grained
navvy of a poem',[5] and his critics have pointed out that the
pen–gun and pen–spade analogies are both somewhat forced.
But his decision to use his pen as a spade rather than as a gun
is nevertheless rich with implications. Firstly, of course, it
implies that Heaney is associating himself with the passive,
rural traditions of Irish history rather than with the fabled
violence of Irish gunmen, however much he might sympathize
with the causes for which those gunmen have fought.
Secondly, he sees himself as continuing (in his own way) the
rural traditions of his family. The poem includes descriptions
of his father digging potatoes and his grandfather cutting peat,
and the last line 'I'll dig with it' is intended to convey
Heaney's determination to carry on with his pen the same
rural traditions to which his father and grandfather
contributed with their spades. Thirdly, he rejects the role of
poet-as-gunman because he sees it as aggressive and self-
willed, and he associates those qualities with the conquering,
sky-worshipping English rather than with the passive, earth-
worshipping Irish. But lastly, he is also making a statement
about the kind of poetry he intends to write: a poetry of
exploration and nurture rather than of assertion and conscious
mastery.

This choice of poetic style is further illuminated by an essay
entitled 'The Fire i' the Flint' (first given as a lecture in 1974),
in which Heaney defines two modes of utterance, the masculine and the feminine:

> In the masculine mode, the language functions as a
> form of address, of assertion or command, and the
> poetic effort has to do with conscious quelling and
> control of the materials, a labour of shaping...
> Whereas in the feminine mode the language func-
> tions more as evocation than as address, and the
> poetic effort is not so much a labour of design as it
> is an act of divination and revelation...[6]

As other essays by Heaney make clear, these ideas about
masculine and feminine modes of utterance are shaped by a
feeling that modern Irish poets must choose between the
examples set by the 'masculine' Yeats—'one is awed by the
achieved and masterful tones of that deliberately pitched
voice'[7]—and the 'feminine' Patrick Kavanagh—'a taker of
verses, a grabber of them' for whom 'The poem is more a
conductor than a crucible'.[8] So far as 'Digging' is concerned,
the 'masculine', Yeatsian mode clearly equates with the poet-
as-gunman, whereas the 'feminine' mode equates with the
poet-as-digger. Furthermore, Heaney associates masculine
utterance with 'conscious quelling and control' and feminine
utterance with 'an act of divination and revelation', so that the
gunman in 'Digging' must be seen as a rational, self-willed
figure, whereas the digger is an intuitive explorer, unsure of
what he is likely to uncover. Thus the act of digging, which
delves into the subsurface of the landscape, becomes associated with the workings of a certain type of poetic imagination,
which finds its inspiration by delving into the unconscious
mind. From this connection Heaney derives the metaphor of
underground-as-memory-and-unconscious which is so important to his early poetry.

Heaney's habit of stacking up symbolic values for a single
aspect of the landscape can sometimes result in a conflict of
meaning within the confines of a single poem. This is the case
with another piece from *Death of a Naturalist*, 'At a Potato
Digging', in which—because the subsurface of the landscape

represents the history of the Irish people as well as their
unconscious paganism—a conflict occurs between the historic
and cyclic views of time. The poem is in four sections. In
the first section, the relationship between the Irish peasants
and the soil on which they live is essentially pagan and suppli-
catory:

> Heads bow, trunks bend, hands fumble towards
> 　　the black
> Mother. Processional stooping through the turf
> Recurs mindlessly as autumn...[9]

Heaney's emphasis on the harshness of rural life in this
poem—which is at variance with more nostalgic or generalized descriptions elsewhere in his poetry—may owe something to the example of Kavanagh's poem 'The Great Hunger'.
But his representation here of the relationship between the
land and the peasants who live on it, with its primitivist undertones, is also reminiscent of the work of R. S. Thomas. Like
Thomas, Heaney sees the work as not only harsh but mindless, and its mindlessness is directly related to its timeless
quality: 'Processional stooping through the turf/Recurs mindlessly as autumn'. Heaney may not use the word 'mindlessly'
with the same approving intonation that we would expect
from Thomas, but the underlying structure of ideas is very
similar nevertheless. The mindlessness of the peasants means
that there is no disruption of natural cycles: the Irish are
dominated by the natural world rather than dominating it; and
as a result there is no notion of progress or of history as a
movement forwards and upwards through time. All activities
are rendered as timeless and cyclic as the recurrence of
autumn itself.

　　The third section of the poem, however, refers to the great
Potato Famine of 1845–49, and here we are presented not with
the cyclic view of time, which tells us that essentially nothing
has ever changed and nothing is ever going to change, but with
the historical view, which tells us that each event is unique,

with its own causes and consequences. The outraged tone in which Heaney describes the famine demonstrates that he is unable to think of it as a natural event which must be accepted as a dispensation of the Earth Goddess:

> Stinking potatoes fouled the land,
> pits turned pus into filthy mounds:
> and where potato diggers are
> you still smell the running sore.

A true primitivist would be inclined to see crop-failures as an unavoidable aspect of the relationship between Man and Nature; but Heaney's knowledge of Irish history tells him that in some way the Famine was an outrage which was the responsibility of the English, who gradually reduced the Irish peasantry to a state of subsistence and almost complete dependence on a single crop for their survival, and who did not take any action to alleviate the crisis for a long while after it had begun.

The cyclic view of time is thus pushed aside in this section of the poem, only to reassert itself at the end, where Heaney describes the potato-diggers flopping down for a rest:

> Thankfully breaking timeless fasts;
> Then, stretched on the faithless ground, [they] spill
> Libations of cold tea, scatter crusts.

Again the primitivist vision is indicated by the use of the word 'timeless', and by the image of the workers making offerings to 'the faithless ground', still unconsciously treating it as a goddess. But as an ending to the poem this is woefully unconvincing. If the ground is the only thing which is 'faithless'—if 'the black mother' is to carry all the blame for the potato famine—then the outraged tone of the third section seems misplaced. But if there are other culprits, then the primitivist view put forward here seems at best a way of missing the point, and at worst a way of dodging the issue. The real problem here is that Heaney has found two different ways of looking at his chosen subject, and he can neither bring himself to abandon one of them in favour of the other, nor work out a way of reconciling them convincingly.

'At a Potato Digging' is unusual for Heaney's early work in that it emphasizes the harshness of rural life and the unreliability of the land as a provider for the peasants who live on it. In other poems with a primitivist slant, where Heaney commits himself more fully to the cyclic view of time and the idea of the earth as a goddess, the 'black mother' becomes both more bloodthirsty and more reliable. But the conflict between two different views of time which is revealed here does not go away. It will eventually re-emerge in *North* and split the book into two halves.

II

The present Troubles in Northern Ireland (which, as I write, seem to have been brought to an end by the IRA's Cessation of Violence in the summer of 1994) began in 1968–69, when Heaney was lecturing at Queen's University, Belfast. He was a supporter of the Catholic civil rights movement, and he writes in *Preoccupations* of the effect that the arrival of British troops on 14 August 1969 had on his poetry:

> From that moment the problems of poetry moved from being simply a matter of achieving the satisfactory verbal icon to being a search for images and symbols adequate to our predicament.[10]

In fact, however, his search for adequate 'symbols and images' was already under way before trouble erupted. His second volume, *Door into the Dark*, which appeared in 1969 only two months after the troops arrived, contains a whole sequence of poems about different features of the Irish landscape—'The Peninsula',[11] 'Whinlands',[12] 'The Plantation',[13] 'Shoreline'[14] and 'Bann Clay'[15]—each of which seems to be striving for symbolic resonance.

Heaney seems to be casting around for a master-symbol that will enable him to express a whole complex of thoughts and feelings about the landscape, history, unconscious urges and present condition of Ireland and the Irish people. The breakthrough comes with 'Bogland', the last poem in the book, which inaugurates a series of poems about bogs and the human remains that have been found in them. For Heaney, the bog with its preserving powers represents history, because it contains so many relics of the past. But it also suggests time-lessness, because those relics are preserved so perfectly, as though the past has been buried alive in the subterranean darkness; and since many of the relics are the corpses of people who were killed hundreds or even thousands of years ago, the bog reminds us that the present-day violence in Northern Ireland is really nothing new. There is a suggestion that violence may recur as timelessly and mindlessly as the seasons and the harvests; and this suggestion allows Heaney, for a while at least, to play down the underlying disparity between the cyclic and historical views of time, by exploring the idea that history is not really linear at all, but as cyclic as the rural calendar—except that the cycles are on a much larger scale. And because the bog contains buried evidence of violence it also comes to symbolize the buried unconscious of the Irish people and of the poet himself, where violent impulses lie concealed. By exploring the bog, Heaney suggests, is may be possible for the Irish people to make contact with the truth about themselves:

> Our pioneers keep striking
> Inwards and downwards,
>
> Every layer they strip
> Seems camped on before.
> The bogholes might be Atlantic seepage.
> The wet centre is bottomless.[16]

Heaney tells us in *Preoccupations* how he came to write 'Bogland':

> At that time I was teaching modern literature in Queen's University, Belfast, and had been reading about the frontier and the west as an important myth in the American consciousness, so I set up— or rather, laid down—the bog as an answering Irish myth.[17]

The contrast is revealing: Heaney is suggesting that the Irish live in a world of stasis and depth, a world which can only be explored and measured properly through downward and inward exploration, rather than through new conquests and the establishment of new frontiers. The American frontiers, he suggests, stand for the urge to break new ground, to leave the past behind and push forward into an unknown future, and thus they lend themselves to the myth of progress. Heaney's 'answering Irish myth' tells us that we can only understand ourselves properly by understanding the past, because the past is still alive. He speaks of the bogland

> Melting and opening underfoot,
> Missing its last definition
> By millions of years.

In such a landscape, the past is never over and done with, and the future will bring nothing new, only further contributions to the timeless depth of the bog. And as in 'Digging', Heaney, by emphasizing a certain aspect of Ireland, is also making a statement about the kind of poetry he wants to write— rejecting ideas of radical newness and the avant-garde in favour of a poetry that explores and makes connections with its own past. Literature itself is seen as a kind of bogland, where the present and the past lie down together.

'Requiem for the Croppies', another poem from *Door into the Dark*, shows how the landscape-symbolism we have examined so far provides Heaney with a language through which to express his nationalism when he retells an incident from Irish history. But it also demonstrates the risk of oversimplification which attends any such attempt to retell historic events in symbolic and mythic terms. Here is the poem in full:

> The pockets of our great coats full of barley—
> No kitchens on the run, no striking camp—
> We moved quick and sudden in our own country.
> The priest lay behind ditches with the tramp.
> A people, hardly marching—on the hike—
> We found new tactics happening each day:
> We'd cut through reins and rider with the pike
> And stampede cattle into infantry,
> Then retreat through hedges where cavalry must be
>   thrown.
> Until, on Vinegar Hill, the fatal conclave.
> Terraced thousands died, shaking scythes at cannon.
> The hillside blushed, soaked in our broken wave.
> They buried us without shroud or coffin
> And in August the barley grew up out of the grave.[18]

The poem refers to the Irish rebellion of 1798. The 'croppy boys' were so-called because they cropped their hair after the manner of the peasants of the French Revolution, but Heaney puns on the name to associate those who took part in the rebellion with their own crops, and thus to emphasize their closeness to the land—'our own country', as the speaker in the poem calls it. He also sets up an opposition between the impulsive actions of the croppies and the organized might which defeats them. The croppies' tactics were never thought out: 'We found new tactics happening each day'. The land seemed to be fighting on their side: they would 'stampede cattle into infantry' (an ancient Irish battle-tactic) or take advantage of 'hedges where cavalry must be thrown'; and when they were defeated, 'The hillside blushed' in sympathy and shame.

Heaney presents them as disorganized, impulsive and at one

with the landscape. By contrast, we assume that their enemies must be ruthlessly well organized. They are described as 'infantry' and 'cavalry', which immediately makes them seem much more like a proper army than the croppies—'A people, hardly marching—on the hike'. But the contrast between the two sides becomes explicit in the line 'Terraced thousands died, shaking scythes at cannon.' The croppies' weapons are not only pathetically inadequate by comparison with the 'cannon' of their enemies; they are also agricultural implements, and thus serve to remind us of their closeness to the land. And this suggestion of an organic connection between the insurgents and their country culminates in the idea that by sacrificing their lives the croppies have renewed the land's fertility—'in August the barley grew up out of the grave'. The barley springs from the seeds the rebels carried in their pockets, but Heaney's intention is to suggest that the croppy boys themselves, like barley, will spring afresh from any grave in which they are temporarily laid low.

The contrast between the croppies and the English-led army that slaughters them is the same as the contrast between the Irish bogland and the American prairie. Heaney is suggesting that the English are frontiersmen, well organized and ruthless, with a cerebral, exploitative attitude towards the lands they conquer; whereas the croppies have an organic, timeless relationship with the country they inhabit, and their impulsive way of fighting reflects their instinctive, almost mindless way of life. The poem thus provides a foretaste of some of Heaney's later work. When he writes of 'The Tollund Man', in one of the later bogland poems from *Wintering Out*,[19] that his body, exhumed from the depths, contains 'His last gruel of winter seeds/Caked in his stomach', the information is meant to link him with the land in just the same way as the croppy boys' pocketfuls of barley. And when he writes in 'Hercules and Antaeus' from *North*[20] that Hercules is 'Sky-born and royal' whereas Antaeus is 'a mould-hugger', he is delineating the same contrast as the one between the croppy boys and the army that slaughters them.

The patterns of symbolism used in 'Requiem for the Croppies' are not entirely unique to Heaney. He describes the genesis of the poem in *Preoccupations*: it was written 'in 1966 when most poets in Ireland were straining to celebrate the anniversary of the 1916 Rising'. Heaney adds that

> The oblique implication [of the poem] was that the seeds of violent resistance sowed in the Year of Liberty had flowered in what Yeats called 'the right rose tree' of 1916.[21]

This reference to Yeats directs us to Yeats's poem 'The Rose Tree' which concludes with the following stanza:

> 'But where can we draw water',
> Said Pearse to Connolly,
> 'When all the wells are parched away?
> O plain as plain can be
> There's nothing but our own red blood
> Can make a right Rose Tree.'

Pearse and Connolly were the leaders of the 1916 rebellion. By suggesting that the Irish landscape was fertilized by the blood of the 1798 rebels, Heaney is consciously echoing Yeats's suggestion that Pearse, Connolly and the other 1916 rebels used their own blood to feed the 'right Rose Tree' of Irish nationalism.

It is also worth remarking that Pearse himself often used the same imagery, as the historian R. F. Foster points out in his book *Modern Ireland*:

> 'Life springs from death, and from the graves of patriotic men and women spring living nations.' Pearse's aesthetic frequently celebrated the beauty of boys dying bravely in their prime...[22]

The 1916 rebellion was originally planned for Easter Sunday—

a deliberate attempt to exploit the Christian myth of self-sacrifice, redemption and rebirth. Heaney's assertion that 'The priest lay behind ditches with the tramp' lends the croppy boys' rebellion a religious dimension in the same way, seizing on the historical fact that some Roman Catholic priests joined the rebellion, and in certain famous examples even took command of the troops. But the link between the croppy boys and the Catholic priesthood is more important in mythological terms than it is historically. The 1798 rebellion became retrospectively associated with the struggles of the Irish Catholics against a social order built on Protestant supremacy, and thus it entered into Irish Catholic mythology. And certainly the symbolic standoff, between organized might and a disorganized peasant rabble, upon which Heaney builds his poem, has the ring of mythological oversimplification to it. The croppy boys have been turned into helpless martyrs. Their opponents have become the faceless agents of depersonalized might. The jumbled messiness and moral uncertainties of real historical events have been cleared away.

The classic account of the 1798 rebellion is Thomas Pakenham's book *The Year of Liberty*. It was published in 1969, so Heaney could not have read it when he wrote 'Requiem for the Croppies'; but all the same, Pakenham's narrative provides a devastating commentary on the clear-cut patterns of the poem. He demonstrates, for one thing, that the forces of Protestant ascendancy, throughout most of the campaign, were every bit as irrational as the rebels. Nor were the rebels very 'quick and sudden' in 'their own country'—they seem to have thrown away most of their early advantages through indecision. For another thing, many of the Loyalist troops were actually Catholics; although some Catholic priests did command rebel troops during the uprising, others were at pains to condemn it; and in the North, many of the rebels (including the leader Henry Monroe) were Protestant dissenters. Furthermore, Vinegar Hill was not the end of the rebellion, as Heaney makes it appear: the Irish insurgency sputtered on for some months after, and later still there was a landing by the French. But the most important point is that although Heaney does acknowledge some violence on the part of the rebels ('We'd cut through reins and rider with the pike') he leaves us with an overwhelming impression of peasants being slaughtered by the impassive cannon-led might of their conquerors. This impression may be reasonably fair as regards the events at Vinegar Hill, but it does not hold good for 1798 as a whole, when terrible atrocities were perpetrated by both sides.

Heaney's reference in *Preoccupations* to the 'right rose tree' of 1916 directs us to the underlying mythologizing tendency which has played such strange tricks (on both sides of the religious divide) with interpretations of Irish history. Heaney himself is seeking to link the rebellion of 1798 with that of 1916, and representing them both as cases of nationalistic martyrs allowing themselves to be slaughtered for the good of their country, so that their blood may fertilize the ground for later generations of free Irishmen. But like the 1798 rebellion, the 1916 uprising itself has become so thoroughly mythologized and impregnated with symbolic meaning that it seems almost impossible to cut away the layers of heroic glamour and see it in more dispassionate, objective terms.

Recent Irish historians have begun a much-needed demythologizing process: here is David Fitzpatrick, in *The Oxford History of Ireland*:

> Joseph Mary Plunkett and Thomas MacDonagh, like Pearse, revelled in the vulgar wartime lie that the shedding of blood was 'a cleansing and sanctifying thing', and imagined that a race of resurrected Gaelic heroes would emerge out of the bloodied gutters of Sackville (alias O'Connell) Street... The main victims of the 'proclamation of the Irish Republic' were... unarmed civilians, whose suffering was compounded by the wreckage of central

> Dublin... Rebels were roughed up on active service
> by enraged women and pelted with tomatoes after
> surrendering...[23]

Fitzpatrick argues that only after the English Government
obliged the rebels by over-reacting to the uprising, were the
ringleaders gradually transfigured into folk-heroes:

> While the new revolutionary elite crystallised in
> detention, a sentimental cult of veneration for the
> martyrs developed outside as after previous failed
> uprisings.

The 'sentimental cult' which came to surround the 1916
uprising certainly owed a good deal to the work of W. B. Yeats;
and there can be little doubt that Heaney is following in the
same tradition by making his own contribution to the 'sentimental cult' of 1798.

Of course, the fact that Heaney simplifies the 1798 rebellion into what he himself has called a 'heraldic murderous
encounter'[24] does not by any means make 'Requiem for the
Croppies' a bad poem in literary terms. But it does demonstrate how tricky it can be to apply ready-made symbolic
systems—systems which seem comparatively innocuous in
the works of R. S. Thomas and Ted Hughes—to the complex-
ities of historical events and present-day political situations.
Whatever it is that separates the country from the city, or a
rationalist from a primitivist, it cannot be tidily equated with
what separates an Irishman from an Englishman or a Catholic
from a Protestant—and this is a conclusion towards which
Heaney himself seems to be working his way in his next two
collections.

III

The most important element that *Wintering Out* (1972) adds to Heaney's developing pattern of landscape-symbolism is the link between landscape and language. One poem to make this link is 'Gifts of Rain'. It describes the River Moyola, beside which Heaney grew up, and which evidently burst its banks and flooded the surrounding countryside at regular intervals. The poem suggests that the local farmers are brought closer to the land by learning to anticipate and deal with the regular floods; and in the third section, Heaney describes how farmers used to be able to tell by the changed sound of the river that a flood was on its way:

> When rains were gathering
> there would be an all-night
> roaring off the ford.
> Their world-schooled ear
>
> could monitor the usual
> confabulations...[25]

Later in the same section, Heaney goes on to imply a link between the voice of the river and Gaelic, the indigenous language of the country:

> I cock my ear
> at an absence—
> in the shared calling of blood
>
> arrives my need
> for antediluvian lore.
> Soft voices of the dead
> are whispering by the shore...

By resorting to the first person in 'I cock my ear at an absence', Heaney separates his own modern awareness from the 'world-schooled ear' of his forefathers. When he listens to the voice of the river he cannot interpret it as they could:

instead he feels a sense of 'absence'. He has been displaced
from 'the shared calling of blood' and feels a 'need/for antediluvian lore', a lore that would reconnect him with the voice
of the river, thus healing his sense of displacement. In the
lines 'Soft voices of the dead/are whispering by the shore',
the voice of the river actually becomes the voice of former
generations, an idea which has already been suggested by the
phrase 'the shared calling of blood'. As he does elsewhere,
Heaney is implying that the Irish landscape contains and
expresses the lives of its former inhabitants.

In 'Gifts of Rain', the ghosts of those former inhabitants
seem to haunt the Moyola, and the river seems to speak with
their voice. So Heaney's inability to understand the voice of
the river involves not only a failure to relate to the landscape
as closely as his forefathers did, but also a failure to make
contact with those forefathers themselves—to understand
their voices and thus share their culture. In part, this failure
results from the fact that Heaney and others of his generation
have broken the old connection with the land in order to
pursue less-rural ways of life—in other words, part of
the feeling in this poem is the familiar nostalgia for the lost
secrets of a more primitive existence; but the sense of broken
connections also has to do with the fact that the Irish
people—especially the Northern Irish Catholics—have been
forcibly separated from the Gaelic language and Gaelic
culture. The language which is whispered by the 'Soft voices
of the dead', a language which has grown organically from the
close relationship between the Irish people and their landscape, is Gaelic; and Heaney cannot understand the voice of
the river as his ancestors could because, unlike them, he has
been brought up to speak not Gaelic but English.

When he writes of his need for 'antediluvian lore' he means
a lore predating the flood of English invasion. In a sense this
lore is not only antediluvian but prelapsarian too, because of
course 'Gifts of Rain' embodies an Irish Nationalist version of
the Eden-myth. There was once an Eden-like Ireland, the

poem would have us believe, where the native Irish lived in such perfect harmony with their surroundings that their language expressed and embodied the impressions those surroundings made on their senses. This Eden-like existence was disrupted by the intrusion of invaders; but even now, if we analyse remaining fragments of the Gaelic language such as old place-names, we can still catch the flavour of the original close connection between language-sounds and physical experiences. Thus, in the last section of the poem, Heaney tells us that

> The tawny guttural water
> spells itself: Moyola...

The voice of the river seems to pronounce its own name—it 'spells itself'. The Gaelic name is thus directly derived from a physical experience of the landscape. Place, language and culture were once organically linked to one another—but the link has been broken by invasion and the near-abolition of the Gaelic language.

Like Heaney's interpretation of the 1798 rebellion, his interpretation of the relationship between Gaelic language and Irish landscape should be set in the context of the historical development of Irish nationalism. Again the remarks of R. F. Foster provide a useful commentary. According to Foster, the Gaelic language had all but disappeared, except from the most underdeveloped parts of Ireland such as Mayo, when the Gaelic League was founded in 1893:

> The League's objective was specifically to revive the
> use of the Irish language, and introduce it into the
> educational curriculum at all levels...[26]

The practice of Irish sectarian societies and political parties adopting Gaelic names dates from this time. When a measure of Irish independence was finally achieved the promotion of the Gaelic tongue became official policy:

> During the 1920s [the era of the Irish Free State]...
> the regime necessarily laid heavy emphasis on the
> 'Gaelic' nature of the new state... most of all, the
> prosecution of the Irish language became the neces-
> sary bench-mark of an independent ethos. In 1911
> those able to speak Irish at all, let alone speaking it
> regularly, had numbered 17.6 per cent of the popula-
> tion...[27]

The appeal of the Gaelic language for Irish nationalists, Foster
implies, can only be partly explained in terms of an enthusiasm for authentic Irish culture. Equally important was the
desire to shut the English out—just as the English themselves
once shut out Gaelic speakers and Roman Catholics.

The Gaelic language helped to define Irishness partly
because it mapped out a territory where the English were
bound to be at a disadvantage. Likewise Heaney, although he
writes in English, salts his poetry in *Wintering Out* with Gaelic
words and allusions which are intended to challenge and
possibly baffle the English reader. Several poems explore
Gaelic place-names and their derivations. 'Broagh', one of
these, ends with a reference to the pronunciation of the word
'Broagh' itself:

> that last
> *gh* the strangers found
> difficult to manage.[28]

The reader is being asked to identify himself: is he a native,
who can pronounce 'that last/*gh*' properly, or is he one of the
'strangers'? The name 'Broagh' apparently derives from
'bruach', which is Gaelic for 'riverbank', and the idea of the
poem is that the word itself enacts the physical experience of a
particular riverbank in Ireland:

> The garden mould
> bruised easily, the shower

gathering in your heelmark
was the black O

in *Broagh*...

If the reader does not happen to know about the derivation of
'Broagh' then the poem may not make much sense to him. It
will shut him out: it will remind him that he is one of the
'strangers'. In this way, Heaney uses the Gaelic language to
challenge his English readers' assumptions of cultural
supremacy, and to reclaim the Irish landscape for the Irish.

IV

North (1975), Heaney's fourth collection, is the one in which
he confronts the Irish Troubles most fully, and for that reason
it is the one which has been most thoroughly discussed by his
critics. The book is divided into two parts, and in them
Heaney seems to approach the Troubles from two different
angles. Crudely speaking, he adopts an ahistorical, mythologizing approach in the first part, whereas in the second part
he focuses more sharply on the here-and-now, and on his own
reactions to the violence as an individual. In the first part, he
uses himself as an everyman-figure, exploring his own unconscious mind along with the subsurface of the landscape, where
macabre evidence of the violence of Irish prehistory lies
buried. When he analyses his own feelings, he does so on the
assumption that they are representative of the Irish people as a
whole: he identifies himself as one of the crowd. But in the
second part of the book he appears as an individual, speaking
for himself: a self-aware artist who stands apart from the
conflict and comments on it from his own point of view. Here
the cyclic view of time is replaced by a sense of history, and
the sense of helpless anonymity is replaced by a feeling of
moral responsibility, an anxiety to do the right thing. But it is
the first part of the book on which I shall concentrate, because

it is there that Heaney's landscape-symbolism seems to complete the line of development it has been following so far.

The title *North* itself can be read in two ways. It refers, of course, to 'the North', modern Northern Ireland: to its separation from the South and the violence of the Troubles. But it also refers to the conflicts and rituals of pre-Christian northern Europe, which Heaney suggests are still being lived out in Ireland today. By turning his attention northwards, Heaney is exploring aspects of Irish history which are sometimes overlooked because of an obsession with Anglo-Irish conflict: the earthbound way of life which Irish peasants share with the primitive peoples of northern Europe, and the *penchant* for endless feuding which they seem to have picked up from their Viking invaders. He is examining historical connections between Ireland and the North in an attempt to uncover hidden aspects of the Irish psyche, and he equates this process of examination with a northern journey, which in turn links metaphorically with a movement from light into darkness, from the present into the past, from the rational mind into the unconscious, from the surface meanings of language to its etymological roots, and from the surface of the landscape to its subsurface.

Thus in 'Funeral Rites' he evokes a northward journey which is also a journey into the past, the purpose of which is to move away from the bitterness of present-day conflict until the origins of violence can be recognized and dealt with:

> we will drive north again
> past Strang and Carling fjords
>
> the cud of memory
> allayed for once, arbitration
> of the feud placated...[29]

And in the title-poem 'North' itself, he again uses the image of northward travel, this time equating it with a 'foray' through inner darkness towards nocturnal illumination:

                    Lie down
    in the word-hoard, burrow
    in the coil and gleam
    of your furrowed brain.

    Compose in darkness.
    Expect aurora borealis
    in the long foray
    but no cascade of light.[30]

The vocabulary in both these poems—'fjords', 'arbitration', 'feud', 'word-hoard' and 'foray'—emphasizes the link with Norse history.

The myth which dominates the first part of *North* is an elaboration of two ideas carried forward from the earlier volumes. The first of them is that bloodletting is an aspect of earth-worship: it arises from an irrational desire to appease the female earth-deity with human blood as a means of persuading her to renew her fertility. Heaney assumes that the Irish people are still essentially earth-worshippers, and that this accounts for their murderous impulses. He takes the boglands of Ireland and northern Europe, and the sacrificial victims which have been exhumed from them, as evidence of the timelessness of such violence.[31] His second idea is that human societies can be divided up into two types—firstly the 'feminine', earth-worshipping, irrational, regressive societies typified by the Irish peasantry; and secondly the 'masculine', sky-worshipping, rational, progressive societies typified by the English.

Heaney plays a series of bewildering variations on these basic ideas, and he often uses them in richly suggestive ways; but as we have already seen from 'Requiem for the Croppies', his determination to deal with the events of the modern Troubles obliquely, via symbolic and mythical systems, can sometimes lead him to oversimplify or misrepresent the situation. One example is the last section of 'Kinship':

Our mother ground
is sour with the blood
of her faithful,

they lie gargling
in her sacred heart
as the legions stare
from the ramparts.[32]

Both sides of Heaney's myth are present here. The idea that
the earth-worshipping Irish slaughter each other in order to
appease the earth-mother is suggested by the phrases 'Our
mother ground', 'the blood/of her faithful' and 'her sacred
heart'. And while the 'mould-hugging' natives 'lie gargling' in
the 'sacred heart' of the landscape (presumably a bog), their
sky-worshipping conquerors, 'the legions', 'stare' down from
a symbolically uplifted position on 'the ramparts', indicative
of the lofty intellectual detachment which has freed them
from the soil and the bloody sacrifices it demands. But these
lines, suggestive though they are, are certainly not an accurate
reflection of the present Troubles, whichever side you look at
the conflict from. The 'faithful' do not simply kill one
another, they kill the 'legions' too; and the 'legionaries' do not
simply stare from their ramparts in aloof astonishment, they
walk the streets with guns in their hands, shooting and being
shot at.

Furthermore, since Heaney's mythic approach is dominated by the cyclic or ahistorical view of time, according to
which individuals are powerless to inaugurate change or
achieve progress, but can only re-enact the lives of their fore-
bears in a timeless ritual, the effect is to make the violence of
the Troubles seem like the inevitable outcome of unconscious
impulses, rather than the result of conscious choices made by
morally responsible individuals. In the poems which describe
bodies exhumed from bogs, this feeling of inevitability manifests itself in a variety of ways. Firstly, there is a suggestion

that the victims have been beatified by their violent deaths, as in 'The Grauballe Man':

> Who will say 'corpse'
> to his vivid cast?
> Who will say 'body'
> to his opaque repose?[33]

Secondly, there is an association of violence with sexuality, as in 'Punishment':

> I can feel the tug
> of the halter at the nape
> of her neck, the wind
> on her naked front.
>
> It blows her nipples
> to amber beads...
>
>
> My poor scapegoat,
>
> I almost love you...[34]

And thirdly, there is the feeling that certain forms of violence may be 'appropriate' in a sense that belies conventional morality—a feeling which emerges in the last lines of 'Punishment', where Heaney, describing the tarring of female Catholics as a punishment for fraternizing with the enemy, admits that although he feels a degree of 'civilized outrage', he also understands 'the exact/And tribal, intimate revenge'.

At times the effect of the poetry in *North* is to provoke a feeling of moral queasiness, but perhaps this is inevitable given Heaney's approach to the subject. Rather than detach himself from the violence of the Troubles completely, adopt a position of 'civilized outrage', and simply condemn the bombings and murderings in Northern Ireland as the incomprehensible acts of monsters or madmen, he prefers to recognize that the violence is both 'tribal' and 'intimate'—it is a part of his culture, and to some extent a part of his own thoughts and feelings. His attempts to understand the Troubles therefore involve delving into his own unconscious mind and the collective unconscious of the Irish people: and since he is searching for the roots of evil, we cannot expect what he comes up with to be particularly pleasant.

It should also be said that Heaney sometimes uses his mythologizing approach as a means of questioning commonly-held assumptions. 'Belderg', for example, describes a discussion between the poet and an archaeologist, on the subject of some ancient quernstones which have been discovered near the archaeologist's home in the county of Mayo in 'the South'. At first the poem seems to be suggesting that these quernstones are 'foreign', and presumably have been brought into the country by invaders; then that they are 'neolithic', and should thus be taken as evidence of 'persistence' and 'A congruence of lives' in that part of Ireland, which is described as 'A landscape fossilized'. Heaney picks up on the second line of thought, and sets out to contrast the undisturbed Irishness of Mayo with the 'forked root' of his own landscape and culture in the North, where English and Irish perspectives exist uneasily side-by-side.

But the archaeologist reminds him that even in the South there have been disturbances, such as the invasions of the Norse, and the landscape is therefore not as unchanged (or 'fossilized') as it may seem:

> 'But the Norse ring on your tree?'
> I passed through the eye of the quern,
>
> Grist to an ancient mill,
> And in my mind's eye saw
> A world-tree of balanced stones,
> Querns piled like vertebrae,
> The marrow crushed to grounds.[35]

As soon as the Norse are mentioned, the quernstones that

seemed 'benign' at the beginning of the poem become more active and malevolent—'an ancient mill', 'A world-tree of balanced stones' and a pile 'like vertebrae'. The world-tree is Yggdrasill, the ash-tree of Norse mythology whose roots hold the earth together—an image which suggests that the quern-stones could be Norse workmanship, without cancelling out the statement that they are 'neolithic', and thus too ancient to be thought of as foreign. A quernstone seems to belong to a culture which concerns itself with the planting and harvesting of wheat—a settled and rural culture, in other words—yet the link with the Norse seems to associate it with a society dedicated to raids and conquests. In this way, by puzzling over the symbolic significance of the quernstones, Heaney seems to be moving towards the idea that settled rural cultures and aggressive, conquering ones may not be as mutually exclusive as they seem.

He also seems to be moving towards a more complex and troubled vision of Irish history than the usual Nationalist Eden-myth, according to which everything was fine until the English came along and spoiled it. In this new vision, aggres-sion and invasion contribute rings of growth to the world-tree, by disturbing a landscape which would otherwise remain 'fossilized'. Heaney seems to be recognizing, in other words, that the Eden-state is a form of stasis, and that disruption of the status quo may be necessary if stagnation is to be avoided. Yet the image of the Norse world-tree crushing the passive Irish to 'grounds' suggests that the growth stimulated by inva-sion must be paid for in oppression and suffering. The invaders grind up the natives until they become 'grounds'—the ground-down produce of the mill, but also the soil itself, and thus the fertility of the country. And this grinding-up process also provides the natives with 'grounds' for resent-ment, grounds for taking revenge on their conquerors. So the poem moves from a simplistic view of Irish history to one where invasion is as much a timeless feature of human behaviour as rural life, and where renewed growth goes hand-in-hand with renewed bloodletting.

The full impact of 'Belderg' can only be appreciated once we have understood the iconic status of the Mayo landscape to which it refers. To begin with, Mayo is in the South, and has thus thrown off the English yoke: so that when Heaney mentions the 'forked root' of his own background, he is comparing the inner conflicts of a Northern Irish consciousness with the (supposedly) purer culture of Eire. But the mention of 'the Norse ring' undermines this assumption of purity. And Mayo is more than just another county in Eire: it lies on the west coast of Ireland, which throughout Irish history has remained the poorest, most underdeveloped and therefore least Anglicized part of the country: almost literally 'a landscape fossilized'. As such, the western side of the country was adopted by the Gaelicist intelligentsia at the turn of the century as the quintessence of true Irishness. Yeats, in his famous poem 'The Lake Isle of Innisfree', is recommending a poverty-stricken Western style of life in the accepted manner (the poem is actually set in County Sligo):

> I will arise and go now, and go to Innisfree,
> And a small cabin build there, of clay and wattles
>   made:
> Nine bean-rows will I have there, a hive for the
>   honey-bee,
> And live alone in the bee-loud glade.[36]

Heaney's suggestion that, despite its comparative freedom from the English taint, the Mayo landscape yields evidence of other invaders, is therefore more iconoclastic than may be immediately apparent.

'Belderg' is a particularly interesting poem because it seems to call into question the Irish Nationalist version of the Eden-myth which Heaney apparently espouses elsewhere, especially in his earlier collections. In this poem, Heaney seems to be suggesting that Ireland never did enjoy an Eden-like state of timeless tranquillity: the archaeological evidence indicates that there have always been invasions, conflict and bloodshed. And in the last analysis, this nagging awareness that primitive life in Ireland was no more idyllic than the present is what separates the primitivism of *North* from the primitivism of R. S. Thomas and Ted Hughes. Like them, Heaney often looks back to a primal state in which Man was content to be ruled by the laws of Nature; but unlike them, he is finally unable to present this primal state as a preferable alternative to the modern world. Instead, the violence of the modern world infects his vision of the primal state, and likewise the mindless compliance of the primal state comes to infect his vision of the modern world. What he finds in the past is an *explanation* for the present, rather than an alternative to it. He certainly does strike a note of wistful nostalgia at times; but this occasional hankering for the past never finally hardens (as it does with the primitivists) into a desire to return to a state of pre-conscious innocence, discarding the values of rationality, progress and moral responsibility. The poems in Part II of *North*—which I shall not examine in any detail, since none of them has much to do with landscape—are one indication of the way in which Heaney eventually edges away from primitivism; but the same point is demonstrated even more clearly by the collections that follow.

V

Field Work (1979) includes three poems—'The Strand at Lough Beg', 'A Postcard from North Antrim' and 'Casualty'[37]—dealing respectively with a cousin, a friend and a drinking-companion of Heaney's, all of them killed in the Troubles. If Heaney can be accused of trying to mythologize the Troubles away in *North*, that accusation cannot be made against *Field Work*, which conveys a much more vivid sense of how they affect everyday life in Northern Ireland, augmented and sharpened by a sense of personal involvement and personal loss.

So far as the treatment of landscape is concerned, *Field Work* is the collection in which Heaney's descriptions seem to find their way from the darkness below the ground to the daylight of the surface. This corresponds with a change of attitude towards the past and the unconscious mind. In the earlier collections, the past seems to have a fateful power over the present: whatever dark evidence is exhumed from below ground is received as evidence about ourselves, evidence of the timeless patterns into which present-day events are bound to fall. But in *Field Work* the past is supposed to teach us about ourselves and about how we should act. As a consequence, the metaphorical link between the darkness of the past and the darkness of the unconscious mind becomes far less important, since both the present and the past are now seen as the products of rational, conscious choices rather than irrational, unconscious impulses; and because Heaney equates the darkness of the unconscious mind with the subsurface of the landscape, his new emphasis on rational self-awareness tends to draw his landscape-descriptions upwards towards the surface and the daylight.

The keynote is sounded by the first poem in the collection, 'Oysters':

> Over the Alps, packed deep in hay and snow,
> The Romans hauled their oysters south to Rome:
> I saw damp panniers disgorge
> The frond-lipped, brine-stung
> Glut of privilege
>
> And was angry that my trust could not repose
> In the clear light, like poetry or freedom
> Leaning in from the sea. I ate the day
> Deliberately, that its tang
> Might quicken me all into verb, pure verb.[38]

Earlier in the poem, we hear that Heaney and his friends are eating oysters as a means of 'laying down a perfect memory'— yet for Heaney the experience is a troubled one. He finds himself unable to enjoy the oysters purely for their own sake, because for him they carry with them a burden of historical associations. He cannot help thinking of them as the 'Glut of privilege'. The oysters enjoyed by the Romans were obviously not native to Italy, but were transported southwards 'Over the Alps' from the more northerly parts of the Empire. The Romans, of course, are sky-worshipping conquerors, and the people from whom they take the oysters must therefore be subservient, 'mould-hugging' peasants. This being the case, Heaney cannot help feeling resentful about the 'privilege' which he associates with the eating of oysters: yet he also feels 'angry' because his awareness of such associations prevents him from experiencing things purely for what they are worth in terms of the here-and-now: '...my trust could not repose/In the clear light...'.

He is constantly being dragged backwards and downwards into the subterranean darkness of the past by the weight of his 'trust', his sense of loyalty to his own people and their burdens: yet in this poem he seems to be making up his mind, not to abandon his 'trust', but to drag it into the daylight. He eats the oysters and 'the day' itself—the sensation of here-and-now, of being alive and experiencing things—as an act of defiance and determination. He wants the 'tang' of the oysters to 'quicken' him 'into verb, pure verb'—to make him active, and thus to grant him power to change the course of history by imposing his own will on the world in which he lives. It is no accident that the atmosphere in these lines is one of 'clear light', 'freedom' and 'day'—it seems to belong to the realm of masculine willpower rather than feminine receptivity. And whereas in previous collections the past was symbolized and brought to mind by exhumed corpses and disused arte-facts from below the ground, inert items which were never-theless endowed with irresistible talismanic power, it is now symbolized by oysters from beneath the sea, a booty which contributes a distinctive 'tang' to the experience of the present day. A past which is homogeneous but all-powerful has been replaced by one which is less powerful but more distinctive.

The choice of sea rather than soil as the storehouse of the past in this poem is noteworthy: as we shall discover, from this point onwards when Heaney wants to use a single image to summarize his impression of the life that surrounds him, he tends to use the ocean rather than the land. The land is static and familiar: it signifies a psychological landscape where inward and downward exploration will reveal a wealth of buried origins. But the sea is mysterious and ever-changing, and represents a world in which there are more questions than answers, which can never be domesticated or humanized by long occupancy, and where each man flounders on his own.

Heaney's movement away from the cyclic view of time in *Field Work* involves a new awareness of change. Various poems in earlier anthologies have shown some appreciation of how technological innovation and urbanization are displacing traditional skills and customs,[39] but the overwhelming feeling is of an Ireland where old-fashioned, rural ways of life still hold sway.[40] But in *Field Work* the force of change seems much more palpable. The second section of 'Triptych' provides one example:

> My people think money
> And talk weather. Oil-rigs lull their future
> On single acquisitive stems. Silence
> Has shoaled into the trawlers' echo-sounders.
>
> The ground we kept our ear to for so long
> Is flayed or calloused, and its entrails
> Tented by an impious augury.[41]

It is unclear whether Heaney is describing the Irish in these lines, or the 'developed' world in general; but the sharp awareness of environmental degradation is something quite new in his poetry. This is a world in which awareness of the weather has been reduced to the status of a conversational gambit: the only thing people really think about is money. The environment only matters in terms of what can be extracted from it—an attitude which is neatly symbolized by the 'single acquisitive stems' of the oil rigs. 'Silence/Has shoaled into the trawlers' echo-sounders' firstly because the seas have been over-fished, and secondly because men can no longer hear the voice of the natural world: 'The ground we kept our ear to for so long/Is flayed or calloused'.

Interestingly, this new awareness of change involves a revival of the Eden-myth which Heaney seemed to set aside in 'Belderg'—although the myth now reappears without its former nationalistic associations. In 'Belderg' the present is neither better nor worse than the past but simply a continuation of the same cycles of invasion and settlement. In this section of 'Triptych', on the other hand, the feeling that men are no longer as responsive to the natural world as they once were seems automatically to suggest that there has been a fall from grace, and that in the past things were better. The same suggestion recurs, on a more personal level, in 'The Harvest Bow'—one of Heaney's most plaintively beautiful poems—where the contemplation of a 'love-knot of straw' woven by his father evokes a feeling of homesickness for a lost rural existence:

> if I spy into its golden loops
> I see us walk between the railway slopes
> Into an evening of long grass and midges,
> Blue smoke straight up, old beds and ploughs in
>   hedges,
> An auction notice on an outhouse wall—
> You with a harvest bow in your lapel,
>
> Me with the fishing rod, already homesick
> For the big lift of these evenings...[42]

The use of half-rhymes is masterly, and adds to the poignancy of the verse. The feeling of impermanence conveyed by 'already homesick' is picked up and strengthened by the details of 'old beds and ploughs in hedges' and the 'auction notice', suggesting that local farmers are selling up. Heaney is homesick because he is leaving to pursue his academic and poetic career; but also because the old way of life, the traditional relationship between the farmer and his land, symbolized by the harvest bow, is disappearing, and can never be recaptured. Thus, at the end of the poem, the harvest bow is 'Like a drawn snare/Slipped lately by the spirit of the corn'.

These signs of a change of outlook should not be taken as evidence that Heaney has turned his back completely on the images and symbols which characterized his earlier poetry. Many of the poems in *Field Work* re-employ motifs from previous collections. One such motif is the interconnection between language and landscape, which is a recurrent theme in the ten 'Glanmore Sonnets'[43] that form the central section of *Field Work*. In the first sonnet of the sequence, Heaney writes:

> Our road is steaming, the turned-up acres breathe.
> Now the good life could be to cross a field
> And art a paradigm of earth new from the lathe
> Of ploughs. My lea is deeply tilled.
> Old ploughsocks gorge the subsoil of each sense...

As in previous collections, fertility can only be renewed by delving into 'the subsoil'—renewing a connection with what lies below the surface. But now this contact with the subsoil no longer involves yielding the self to the control of dark subterranean powers. Instead, the farmer seems to remake the land in a new form ('earth new from the lathe/Of ploughs') and the poet, by implication, remakes language in the same way. Furthermore, the balance of power between land and language seems to be changing. In earlier collections it is the land which Heaney sees as the fundamental reality: language grows organically from the landscape and is at its most meaningful when it reminds us of the physical experience of being in a particular place. But now Heaney suggests that 'art' is 'a paradigm of earth', rather than earth being a paradigm of art; language comes first, the world comes after.

Throughout 'The Glanmore Sonnets' there is a new sense that the external world is slippery and untrustworthy, a chaos which can only be conjured and controlled through the power of language. The most euphoric expression of this new faith in words is the seventh poem in the sequence, which reads as follows:

> Dogger, Rockall, Malin, Irish Sea:
> Green, swift upsurges, North Atlantic flux
> Conjured by that strong gale-warning voice
> Collapse into a sibilant penumbra.
> Midnight and closedown. Sirens of the tundra,
> Of eel-road, seal-road, keel-road, whale-road, raise
> Their wind-compounded keen behind the baize
> And drive the trawlers to the lee of Wicklow.
> *L'Etoile, Le Guillemot, La Belle Helene*
> Nursed their bright names this morning in the bay
> That toiled like mortar. It was marvellous
> And actual, I said out loud, 'A haven,'
> The word deepening, clearing, like the sky
> Elsewhere in Minches, Cromarty, The Faroes.

Here the external world is an almost formless 'flux' which can only be controlled or 'conjured' by language. Significantly, this is one of the poems in which Heaney represents external reality as an ocean rather than a landscape—an ever-changing unfamiliar element rather than a static and intimately-known one. He dramatizes the struggle between the knowable, named world and the unknowable, chaotic, nameless one by describing the overthrow of order by a stormy night, and its rebirth on the following calm day. The list with which the poem begins is a shipping forecast, given in a 'strong gale-warning voice' which seems almost capable of controlling the storm through the power of language. But this feeling of control is illusory: the gale-warning is succeeded firstly by 'Collapse into a sibilant penumbra', then by 'Midnight and closedown', and eventually by the 'sirens of the tundra'.

The voice of civilization and science gives way to the more primitive wordless sounds of the elements, and the second list of the poem is correspondingly more primitive-seeming than the first: 'eel-road, seal-road, keel-road, whale-road'. The epithets are recognizably Norse in style, and therefore suggestive of a seafaring culture in which the chaotic power of the elements was both celebrated and feared. And that same chaotic power is still enough to 'drive the trawlers to the lee of Wicklow'. When Heaney sees them there the next morning, it strikes him that they are protecting their names from the storm as much as their physical integrity: he tells us that 'they nursed their bright names this morning in the bay'. The names are literally 'bright': they remind us respectively of a star, a seagull and the legendary Helen. Language is used here, in the boats' names, to suggest images of beauty, to give the boats separate identities, and thus to establish a sense of their value and importance. In a sense language is a protection against the elements, yet the element which has threatened the boats with nameless and wordless destruction—the water of the bay—is also what buoys them up and links them together, which is why it is 'like mortar'. This relationship between the nameless and the named, the chaotic and the fixed, is part of what Heaney finds 'marvellous/And actual'. The poem ends with a reassertion of the power of language—Heaney's utterance of the word 'haven' seems to have the effect of conjuring an end to the storm; and in the last line there comes another weather-forecast list, this time reversing the effect of the first one, by announcing the progress of a calm rather than a storm.

VI

The concern with the relationship between language and the external world which characterizes the 'Glanmore Sonnets' is also a feature of Heaney's second collection of critical essays, *The Government of the Tongue* (1988). Almost every essay in this collection expresses in one form or another the same belief: that if the poet is to give utterance to any truth at all, then it must be a truth which he has discovered through his art—through his exploration of the mysteries of language itself. He must not allow himself to be tyrannized either by predetermined systems of ideas or by the physical presence of the external world.

These ideas, and their implications for Heaney's view of the landscape, are elaborated in an essay from *The Government of the Tongue* entitled 'The Placeless Heaven: Another Look at Kavanagh'. Heaney begins the essay with a story about a chestnut tree, which, he tells us, was planted at Mossbawn in the year of his birth. Because he and the tree were always the same age, he came to associate himself with it. When his family moved, the new owners of the farm cut the tree down; but that was not the end of the matter, because after a while Heaney began to associate himself with 'the space where the tree had been or would have been... The new place was all idea, if you like; it was generated out of my experience of the old place but was not a topographical location.'[44] He goes on to compare the early and late poetry of Patrick Kavanagh with the real tree and the invisible tree. Kavanagh's early poetry arises from 'an imagination which is not yet weaned from its origin',[45] and at this stage 'Kavanagh is pervious to the world's spirit more than it is pervious to his spirit'.[46] But in the later poems, 'We might say that now the world is more pervious to his vision than he is pervious to the world. When he writes about places now, they are luminous spaces within his mind.'[47] Heaney calls this second type of poetry the poetry of 'inner freedom' and ends by stating: 'I have learned to value this poetry of inner freedom very highly.'[48]

The importance of this essay is indicated by the fact that the invisible tree symbol appears twice in Heaney's later poetry; firstly in *Station Island*, in the third section of the title-poem:

> I thought of walking round
> and round a space utterly empty,
> utterly a source, like the idea of sound...[49]

The connection of these lines with the image of the invisible tree is not immediately clear, but it becomes evident when they are compared with the following from the last section of 'Clearances', a sonnet sequence from *The Haw Lantern* which commemorates the death of Heaney's mother:

> I thought of walking round and round a space
> Utterly empty, utterly a source
> Where the decked chestnut tree had lost its place
> In our front hedge above the wallflowers.[50]

The above lines attempt to summarize Heaney's feelings about his own activities both as a man and a poet. He sees himself circling round and round an idea derived from a reality that has itself been lost. There seems to be a pang of regret at the way in which the world of Heaney's boyhood has disappeared, but there is also a sense that the individual who comes to trust his own vision of the world rather than the world itself has achieved a degree of inner liberty.

The external world is always in a state of flux; people die and trees are cut down; but the idea of a tree or of a person, like 'the idea of sound', is in a sense more spiritually significant, more 'utterly a source', than the thing itself, because it can be treasured up in the mind and used to reilluminate the world of externalities. And by emphasizing the importance of ideas rather than things, Heaney is making a plea for the individual and for personal interpretation. He is saying that each individual—particularly if he is an artist—must be free to formulate and express his own private vision. This corresponds with his new enthusiasm for a 'poetry of inner freedom', and with his insistence that poetry's first duty is to itself, not to this or that aspect of the external world, or to any given ideology, or even to the poet's own desire for self-expression. As Heaney puts it in another essay from *The Government of the Tongue*:

> The fact is that poetry is its own reality and no matter how much a poet may concede to the corrective pressures of social, moral, political and historical reality, the ultimate fidelity must be to the demands and promise of the artistic event.[51]

Although Heaney is arguing that the poet must express his own personal vision, this does not mean that he is recommending poetry which is 'personal' or 'confessional' in a narrow sense. He believes that the poet must explore the 'subsoil' of meaning that lies within and below normal everyday language until it begins to yield universal truths.

In order to do this properly, he must lay his personal problems and circumstances aside. He must

> get beyond ego in order to become the voice of more than autobiography. At the level of poetic speech, when this happens, sound and meaning rise like a tide out of language to carry individual utterance away upon a current stronger and deeper than the individual could have anticipated.[52]

This account of poetic inspiration may seem to bear out the insistence of a primitivist such as Ted Hughes that the individual must learn to abandon his rational self in order to re-establish contact with the torrent of universal life-force which pours through his unconscious mind; but although Heaney agrees that there are powers beyond the rational mind that must be given a voice if the poet's utterance is to go beyond the level of mundane self-expression, he does not believe that these powers can only be contacted if the rational self is abandoned. He ends *The Government of the Tongue* as follows:

> Wordsworth declares that what counts is the quality, intensity and breadth of the poet's concerns between writing... This is what determines the ultimate human value of the act of writing. That act remains free, self-governing, self-seeking, but the worth of the booty it brings back from its raid upon the inarticulate will depend upon the emotional capacity, intellectual resource and general civilization which the articulate poet maintains between the raids.[53]

For Heaney, poetry may well be a 'raid upon the inarticulate', but it does not follow that the poet—let alone the rest of humanity—should attempt to live life entirely on that level. He borrows primitivist ideas about the importance of the inarticulate, inner life because he wants to set the creative act free from conscious control, and thus allow it to be entirely 'self-governing' and 'self-seeking'. But he is aware that a wholehearted espousal of primitivist ideas would itself require him to write poetry in a certain style and see the world from a certain angle. He therefore balances his insistence on the importance of 'the inarticulate' with an equal insistence on the importance of 'intellectual resource and general civilization'. This balance allows the autonomy of the poetic act to go unchallenged.

Reading rather cynically between the lines, it is easy to discover, in all this talk of 'inner freedom' and the autonomy of the act of writing, an undeclared urge on Heaney's part to distance himself from his 'roots'. Clearly he does not want to spend the rest of his life feeling obliged to act as a spokesman or apologist for the Northern Irish Catholics. He is claiming the right to speak for himself and nobody else. But the emphasis on 'inner freedom' and the image of the invisible tree are also connected with his changing views about time and individual responsibility. In his later poetry Heaney seems to be increasingly preoccupied, not with 'persistence' and 'congruence of lives', but with the importance of change. Too strong a connection with the past can only mean that the same patterns will repeat themselves over and over again for ever; and obviously, so far as Northern Ireland is concerned, this is not to be desired. If there is ever to be an end to the violence, then all parties in the province must be prepared to put the past behind them to some extent, and make a fresh start. They must be prepared to act out of a sense of 'inner freedom' rather than a slavish adherence to traditions and party lines.

The evolution of Heaney's views about his own role as a poet, about time, and about individual responsibility seems to be closely connected with his changing view of the political situation, both in Northern Ireland and in the world as a whole. Certainly his latest poetry, with its sense of miraculous possibilities, must be set in the context of such events as the collapse of the Soviet Union, the tearing down of the Berlin Wall, the first moves towards democracy in South Africa, the first foreshadowings of the establishment of a Palestinian homeland, and so on. The peace which has now broken out in Northern Ireland has in part been made possible and inspired by these other events; and Heaney's poetry, always politically aware, reflects his feeling that he is living in a world where sudden and sensational changes in the course of history have become possible.

In *Station Island* (1984), Heaney's new insistence on poetic autonomy makes itself felt through a whole sequence of images showing the poet as an isolated character striking out on his own or observing society from afar. The whole 'Sweeney Redivivus' section, which forms the last part of the book, is concerned with this kind of poetic isolation.[54] The first poem in the section, 'The First Gloss', reads as follows:

Take hold of the shaft of the pen.
Subscribe to the first step taken
from a justified line
into the margin.[55]

The shaft of the pen is a reminder of the pen-as-spade image
in 'Digging', but the note of deliberate deviation in this poem
is new. In 'Digging' Heaney converted his pen into a spade in
order to express solidarity with his father and grandfather and
the rural traditions they represented. Here, he takes hold of
the shaft in order to guide his pen away from 'a justified
line'—the trim edge of the type on the printed page—and
'into the margin'. A 'gloss', of course, is a marginal note
explaining or interpreting what is written in the main body of
a text. Heaney is characterizing his own poetry as such a
'gloss'—something that stands to one side, commenting on
the contents of a 'justified' text without allowing itself to be
subsumed. A 'gloss' can only serve its purpose if it remains
separate from the text to which it refers.

Whereas 'Digging' aligned Heaney's poetic ambitions with
his desire to continue the rural traditions in which he was
brought up, 'The First Gloss' suggests that the poet must
abandon conformity and venture 'into the margin'. The
'Station Island' sequence itself confirms this move away from
rural experience towards a more purely poetic outlook. It
describes a series of dream-encounters between Heaney and
figures from his own past or from literature, all of whom have
been important influences on him at one time or another in
his life. Through these encounters he is able to revisit his own
past, to meditate on the ways in which it has shaped him, and
to reconsider where he should go from here. The poem begins
and ends with oracular individuals, both of whom advise
Heaney to ignore other people and go his own way—but the
first piece of advice comes from a tinker, who prefers the
freedom of primitive country life to the conformity of settled
society; whereas the second comes from James Joyce, who is

urging the virtues of artistic independence. The poem as a whole, moving between these two voices, therefore follows the path which Heaney maps out for both Patrick Kavanagh and himself in *The Government of the Tongue*—away from an intense preoccupation with the here-and-now, and towards the 'inner freedom' of the 'invisible tree'.

The tinker is Simon Sweeney, whom Heaney used to know as a child. It is Sunday, but Sweeney is cutting hazel branches in the hedgerows instead of responding to the church bells. He carries a bow-saw 'held/stiffly up like a lyre', which suggests a connection with music or poetry; but the suggestion remains undeveloped. Heaney greets him:

> "I know you, Simon Sweeney,
> for an old Sabbath-breaker
> who has been dead for years."[56]

At the end of the section, Heaney finds himself being drawn forward to join a band of pilgrims who are passing through the field in answer to the communion bell. Sweeney warns him against losing his independence:

> 'Stay clear of all processions!'
>
> Sweeney shouted at me
> but the murmur of the crowd
> and their feet slushing through
> the tender, bladed growth
> opened a drugged path
>
> I was set upon.[57]

Clearly this Simon Sweeney is close in spirit to his counterpart, Sweeney the mad Irish bird-king who is the protagonist of both the 'Sweeney Redivivus' poems in this collection, and the medieval *Buile Suibhne* to which they refer. Heaney, who published a translation of the *Buile Suibhne* in 1983, describes King Sweeney as 'the green spirit of the hedges'[58]—he is a spirit of pagan wildness which rejects the conformity of the

Catholic Church. Likewise the Simon Sweeney of the 'Station Island' sequence prefers the life of an outcast of the hedgerows to the 'drugged' conformity of churchgoers: and the bow-saw-as-lyre image suggests that this isolation contains at least the potential for poetic self-expression. The idea that the Marian tradition of Catholicism is a continuation of pagan earth-worship, and thus represents a continued closeness to the soil, seems to have been discarded or devalued: the man who is truly close to Nature now is not the Catholic farmer but the pagan tinker.

But although Heaney wants to draw inspiration from the natural world, he does not want to become a tinker himself: so 'Station Island', which begins with 'the green spirit of the hedgerows', ends with the spirit of independence in literature: James Joyce. Joyce gives Heaney much the same advice as Simon Sweeney—he tells him to stay independent—but with more emphasis on the importance of self-expression:

> 'Keep at a tangent.
> When they make the circle wide, it's time to swim
>
> out on your own and fill the element
> with signatures on your own frequency,
> echo soundings, searches, probes, allurements,
>
> elver-gleams in the dark of the whole sea.'[59]

This is one of the moments in Heaney's later poetry where the sea takes over from the land as the image he uses to epitomize his world-view. A shared depth, mysterious but unchanging, of memories and unconscious impulses is replaced by a world of unknowable flux. In this world it is not enough for the individual to explore the element that surrounds him and announce the results of his explorations: he must 'fill the element/with signatures', as well as examining it with 'echo soundings, searches' and 'probes'. In other words he must to some extent make his own reality, as well as using his own personal vision as a kind of sonar. He must aim for that state in which, as Heaney says of Kavanagh, 'the world is more pervious to his vision than he is pervious to the world'.

Two other passages from 'Station Island' further illustrate Heaney's new attitudes towards the natural world and the necessity for self-expression. In the second section of the poem he encounters William Carleton, a nineteenth-century Irish writer who renounced his own Catholicism and wrote unromantic descriptions of Irish rural life and the superstitions of the Irish peasantry. Carleton's advice to Heaney is

'Remember everything and keep your head.'

'The alders in the hedge,' I said, 'mushrooms,
dark-clumped grass where cows or horses dunged,
the cluck when pith-lined chestnut shells split open
in your hand, the melt of shells corrupting,
old jampots in a drain clogged up with mud—'

But now Carleton was interrupting:

'All this is like a trout kept in a spring
or maggots sown in wounds—
another life that cleans our element...'[60]

Carleton's instruction to 'remember everything' sends Heaney off into recollections of the rural world in which he was brought up. The lines that follow—crammed with onomatopoeic words and phrases such as 'dunged', 'cluck', 'pith-lined', 'melt' and 'clogged up with mud'—are a deliberate pastiche of his own early poetry. Carleton reacts impatiently: 'All this is like a trout kept in a spring'. A vivid apprehension of the external world does serve a purpose in that it 'cleans our element'—it chastens and invigorates us by taking us out of ourselves—but the artist should not abandon himself to it completely. Heaney is obeying one half of Carleton's instruction, to 'remember everything', but not the other half, to keep his head. It is not enough to be intensely aware of the external

world and responsive to it: the poet must also be self-aware
and self-expressive.

In section nine of the poem this change from passive recep-
tiveness to self-assertion and self-expression is described by a
dream-sequence which reuses the symbolism of masculinity
and femininity from Heaney's earlier collections:

> I dreamt and drifted. All seemed to run to waste
> As down a swirl of mucky, glittering flood
> Strange polyp floated like a huge corrupt
> Magnolia bloom, surreal as a shed breast,
> My softly awash and blanching self-disgust.
> And I cried among night-waters, 'I repent
> My unweaned life that kept me competent
> To sleepwalk with connivance and mistrust.'
> Then, like a pistil growing from the polyp,
> A lighted candle rose and steadied up
> Until the whole bright-masted thing retrieved
> A course and the currents it had gone with
> Were what it rode and showed. No more adrift,
> My feet touched bottom and my heart revived.[61]

The 'mucky, glittering flood' is the flow of time or events. At
first Heaney is passively carried along by it, and his passivity is
identified as feminine by the images of 'shed breast' and
'unweaned life'. In the second half of the passage, however,
self-control and masculinity take over. The 'pistil', 'lighted
candle' and 'bright-masted thing' are all phallic. This new
masculinity leads to the statement that Heaney has 'retrieved
a course'—'No more adrift,/My feet touched bottom'. It is
true that the relationship between the illuminated, masculine
self and the flow of events remains ambiguous: 'the currents it
had gone with/Were what it rode and showed'. The new
feeling of autonomy may be an illusion: the candle illuminates
the currents on which it rides, but it is still at their mercy for
all that. Nevertheless Heaney's choice is clear: he now prefers
riding to floating, and the masculine, self-illuminated state to

the feminine 'unweaned life' to which he seemed to pledge himself in his earlier books. From now on the external world will be 'another life that cleans our element', not a goddess with fateful powers over her almost-mindless children; and Heaney's allegiance will be to the invisible tree that represents the idea of a place, rather than to the real tree that represents the place itself.

VII

The same transfer of allegiance, from received experience to the internalized image of that experience, reappears in 'Alphabets', which is the first poem in *The Haw Lantern* (1987). The poem begins by describing how a child is taught to connect symbols with the realities they are supposed to represent:

> A shadow his father makes with joined hands
> And thumbs and fingers nibbles on the wall
> Like a rabbit's head.[62]

When the boy goes to school and begins to learn how to write, he memorizes the different shapes of letters and numbers by comparing them with familiar sights from his rural upbringing. He

>   draws the forked stick that they call a Y.
> This is writing. A swan's neck and a swan's back
> Make the 2 he can now see as well as say.
>
> Two rafters and a cross-tie on the slate
> Are the letter some call *ah*, some call *ay*.

At the beginning of our lives, Heaney seems to be saying, we do not conceptualize about our experiences, we simply drink them in; but when our education begins, we learn systems of abstract signs and concepts that will enable us to reorganize our experiences into new equations and categories.

At the end of the poem, the process is taken a stage further, and Heaney describes how adults come to interpret completely new experiences in terms of the categories, signs and concepts which they already hold in their heads:

> As from his small window
> The astronaut sees all he has sprung from,
> The risen, aqueous, singular, lucent O
> Like a magnified and buoyant ovum...

The astronaut copes with something he has never seen before by comparing it to a letter of the alphabet, a 'lucent O', whereas the farm-boy learned the letters of the alphabet by comparing them with objects from his rural background. Systems of abstract concepts, once learned, can be reused to cope with even the most staggeringly unfamiliar of experiences. The astronaut himself symbolizes the achievements made possible by this gift of conceptualization: he is able to see 'all he has sprung from' through 'a small window'. On the other hand, the smallness of the window possibly signifies Heaney's awareness that conceptualization is limiting as well as enabling. But the poem is by no means a lament for the way in which abstract ideas come to triumph over raw experiences—it would seem that Heaney views this process as an inevitable and indispensable part of growing up.

A number of pieces in *The Haw Lantern* demonstrate Heaney's new recognition that—from an artistic point of view at least—our ideas about a place are just as important as our physical apprehensions of it. There is a whole sequence of poems that pretend to be about places but are in fact quasi-allegorical descriptions of states of existence. The titles themselves are indications of the style in which these poems are written: 'From the Frontier of Writing', 'Parable Island', 'From the Republic of Conscience', 'From the Land of the Unspoken' and 'From the Canton of Expectation'. 'From the

Republic of Conscience', for example, is about the way in which older generations attempt to impose their own values and traditions on their children, especially in Ireland. The poem begins:

> When I landed in the republic of conscience
> it was so noiseless when the engines stopped
> I could hear a curlew high above the runway.
>
> At immigration, the clerk was an old man
> who produced a wallet from his homespun coat
> and showed me a photograph of my grandfather.[63]

In Heaney's early poetry, his technique is to convince us of the validity of his descriptions first, and then to attach symbolic meanings to them. Here, on the other hand, he starts from an idea about a place; he illustrates it with images, either realistic (like the lark above the runway) or symbolic (like the clerk in the homespun coat who produces a photograph of the poet's grandfather); and he leaves the reader to decide for himself which place is being alluded to.

Another poem from *The Haw Lantern*, 'The Disappearing Island', takes a fresh look at the relationship between the Irish and their landscape. It reads as follows:

> Once we presumed to found ourselves for good
> Between its blue hills and those sandless shores
> Where we spent our desperate night in prayer
> and vigil,
>
> Once we had gathered driftwood, made a hearth
> And hung our cauldron like a firmament,
> The island broke beneath us like a wave.
>
> The land sustaining us seemed to hold firm
> Only when we embraced it *in extremis*.
> All I believe that happened there was vision.[64]

Once again, the sea has displaced the land as the crucial

image—in fact this poem dramatizes the very moment of displacement: 'The island broke beneath us like a wave'. The island can only retain the reliable stability of common ground as long as 'The land sustaining us' completely dominates the lives and thoughts of its inhabitants. But both the Irish people as a whole and Heaney as an individual have grown away from this state of domination. In Heaney's early collections the landscape itself is the ultimate value of the Irish people: it is their goddess and they are its children. But he now sees this state as a 'desperate night' of 'prayer and vigil'. Once the people have become self-reliant and presumptuous enough 'to found' themselves 'for good' on the land—to assume that their residence will be permanent, and to take the first civilized steps of building a hearth, lighting a fire and hanging up a cauldron—then the land's stranglehold on their attention is broken. The suggestion that the cauldron is 'like a firmament' indicates that the people are now beginning to lift their eyes from the ground towards the sky; but as soon as they transfer their attention the land ceases to exist, and the sea takes its place.

The parallel is with the Eden-like lost island of Atlantis, which was swallowed by the sea. The land lost in this poem was no Eden, but the fact that it has been lost confers on it the status of a vision. At least it represented the certainty of absolute stasis and consensus, whereas the sea represents a wilderness of perpetual uncertainty and change. In fact what Heaney is doing, probably unconsciously, is rewriting the story of the Tower of Babel, which shows how Man brings confusion on himself by attempting to raise himself up from the lowly state to which he is born. The last line of the poem, 'All I believe that happened there was vision', is ambiguously phrased. It suggests that everything which seemed to happen on the island was mere 'vision' or illusion, but it also suggests that all the poet's beliefs—'All I believe'—are based on that experience, illusory or not. The island seems to be the most important thing in his life, the foundation of all his thoughts, but it has been lost in the sea, and it may have never been anything more than a mass hallucination.

It is worth saying a few words about the style in which this poem is written. The only directly descriptive phrases are 'blue hills' and 'sandless shores'. It deals with ideas about a landscape rather than attempting to suggest the physical presence of the landscape itself. The language lacks either the rich onomatopoeia of Heaney's early poetry or the bewildering references to literature, Irish history and the Gaelic tongue which often festoon the poems of his middle period. It is written in simple, almost prosaic language, but it nevertheless expresses complex ideas. The delight in paradox is almost metaphysical; and it allows Heaney to give us the most subtle and ambiguous version of the Eden-myth we have yet encountered. The simplicities of his old nationalist vision have now evolved into something very different.

Ireland is no longer an Eden ruined by the intrusion of the English, but a mass hallucination broken by the inevitable desire of the Irish themselves to escape the desperation of complete dependence on the land. Yet the poem accommodates an awareness of the importance of the Eden-myth: the 'desperate night' of 'prayer and vigil' which made the island real may have been undesirable as a lived reality, but once lost the island acquires a new importance as a 'vision' which can help to make sense of the chaotic ocean where the islanders now find themselves. In 'The Disappearing Island' Heaney is able to stand back from the Eden-myth and see it from the outside, with an ironic awareness of its paradoxes and self-contradictions, but also with an appreciation of its immense importance. This ability to put the myth into perspective is the reward he collects for having first embraced and then re-examined his own nationalist and primitivist version of it.

VIII

Heaney's next book, *The Cure at Troy*, published in 1990, is a play based on Sophocles' *Philoctetes*. Philoctetes is a Greek archer, marooned on the island of Lemnos at the beginning of the Trojan War; but now the Greeks have discovered that the war can never be won unless he fights on their side, and they have come to seek his help. At first he only wants revenge on them and refuses to accept their offer of reconciliation, but eventually he realizes that by abandoning his desire for vengeance he will be able both to put an end to his own suffering and to bring the Trojan War itself to a conclusion. One of the play's central themes is a belief in the possibility of unlooked-for redemption and rebirth through change:

> History says, *Don't hope*
> On this side of the grave.
> But then, once in a lifetime
> The longed-for tidal wave
> Of justice can rise up,
> And hope and history rhyme.
>
> So hope for a great sea-change
> On the far side of revenge.[65]

The relevance of these lines to the Troubles is obvious; but they also imply a change of attitude on Heaney's part towards Irish history and the Irish landscape.

In 'The Disappearing Island', as we have just seen, the tyranny of an earthbound existence is replaced by the uncertainty of the ocean. The poem balances these two alternatives against one another without making it obvious which of them is to be preferred. But in *The Cure at Troy* Heaney seems to be arriving at a new conviction that change is essential and that stultification and stasis must be avoided—that the sea must be let in. If we are ever to change things for the better, he seems to be saying, we must be prepared to make a decisive break with the past when the opportunity presents itself: to leave behind a tortured but familiar and therefore comforting set of circumstances, for the sake of a more uncertain but also more hopeful future. Philoctetes loathes his island exile, but he has come to rely on it too, and there are moments in *The Cure at Troy* when he almost misses his chance of escape and redemption because the thought of change seems to be too much for him to cope with. Even when he does finally make up his mind to leave, he makes it clear that he is not renouncing his past, or the landscape which embodies it:

> But I can't believe I'm going. My head's light at the thought of a different ground and a different sky. I'll never get over Lemnos; this island's going to be the keel under me and the ballast inside me.[66]

Yet he leaves the island, and he does not intend to return. He does not want to abandon or forget what the island has taught him; but neither does he want to tie himself to it forever. The idea of Lemnos, which can be carried away from it, is more important to him than the place itself.

The importance of change is a theme that resurfaces in *Seeing Things*, published in the early summer of 1991. The book is divided into two parts: the first part is a miscellany, although many of the poems there are concerned with the talismanic power of personal memories; but the second part is one long sequence of forty-eight poems (all in the same twelve-line format) entitled 'Squarings'.

The last poem in the first part is called 'Fosterling', and it describes the way in which a certain type of landscape can have a limiting effect on the lives and thoughts of its inhabitants:

> I can't remember never having known
> The immanent hydraulics of a land
> Of *glar* and *glit* and floods at *dailigone*.
> My silting hope. My lowlands of the mind.

Heaviness of being. And poetry
Sluggish in the doldrums of what happens.
My waiting until I was nearly fifty
To credit marvels...[67]

As in his earlier collections, Heaney is making a connection
between the physical presence of a landscape and the inner life
of its inhabitants. The land seems to influence the culture,
language and feelings of its people until a lowland country
creates a 'lowlands of the mind' in those who live there. The
language of 'glar' and 'glit' and 'dailigone', which reflects a
certain physical environment, also corresponds with 'silting
hope', 'Heaviness of being' and the inability to 'credit
marvels'. Circumspect as always, Heaney prefers to measure
the dampening effect of the landscape on himself rather than
risk openly accusing his fellow-lowlanders of the same slug-
gishness. But it seems clear that with hindsight he finds
himself wishing he had been able to 'credit marvels' earlier,
instead of spending so many years 'Sluggish in the doldrums
of what happens'. By inference, he is wishing that he had
earlier been able to extend his own mental horizons beyond
the horizons of his native landscape—and since place, in
Heaney's poetry, is so often involved with history and culture,
he seems to be lamenting the limitations imposed on him by
his cultural background too.

A world full of 'marvels', 'tidal waves' and 'sea changes', of
course, is a long way from the changelessly cyclic world of
Heaney's earlier collections; but it must also be distinguished
from the deterministic and linear idea of time which often
dominates conventional history and politics. 'History says,
Don't hope/On this side of the grave', and the world of history
emphasizes 'the doldrums of what happens'. The linear view
of time may be dynamic, whereas the cyclic view is static, but
in some ways it is just as incapable of escaping from the past,
because it makes every new situation seem dominated and
limited by the power of what has gone before. Development

only appears to be possible in straight lines; new starts and sideways jumps seem out of the question. Yet these lateral movements are precisely the 'marvels' which Heaney is now persuading himself to credit.

In 'Squarings', the sequence of forty-eight poems which makes up the second half of *Seeing Things*, there is again an insistence on the importance of unexpected and miraculous occurrences, and a corresponding reassessment of the relationship between the potentially dynamic world of the human spirit, and the sometimes limiting external world of things and places. In section xxxvii, for example, Heaney writes:

> In famous poems by the sage Han Shan,
> Cold Mountain is a place that can also mean
> A state of mind. Or different states of mind
>
> At different times, for the poems seem
> One-off, impulsive...[68]

The success of Han Shan's poems, Heaney suggests, lies in his refusal to limit himself to a fixed interpretation of the mountain he describes. Every time he comes to the subject he makes a fresh response, 'One-off, impulsive...'. To achieve this, he transforms the mountain from 'a place' into 'a state of mind' so that, as Heaney puts it in *The Government of the Tongue*, the world becomes 'more pervious to his vision than he is pervious to the world'.

So far as Heaney's attitudes towards his native landscape are concerned, three of the last poems in the 'Squarings' sequence—sections xli, xlii and xliii—are of particular interest. In the first of the three, Heaney describes himself revisiting the haunts of his childhood:

> The places I go back to have not failed
> But will not last. Waist-deep in cow-parsley,
> I re-enter the swim, riding or quelling
>
> The very currents memory is composed of...

> Lick of fear. Sweet transience. Flirt and splash.
> Crumpled flow the sky-dipped willows trailed in.[69]

The river-imagery is used to suggest the flow of time, 'sweet transience', a continuous onrush in which the beauty of 'crumpled flow' and 'sky-dipped willows' is accompanied by a 'lick of fear'. Clearly there is a note of regret when Heaney, introducing the theme of transience, acknowledges that the world of his childhood 'will not last'; yet at the same time, his insistence that he is 'riding or quelling' his memories rather than surrendering to them indicates a refusal to give in either to nostalgia or to a hopeless desire to preserve the status quo forever.

The imagery here—riding or quelling the flow of a stream— seems to echo Section IX of 'Station Island':

> the whole bright-masted thing retrieved
> A course and the currents it had gone with
> Were what it rode and showed.

In that poem, it will be remembered, the 'bright-masted' or phallic self-image was used to suggest Heaney's new 'masculine' urge to ride the currents of life rather than simply allowing himself to be swept along by them; and in this section of 'Squarings', likewise, he seems to be committing himself to masculine self-assertion rather than feminine receptivity—and thus to an appreciation of the beauties of 'sweet transience' rather than a doomed attempt to keep things as they are. As ever with Heaney, however, the message is a complex one: he is not simply extolling the virtues of masculine self-assertion or an acceptance that things must change. The images he uses to express what he means by 'sweet transience' are all recognizably rural—the 'Waist-deep... cow-parsley', the 'Flirt and splash' and 'Crumpled flow' of the river, and 'the sky-dipped willows'. They seem to belong as much to the old-fashioned way of life which 'will not last' as to the forward-looking way of thought which can perceive the beauty of change. Regret and optimism go hand-in-hand.

In the next section of the poem, section xlii, Heaney looks again at the last remnants of the Ireland he knew as a boy:

The same yet rarer: fields of the nearly blessed

Where gaunt ones in their shirtsleeves stooped
    and dug
Or stood alone at dusk surveying bog-banks—
Apparitions now, yet active still

And territorial, still sure of their ground,
Still interested, not knowing how far
The country of the shades has been pushed back...[70]

Again, the tone is ambiguous. The men who inhabit this land-scape are 'nearly blessed', but they also seem stranded by their own refusal to change. They are 'active still', 'still sure of their ground' and 'Still interested', yet they have failed to notice 'how far/The country of the shades has been pushed back'. The territory of which they seem so sure has been sidelined and diminished by the passage of years. They have apparently been consigned to the underworld—reduced to the status of 'apparitions'—but they are unaware that any change has taken place. In fact, if Heaney was thinking of Dante's cosmos when he wrote the phrase 'fields of the nearly blessed', then he is identifying the stasis of this rural scene with the stasis of Limbo, where dwell the souls of those dead who have committed no sin, but who have not been redeemed through Christ, and who can therefore never enter Paradise. Furthermore, in the context of the previous poem, the state-ments that the farmers are still 'territorial' and 'sure of their ground' suggest that they have chosen to stay on the solid earth rather than commit themselves to the risks and possi-bilities of the river. So although Heaney notes 'how far/ The country of the shades has been pushed back' in an unmis-takable tone of regret, he also notes the extent to which the shirtsleeved farmers have brought their fate upon themselves by separating themselves from the onward flow of events. They have, in effect, transformed themselves into powerless ghosts.

The next poem in the sequence takes us a step further:

> Choose one set of tracks and track a hare
> Until the prints stop, just like that, in snow.
> End of the line. Smooth drifts. Where did she go?
>
> Back on her tracks, of course, then took a spring
> Yards off to the side; clean break; no scent or sign.
> She landed in her form and ate the snow.
>
> Consider too the ancient hieroglyph
> Of 'hare and zig-zag', which meant 'to exist',
> To be on the *qui vive*, weaving and dodging
>
> Like our friend who sprang (goodbye) beyond our
>   ken
> And missed a round at last (but of course he'd
>   stood it):
> *The shake-the-heart, the dew-hammer, the far-eyed.*[71]

In this section Heaney is comparing the linear view of time with the alternative notion of development through a series of sudden lateral movements, epitomized by the miraculous sideways leaps of the hare. These sudden changes and transformations can be destructive as well as creative: at the end of the poem they are associated with death, the sudden removal of a 'friend' to a realm 'beyond our ken'. As before, 'sweet transience' is being associated with the 'lick of fear'. But change is associated with life too, as indicated by the 'ancient hieroglyph' which portrays life not as a still point or a straight line but as a zig-zag. 'To be on the *qui vive*', Heaney implies, is bound to involve some 'weaving and dodging'; and those who shrink from this activity are in effect marginalizing themselves, refusing the possibility of further development, like the shirtsleeved farmers of the previous poem, who are privileged or condemned to be 'nearly blessed' throughout eternity.

Heaney's new emphasis on the importance of change can be interpreted in a number of ways. It can be related to his own development as a poet, which has been marked by several conscious changes of direction since the rural primitivism and nationalism of his early poems. It can also be related to the poetic style in which 'Squarings' is written, for as the three poems quoted above indicate, he develops his themes laterally rather than in a linear fashion, introducing new images without warning and moving nimbly from one aspect of his subject to another, rather than attempting to follow a single thread of ideas. In this way the concern with change becomes a poetic method as well as a philosophical theme. But for the purposes of the present thesis, the most challenging aspect of Heaney's new eagerness for change is the way in which it affects his attitude towards the landscape. Whether consciously or unconsciously, he seems to be swimming against the increasingly strong tide of 'light green' conservatism which tends—often in a rather simpleminded manner—to look on any change as an evil and to attribute virtue to any old-fashioned way of life. Of course he is aware of the beauties of rural existence, and cannot contemplate their passing without regret; but this does not prevent him from recognizing that too slavish an attachment to the past can be stultifying, and that change for the better cannot be achieved by those who are too timorous or set in their ways to risk entering 'the swim' of events.

Perhaps the crucial point here is that in his later writings Heaney's attitude towards time seems different from the attitudes of the other four poets I have examined. Larkin, Thomas, Tomlinson and Hughes all associate involvement with the natural world with a desirable sense of timelessness. They assume that Nature exists exclusively in the here-and-now, untroubled by either the loss of the past or the onrush of the future, and thus free from the fear of mortality which seems to haunt Man's rational, self-aware existence. They seek to merge themselves with—or poise themselves against—the natural world, in order to catch at least a flavour of this freedom. But Heaney seems to be suggesting in his later poetry that such an escape is a retrograde step. He encourages us to ride and quell 'The very currents memory is composed of' in a masculine, self-assertive way rather than submerge ourselves within them in a feminine, receptive way; and to accept and value the sudden transformations that come to those who live their lives in this manner, even though they involve the 'Lick of fear' and include the transformation of death.

Heaney's feeling that the internal world of ideas must be given precedence over the external world of things and places takes us at last beyond the confines of the Eden-myth. For Heaney, the ability to conceptualize about our experiences and to form abstractions out of them is not unnatural, even though it brings about our separation from the 'natural' world. He understands the value of the past and of Nature, but he also understands the power and appropriateness of the instincts that drive us away from them. He acknowledges both the desire for stasis and the need for change; but in his later work he suggests that our nostalgic impulse to keep things as they are, or even to put them back as they were, must never be allowed to smother the contrary urge to break with old habits and move on.

NOTES

1. Heaney, *Preoccupations* (Faber, 1980), pp. 132–33.
2. *Ibid.*, p. 134.
3. 'Unhappy and at Home', interview with Seamus Deane, in *The Crane Bag*, vol. 1, no. 1 (1977).
4. Heaney, *Death of a Naturalist* (Faber, 1966), p. 13.
5. Heaney, *Preoccupations*, p. 43.

6. *Ibid.*, p. 88.

7. *Ibid.*, 'Yeats as an Example?', p. 109.

8. *Ibid.*, 'From Monaghan to the Grand Canal', p. 118.

9. Heaney, *Death of a Naturalist*, pp. 31–33.

10. Heaney, *Preoccupations*, p. 56.

11. Heaney, *Door into the Dark* (Faber, 1969), p. 21.

12. *Ibid.*, pp. 47–48.

13. *Ibid.*, pp. 49–50.

14. *Ibid.*, pp. 51–52.

15. *Ibid.*, pp. 53–54.

16. *Ibid.*, pp. 55–56.

17. Heaney, *Preoccupations*, p. 55.

18. Heaney, *Door into the Dark*, p. 24.

19. Heaney, *Wintering Out* (Faber, 1972), p. 47–48.

20. Heaney, *North*, pp. 52–53.

21. Heaney, 'Feeling into Words', *Preoccupations*, p. 56.

22. R. F. Foster, *Modern Ireland 1600–1972* (Allen Lane, 1988; Penguin, 1989), p. 477.

23. David Fitzpatrick, 'Ireland Since 1870', in R. F. Foster (ed.), *The Oxford History of Ireland* (Oxford University Press, 1989, 1992), pp. 198–99.

24. Heaney, *Preoccupations*, p. 56.

25. Heaney, *Wintering Out*, pp. 23–25.

26. Foster, *Modern Ireland*, p. 448.

27. *Ibid.*, p. 518.

28. Heaney, *Wintering Out*, p. 27.

29. Heaney, *North*, p. 17.

30. *Ibid.*, p. 20.

31. Many of Heaney's ideas about the bogland of Northern Europe are derived from his reading of P. V. Glob's book *The Bog People*, which gives detailed accounts of the bodies exhumed from various bogland sites. Glob argues that 'At the beginning of the era of the bog people... a female god was dominant; and her servant, who fulfilled the role of the male deity, had to be sacrificed at the completion of the journeyings so that the cycle of nature might be completed and helped forward' (P. V. Glob, *The Bog People* (Trans. R. L. S. Bruce-Mitford; Faber, 1969), p. 190).

Several of Heaney's bogland poems, both in *North* and *Wintering Out*, refer directly to photographs and descriptions in Glob's book: 'The Tollund Man' and 'Nerthus' from *Wintering Out* (pp. 47–48 and 49), and 'Bog Queen', 'The Grauballe Man', 'Punishment' and 'Strange Fruit' in *North* (pp. 32–34, 35–36, 37–38 and 39).

32. Heaney, *North*, p. 45.

33. *Ibid.*, p. 36.

34. *Ibid.*, pp. 37–38.

35. *Ibid.*, pp. 13–14.

36. Yeats, *Collected Poems* (Macmillan, 1933, 1950), p. 44.

37. Heaney, *Field Work* (Faber, 1979), pp. 17–18, 19–20 and 21–24.

38. *Ibid.*, pp. 11–12.

39. For example, in 'The Forge' from *Door into the Dark* (p. 19) and in the first section of 'A Lough Neagh Sequence' (*ibid.*, p. 38).

40. To pick up the two examples from the previous note, the smith in 'The Forge' seems to be in no danger of losing his livelihood even though the horses he once shod have been replaced by motor-cars; and 'A Lough Neagh Sequence', having made its nod in the direction of modern developments, goes on to ignore them for the bulk of its six sections. Furthermore, aside from these two examples, there are numerous poems in the early anthologies which celebrate traditional rural pursuits such as peat-cutting, blackberry-picking, churning, water-divining, thatching and cairn-building.

41. Heaney, *Field Work*, pp. 12–14.

42. *Ibid.*, p. 58.

43. *Ibid.*, pp. 33–42.

44. Heaney, *The Government of the Tongue* (Faber, 1988), pp. 3 and 4.

45. *Ibid.*, p. 4.

46. *Ibid.*, p. 6.

47. *Ibid.*, p. 5.

48. *Ibid.*, p. 14.

49. Heaney, *Station Island*, p. 68.

50. Heaney, *The Haw Lantern* (Faber, 1987), p. 32.

51. Heaney, *The Government of the Tongue*, p. 101.

52. *Ibid.*, p. 148.

53. *Ibid.*, p. 170.

54. Sweeney was a mad Irish king whose story is told in the *Buile Suibhne*, a medieval Irish poem which Heaney translated and published as *Sweeney Astray* (Faber, 1983). The hero, a pre-Christian figure, quarrels with Ronan, who represents the early Church. Ronan curses him, whereupon Sweeney sprouts feathers and begins to behave like a bird, performing magical feats of leaping and floating and refusing to have anything to do with human society, much as he sometimes longs to rejoin it. He utters a series of laments: many of them are concerned with the beauties of the Irish landscape, while others voice his grief at having been cut off from his fellow-men. The poem can thus be read as a mythical account of how Christianity civilized the Irish and broke the old connection between Irishmen and the natural world. Sweeney, the only character in the poem who resists Christianity and retains his love of Nature, is transformed into a mad bird-man and driven into the wilderness, where he finally perishes. Graves refers to this myth in *The White Goddess*, where he takes Sweeney to represent the poet and his isolation from others (pp. 450–58).

55. Heaney, *Station Island*, p. 97.

56. *Ibid.*, p. 61.

57. *Ibid.*, p. 63.

58. Heaney, *Sweeney Astray*, Introduction. See also note 54 above.

59. Heaney, *Station Island*, pp. 93–94.

60. *Ibid.*, p. 66.
61. *Ibid.*, p. 85.
62. Heaney, *The Haw Lantern*, pp. 1–3.
63. *Ibid.*, pp. 12–13.
64. *Ibid.*, p. 50.
65. Heaney, *The Cure at Troy* (Faber, 1990), p. 77.
66. *Ibid.*, p. 80.
67. Heaney, *Seeing Things* (Faber, 1991), p. 50.
68. *Ibid.*, p. 97.
69. *Ibid.*, p. 101.
70. *Ibid.*, p. 102.
71. *Ibid.*, p. 103.

Chapter Seven
Conclusion

I

I began my Introduction by arguing that the environmental crisis, as it deepens, is sure to make us think about the relationship between Man and Nature in new terms. Images of separation will be replaced by images of interconnection and interdependence. Man must begin to see himself as a part of the natural world, instead of imagining himself to be separate from it, superior to it in some ways and inferior in others. Yet a great deal of my book has been devoted to an examination of the Eden-myth, which implies that we are separated from the non-human universe by our reliance on rational thought. From the literary evidence I have been examining, it would seem that the old separatist view is still very much a force to be reckoned with. Evidently, if the attitudes of my five poets are at all representative, we are still inclined to regard ourselves as the odd species out, the only 'unnatural' creatures on the face of a natural world. Furthermore, we believe our unnaturalness to be something that we have brought upon ourselves through our own wilfulness; and like naughty children, even though we can see that things are going wrong, we are too stubborn to mend our ways. We have turned our backs on Nature; we have abandoned our old-fashioned rural ways of life; we have bricked ourselves up in towns and cities; and now we are simply making things worse and worse with our machines, our oil-wells, our pollution, our rapacity and our self-obsession.

All of these ideas emerge (to a greater or lesser degree, and with variations of emphasis and interpretation) from the

269

landscape poems of the five poets I have been examining. But, as I remarked in my Introduction, the feeling that our present destructive relationship with the natural world has come about through some kind of fall from grace is not confined to the realms of creative writing alone. The outlines of the Eden-myth can also be discerned in the works of environmentalist writers. Yet in some ways the persistence of this myth, and of the various subordinate ideas which are generally associated with it, seems incongruous and unaccountable.

Take, for example, the notion that country life is somehow 'better' than city life, whether by 'better' we mean 'more aesthetically pleasing' or 'more morally virtuous'. A Marxist commentator would not find it at all difficult to account for this bias in favour of rural life, or to point out the inadequacies of understanding which such a bias may conceal. After all, there are obvious reasons why, in Britain at least, the country-side should be thought more congenial than the city: it is less congested, less obviously polluted, less violent and often less socially deprived. But these differences are merely the outward expressions of an underlying principle of organiza-tion.

Since the Agrarian Revolution there has been no need for a large labouring population in the rural parts of our land-scape. The countryside has therefore become depopulated—a process that was greatly accelerated by Enclosure—and large tracts of farmland have been controlled by a comparatively small number of landowners and their managers. Since the Industrial Revolution, on the other hand, cities have come to function as vast pools of labour for the benefit of the manufacturing industries, and it is in the cities that the labourers displaced from the countryside by Enclosure have accumulated. In recent years, of course, this picture has been complicated by various factors, most notably the increasing availability of fast personal transport in the shape of the motor-car, which has encouraged people to live in one place and work in another. But our culture and our aesthetic judgements are still influenced by the traditional assumption that the work is done in the towns and cities, while the benefits are enjoyed in the country.

Country life has become a symbol of bourgeois success, symbolizing an ability to detach oneself from the squalid urban centres of capitalist production. A residence in the countryside is desirable because it advertises the fact that its occupier is either an owner or an administrator rather than a labourer; and the labourers themselves, whether they wish for this type of success or not, are attracted towards an idealized vision of rural life simply because it seems to represent an alternative to the all-too-familiar alienation and exploitation of the city. But once we leave these acquired prejudices on one side and begin to analyse the landscape in social and economic terms, it soon becomes apparent that the dividing-line which separates the town from the country is impossible to draw with any degree of accuracy. Rural life and urban life are actually interrelated parts of a single all-embracing economic system. The countryside provides the towns and cities with food, raw materials, cheap labour, scope for further expansion, and a dumping-ground for their waste. Towns and cities, on the other hand, provide the countryside with its manufactured goods, with large-scale marketplaces in which to buy and sell, and with nerve-centres of economic, administrative, cultural and religious power. The image of the city as a monster devouring and destroying the countryside—an image which, as we have seen, is particularly prominent in the works of R. S. Thomas—is a half-truth.

In Britain we often tend to think of towns and cities as products of the Industrial Revolution; we think of belching chimneys, huge factories, black canals, railways, terraced houses, slag-heaps and all the other paraphernalia of the industrial age. In a sense this is understandable, because many of our cities were created almost out of nothing within the space of a few decades, as a part of the tremendous transformation which the Industrial Revolution brought about. But this circumstance has helped to foster the illusion that the life of a town or a city is completely different from—and unconnected with—the life of the countryside. Of course we all know that the towns and cities could not survive without the fields and farms beyond: the food has to come from somewhere, after all. But isn't it true that the countryside could get along perfectly well without the towns and cities? Don't the towns and cities live off the countryside, sucking out all of its goodness without giving back anything other than trash?

The answer is no. Towns and cities will arise in any landscape where people are buying and selling things to make their livings, rather than existing in entirely self-sufficient communities, eating and wearing and using only those things which they can make for themselves. As soon as goods for sale or barter begin to move backwards and forwards across a landscape, the traffic will automatically begin to accumulate at certain points—where a road crosses a river, or where a river reaches the sea. Storehouses, inns, marketplaces, wharves, boats, wheelwrights and shipbuilders will appear. A town will spring up, and if the conditions are right then the town will become a city. Money will accumulate there; banks and exchanges will be established; and once the importance of the place has been commonly recognized, it will acquire administrative, cultural and religious power too. Lawyers and bureaucrats will set up their offices. Theatres and churches will be built. If the town thrives, then the life which goes on there will soon seem very different from the life of the countryside; yet it will have arisen from it quite naturally, and it will be performing various basic functions without which the countryside could not exist in the form we know, because it could not acquire goods from any distance away, and it could not sell off its surplus produce.

The urban and rural ways of life are not really fundamentally separate and opposed to one another, although it is easy to understand the temptation to see them as such: they are different aspects of a single system. And it is not the urban way of life which is devouring and destroying the natural world, but the system as a whole. So people who move from the city to the countryside cannot claim to have abandoned a set of false values in favour of a more virtuous lifestyle, as long as they still draw their electricity from the national grid, still make use of the water and sewage network, still carry money in their pockets or accumulate it in their bank-accounts, and still enter the capitalist marketplace to sell their labour or their produce and to buy their material goods.

If we observe the landscape in terms of its economic geography, then, the conceptual boundary which sometimes appears to separate the town from the countryside soon begins to fade. But the matter does not end there. If we observe the landscape from a scientific point of view—especially in the light of post-Darwinian evolutionary theory—the boundary which seems to separate the human world from the natural world soon begins to fade too.

The unspoken assumption that underlies my five poets' reactions to any given landscape is that there is a fundamental and qualitative difference between the works of Man and the works of Nature. This assumption is best explained by reverting to our examination of the Fall-myth, which tells us that Man fell from grace when he contravened one of God's instructions—in other words, when he chose to separate his own will from God's. This act of rebellion symbolizes Man's apparent refusal to accept the dictates of natural law. By separating himself from God and Nature, the myth tells us, Man has become responsible for his own actions in a way that no denizen of the natural world shares. The stars, plants, animals and so on all continue to act in accordance with God's commands, and in this sense the natural world— even when it is at its most destructive—remains sinless. The historian Keith Thomas, in his classic book *Man and the Natural World*, writes as follows:

> It was a humanist commonplace that man's very
> possession of reason and free choice enabled him to
> descend to infinitely greater moral depths than
> could the brute; so-called animal instinct was much
> less fallible than reason.[1]

Only Man, having separated himself from God, is burdened
with the need to make rational decisions, to choose between
one course of action and another, and thus to risk making the
wrong choice. It is our sense of our own freedom to make
morally-significant choices which leads us to pass judgement
on the works of Man in terms that we would never dream of
applying to the works of Nature. The scars left by bombs,
road-builders or peat-diggers attract our disapproval in a way
that the scars left by volcanic eruptions, flood or plagues of
locusts do not, however much we may lament the effects of
such natural disasters. We can only begin to apply moral
judgements to these 'acts of God' if we can somehow find
ways of connecting them with the human world—for example
by blaming a plague of locusts on the sinfulness of the nation
which is afflicted by it, or by interpreting spells of abnormal
weather as the results of global warming.

Yet if we consider our relationship with Nature dispassion-
ately and scientifically, we may find ourselves wondering
whether the differences between the human and non-human
worlds are really as fundamental as these double standards
might suggest. Evolutionary theory teaches us that the
rational mind is simply a product of the struggle for survival.
Man can no more be held responsible for his ability to think
and reach decisions than a fish can be held responsible for its
ability to swim. Nor does Man's rational mind detach him
from the struggle to survive, or free him from the instincts
and desires which control the actions of the beasts. Rational
thought is simply the medium through which these instincts
and desires express themselves in our case. So, if our natural
urge to live as long and as comfortably as possible, operating

through our rational minds and our creative and mechanical abilities, has resulted in the building of towns and cities, we are in a sense mistaken to condemn these developments as 'unnatural'. Man uses his rational mind to alter his environment to his own advantage instinctively and naturally, just as the fish uses its swimming ability to search for food, or to escape from environments which it finds unpleasant. Even if Man's attempts to 'improve' his environment result in a partial destruction of the natural world, or of the human race itself, there is no objective or scientific reason for thinking of this outcome as 'unnatural'.

Our disapproval of Man's disruptive effect on Nature often reflects the questionable assumption that, were it not for Man, the natural world would remain unchanged throughout eternity—infinitely complex, delicately balanced, always in motion yet essentially static, like an enormous watch that would never need to be wound. Instead of seeing Man as part of the watch, we imagine him arriving from outside and impetuously beginning to tinker with the mechanism in order to 'improve' it, oblivious to the fact that his 'improvements' are permanently damaging an irreplaceable artefact, which had been functioning perfectly for millions of years before his arrival. But Man belongs inside the mechanism rather than outside it, and the mechanism itself is not as static as the watch-image suggests. If the natural world were really in a state of perfect harmony and balance, then there would be no such thing as evolution. The theory of evolution argues that the first law of Nature is not perfect equilibrium but constant change. Disruptions such as ice-ages, earthquakes and volcanic eruptions occur regularly; mountain-ranges are thrown up and flattened; continents change their shapes and drift slowly from one part of the globe to another; and new life-forms appear, enjoy a spell of success, then either mutate or disappear. There are no guarantees of survival. The hills are full of the fossilized remains of unsuccessful experiments. Man must be seen as part of this evolutionary turmoil:

whether he survives or perishes, his fate will be encompassed by the evolutionary pattern as a whole, and there will be nothing 'unnatural' about it.

From a scientific point of view, then, the boundary which separates Man from Nature is non-existent; and likewise, from a socio-economic point of view, the boundary that divides the country from the city is non-existent. Yet these boundaries evidently persist in the minds of readers and writers alike. Just why this should be so is a difficult question to answer, but perhaps the problem becomes somewhat clearer if we follow Carl Jung in making a distinction between physical (or scientific) facts and psychological truths. As Jung writes in the 'Lectori Benevolo' with which he prefaces his book *Answer to Job*:

> 'Physical' is not the only criterion of truth: there are also *psychic* truths which can neither be explained nor proved nor contested in any physical way. If, for instance, a general belief existed that the river Rhine had at one time flowed backwards from its mouth to its source, then this belief would in itself be a fact even though such an assertion, physically understood, would be deemed utterly incredible. Beliefs of this kind are psychic facts which cannot be contested and need no proof.
>
> ...Although our whole world of religious ideas consists of anthropomorphic images that could never stand up to rational criticism, we should never forget that they are based on numinous archetypes, i.e., on an emotional foundation which is unassailable by reason. We are dealing with psychic facts which logic can overlook but not eliminate.[2]

Perhaps the Eden-myth, and the ideas associated with it about Man's separation from Nature, are 'psychic facts' of this type. They may not seem to hold very much water from a purely rational point of view, but to expose their shortcomings as descriptions of the 'real world' is to miss the point about them. What we need to ask ourselves is not whether they are scientifically true, but what they are expressing—what they can tell us about ourselves. If their roots go deep enough, then no amount of purely scientific or rational analysis will ever be able to eradicate them. No matter how often they are cut down, they will always reappear—in our literature, in environmentalist tracts, or in our unconscious thoughts and feelings. And there is one piece of evidence which does seem to indicate that the old-fashioned view of Man and Nature really is too deep-rooted to be wiped out by modern theories or scientific advances: namely, the way in which our literary traditions on this subject have withstood the advent of evolutionary theory, which at one point seemed set to overwhelm them.

II

In the mid-nineteenth century, certain members of the scientific community began to publish the geological findings and evolutionary theories which were eventually to revolutionize the scientific view of creation. It is now commonly accepted that these ideas also constituted a shattering challenge to the traditional Christian view of the universe, based as it was on a literal interpretation of the biblical creation narrative; and the consternation which they could cause amongst the British literary community of the day is famously exemplified by Section LVI of Tennyson's long poem *In Memoriam*.

The poem as a whole, of course, was occasioned by the sudden death in 1833 of Tennyson's close friend Arthur Hallam. It must therefore be seen as an account of—and response to—a period of intense personal grief, rather than as a discussion of the scientific discoveries of the day. It should also be remembered that *In Memoriam*, published in 1850, actually predates Darwin's book *The Origin of Species by*

Means of Natural Selection, which did not appear until 1859.
But geological discoveries, especially those arising from the
investigation of fossils, were already revolutionizing the scientific view of creation. They indicated that the history of the
world was a matter of millions rather than thousands of years,
and that during this period certain species, once flourishing,
had vanished from the earth forever. In this way the foreshort-
ened view of history encouraged by a literal reading of the
Bible was challenged: the idea that the world was created at a
given moment a few years before the dawn of Israelite history,
and thus a finite number of generations before the birth of
Christ, began to seem unscientific. Perhaps more importantly,
so did the idea that God had created the natural world in a
perfect and immutable form, designed to last unchanged
throughout eternity, and in fact only fundamentally changed
once, by the impact of Original Sin. It began to seem that
perhaps the natural world itself was imperfect and mutable.

Tennyson was obviously familiar with these new ideas, and
In Memoriam records how they intensified and deepened the
pangs of religious doubt brought on by Hallam's sudden
death. In place of the old idea that the natural world, by and
large, retains its original virtue because it has never deliberately rejected the laws of God, Tennyson finds himself
contemplating a new image of Nature, a Nature without
mercy or morality, governed only by laws of strength and
endurance. If Nature is subject to change, then it can only
mean that the natural world is less than perfect; and if it is less
than perfect then it cannot be the creation of God. Can
Nature have somehow escaped from God's control and
rebelled against his wishes? Tennyson writes in Section LV of
his poem—

> Are God and Nature then at strife,
>   That Nature lends such evil dreams?
>   So careful of the type she seems,
> So careless of the single life;

That I, considering everywhere
    Her secret meaning in her deeds,
    And finding that of fifty seeds
She often brings but one to bear,

I falter where I firmly trod...
                (Tennyson, In Memoriam, LV, *ll. 5–13)*

Early Romantic primitivists such as Wordsworth were
inclined to believe that only Man was affected by the Fall and
that the natural world was still suffused by the spirit of God.
They therefore suppressed their own awareness of Nature's
uglier and crueller aspects. But as soon as the connection
between God and Nature is called into question, the ugliness
and cruelty reappear: this is what is happening in the lines
above. Yet the idea that Nature is merely ruthless and amoral
is still held in check by the thought that although she is clearly
'careless of the single life', she may still be 'careful of the
type', or species. In other words, Nature's apparent cruelty to
individuals may be caused by the fact that she is working on
too large a scale to take account of personal feelings. The
underlying pattern, despite the disappointments and sufferings of numerous individuals, may still be governed by a
framework of moral values. But during Tennyson's lifetime
geological discoveries and the analysis of fossils were
providing more and more emphatic evidence that nature was
as careless of 'the type' as she was of 'the single life'. Scientists
were uncovering the buried remains of species which had once
flourished only to be completely wiped out.

Perhaps even Man himself was destined one day to become
extinct in his turn. It is this profoundly un-Christian thought
which lies behind the slightly hysterical language of Section LVI:

'So careful of the type?' but no.
    From scarpèd cliff and quarried stone
    She cries, 'A thousand types are gone:
I care for nothing, all shall go.

Thou makest thine appeal to me:
    I bring to life, I bring to death:
    The spirit does but mean the breath:
I know no more.' And he, shall he,

Man, her last work, who seem'd so fair,
    Such splendid purpose in his eyes,
    Who roll'd the psalm to wintry skies,
Who built him fanes of fruitless prayer,

Who trusted God was love indeed
    And love Creation's final law—
    Tho' Nature, red in tooth and claw
With ravine, shriek'd against his creed—

Who loved, who suffer'd countless ills,
    Who battled for the True, the Just,
    Be blown about the desert dust,
Or seal'd within the iron hills?

No more? A monster then, a dream,
    A discord. Dragons of the prime,
    That tare each other in their slime,
Were mellow music match'd with him...
        (Tennyson, In Memoriam, LVI, *ll. 1–24)*

Just for a moment Tennyson sees Man from a scientific perspective, not as something separate from Nature, but as one of Nature's creations: 'her last work, who seem'd so fair'. But the vision falls apart at once. Ostensibly this is because Tennyson cannot reconcile the geologists' view of Nature with his preconceptions about the existence of a beneficent God who commands that 'love' must be 'Creation's final law'; but in reality what he cannot accept is the idea of a completely unified world, a world in which good and evil simply co-exist instead of doing battle with one another, a world shorn of moral purpose, a world which exists for the sake of existing and may continue to do so forever, a world in which 'The spirit does but mean the breath'. Tennyson needs dividing-lines—balance—the drama, dynamism and symmetry of conflicting opposites. If he cannot have his separatist vision in one form then he will (perhaps unconsciously) recreate it in another. If Nature cannot be aligned with God, and sinful Man aligned with the Devil, then the same symmetrical pattern must be rebuilt in a new form.

Man is suddenly purged of his sin and becomes a suffering Christ-figure—'Who loved, who suffer'd countless ills,/Who battled for the True, the Just'—while Nature, suddenly hideous and evil rather than beautiful and virtuous, aligns herself with the Devil—'Nature, red in tooth and claw/With ravine, shriek'd against his creed'. 'His creed' means here both the creed of Man and of God—the idea that 'love' should be 'Creation's final law'. The natural world is transformed into a barren, merciless realm of 'wintry skies', 'desert dust' and 'iron hills', enlivened only by 'ravine', 'dragons' and 'slime'. Correspondingly, Man becomes an angelic creature 'who seem'd so fair', with 'Such splendid purpose in his eyes'. In other words, Tennyson stands the conventional Fall-myth on its head, so that Man becomes the unfallen part of creation and the natural world becomes the repository of violence and evil—but at least the dividing-line between the two is preserved.

Tennyson was not the only Victorian poet who coped with a renewed awareness of the cruelty and mutability of the natural world by describing Man as a sinless, suffering, aspiring figure whose one desire is to transcend the evils of his material existence. Matthew Arnold's early sonnet 'In Harmony with Nature' (published in 1849 but probably written 1844–47) also retains the old opposition between Man and Nature in a reversed form:

> Nature is cruel, man is sick of blood;
> Nature is stubborn, man would fain adore;

Nature is fickle, man hath need of rest;
Nature forgives no debt, and fears no grave;
Man would be mild, and with safe conscience blest.
                (*Arnold, 'In Harmony with Nature', ll. 7–11*)

The familiar notion that God made the country and the
natural world, whereas Man made towns and cities and all the
evils and inadequacies of human life, was thus occasionally
replaced by the idea that Nature—standing in for the Devil—
made the bloodthirsty world of the beasts, whereas God made
Man. Of course this idea was far from new: dislike of 'beast-
liness' has long been a facet of human self-awareness, and
one of the ways in which the people of the West are taught
to define themselves as human beings is by ritualistically
separating themselves from 'beastly' behaviour.

But in some ways a vision of noble and heroic Man struggling to rise above the toils of a mindlessly violent natural
world is even more difficult to sustain than the early Romantic
alternative of a tranquil, Eden-like, God-suffused natural
world from which only Man has been excluded. For one thing,
if Nature is to be shown as 'red in tooth and claw' then the
poet must turn his back on all the images of tranquillity and
fertility with which the literary tradition supplies him. The
British poet must also find a way of getting beyond the apparently calm prettiness of his own domesticated countryside.
Tennyson, in the passage quoted above, is obliged to draw his
imagery from foreign countries and prehistoric times; and if
the resulting picture seems a little overstated or even hysterical, then this is at least partly because our own awareness of
the traditions of British 'nature poetry' will not quite let us
forgive him for ignoring those aspects of the natural world
with which other poets—and even Tennyson himself at other
times—have made us more familiar. If this kind of imagery
were sustained for a long period we might begin to accuse the
poet of wilful misrepresentation. In our own century poets
such as Ted Hughes have managed to find ways of describing

the British countryside so as to reveal the struggle for life going on beneath its apparently calm and benign surface; but it should be noted that Hughes himself has not escaped accusations of wilful misrepresentation, despite our supposed acceptance of the Darwinian view of Nature.

But the more obvious weakness of a world-view which opposes bestial and diabolical Nature against noble and blameless Man is that we are more acutely aware of our own faults than we are of the faults of the natural world, and for this reason we cannot accept such an idealized portrayal of the human race as anything but a partial truth. We can scarcely read Arnold's line 'Nature is cruel, man is sick of blood', for example, without a mental protest.

Whatever the reasons, the traditional patterns of the Fall-myth—sinless Nature opposed to sinful Man—were to reassert themselves. By the end of *In Memoriam* Tennyson has begun to describe the natural world in conventional pastoral terms again, without ever having offered a convincing rationale for doing so:

> Now rings the woodland loud and long,
>   The distance takes a lovelier hue,
>   And drown'd in yonder living blue
> The lark becomes a sightless song.
>   *(Tennyson,* In Memoriam, CXV, *ll. 5–8)*

In this respect, as in others, the poem is prophetic. Tennyson at least has the wit to confess openly that he is allowing his heart to rule his head:

> The hills are shadows, and they flow
>   From form to form, and nothing stands;
>   They melt like mist, the solid lands,
> Like clouds they shape themselves and go.
>
> But in my spirit will I dwell,
>   And dream my dream, and hold it true;

> For tho' my lips may breathe adieu,
> I cannot think the thing farewell.
>   *(Tennyson,* In Memoriam, CXXIII, *ll. 5–12)*

He refuses to accept that the life of the spirit is a mere side-effect of the development of the material universe, or that the obliteration of individuals and species alike is unredeemed by any guarantees of later rebirth—not because he can find any rational means of refuting these ideas, but because he simply 'cannot think' them. His imagination cannot cope with them.

In fact Tennyson manages in the two stanzas given above to sidestep the scientific world-view whilst seeming to accommodate it. His imagery draws on the long perspective of the geologists, which suggests that the forms of the landscape are not as stable as they might seem, but mere 'shadows' which 'flow/From form to form'. But whereas this perspective might prompt a scientist to reflect that the history of the earth seems to be controlled by physical laws rather than moral ones—by an interplay of unconscious forces rather than by the guiding hand of a creative deity—the effect on Tennyson is just the opposite. The geological perspective allows him to imagine the hills in motion, and he automatically equates this motion with life and self-awareness. Thus the effect of the line 'Like clouds they shape themselves and go' is to make the hills seem self-motivated: they decide on their own shapes, and move on from one place to another at least partly of their own accord. This does not dispel the impression of impermanence, but it does suggest that spiritual self-awareness, far from being a mere side-effect in a world governed by mechanistic forces, actually suffuses the entire universe. Man is surrounded by other beings that feel and persish just as he does himself, but on a different time-scale. There is even a suggestion that these elemental being are able to metamorphose from one form to another—to 'flow/From form to form'—without suffering the pangs of death and without losing control of their own destinies—they *'shape themselves* and go'. So although Tennyson is adopting elements of the scientific world-view, the picture into which he incorporates them is pseudo-scientific at best. In this respect he is prophetic again. The use of pseudo-scientific imagery and language has become a commonplace of the modern landscape poet's reaction to—and defence against—the scientific world-view.

Matthew Arnold, like Tennyson, soon overcame his temporary aversion to the natural world, and like Tennyson he went on to write of the relationship between Man and Nature in a manner which incorporates elements of the scientific vision, without adopting that vision as a whole. In a later sonnet, 'Quiet Work' (published at the same time as 'In Harmony with Nature', but probably composed three or four years later), Arnold compares the achievements of Man with the achievements of Nature; and concludes by addressing Nature as follows:

> Yes, while on earth a thousand discords ring,
> Man's fitful uproar mingling with his toil,
> Still do thy sleepless ministers move on,
>
> Their glorious tasks in silence perfecting;
> Still working, blaming still our vain turmoil,
> Labourers that shall not fail, when man is gone.
> *(Arnold, 'Quiet Work', ll. 9–14)*

Again, the last line of the poem suggests a long scientific perspective, which allows Arnold to foresee a time when Man will have vanished like many other species before him. Such a thought would have been almost unthinkable before the nineteenth century, and in this way the poem registers the impact of contemporary geological discoveries and new ideas about the mutability of species. But instead of encouraging Arnold to think of Man as part of the natural world, these scientific ideas seem to have inspired him to describe the old separation of Man and Nature from a new angle. The mutability that will eventually silence 'Man's fitful uproar' will not, it seems, have the same effect on Nature—her labourers 'shall not fail, when man is gone'.

Instead of concluding from the scientific evidence that both Man and Nature are subject to the same laws of imperma-nence, Arnold seems to have concluded that Man's life of 'discords', 'uproar' and 'vain turmoil' will result in his eventual extinction, whereas Nature's steadiness and 'silence' will guar-antee her continued—and apparently unchanged—existence. Man is the only mortal exile from a natural world character-ized by its immortal tranquillity. In a later poem, 'The Youth of Nature' (published in 1852), Arnold makes a very similar point. He ends the poem by putting the following words into Nature's mouth:

> 'Race after race, man after man,
> Have thought that my secret was theirs,
> Have dream'd that I lived but for them,
> That they were my glory and joy.
> —They are dust, they are changed, they are gone!
>   I remain.'
>   (*Arnold, 'The Youth of Nature', ll. 129–34*)

The size of the timespan suggested by these lines may repre-sent a new development in Western literature, but the asser-tion that man is incapable of encompassing Nature or learning her secrets is unchanged since the Book of Job.

Of course the poems that I have examined up until now were all published before the appearance of *The Origin of Species* in 1859, and it could therefore be argued that they do not represent the conflict between scientific and Christian ideas at its climax; but it is undeniable that by the late 1840s and early 1850s the literary community had already begun to recognize the force of the new scientific ideas and to find ways of coping with them. The pattern was already estab-lished: fragments of the scientific world-view would be absorbed, but the idea that Man must be seen as a part of the natural world would be either consciously or unconsciously resisted. The separatist vision was not to be destroyed by mere weight of scientific evidence and logical argument. Darwin's theories did nothing to change this pattern.

Hardy is perhaps the exception that proves the rule. It is true that in Hardy's nature-poems there is a new sense that Man and the 'lower' denizens of the natural world are in much the same boat: his poem 'The Caged Thrush Freed and Home Again' is one example of this. The thrush, back among the other 'birds in brown', tells them that when he was carried off to live with men he 'hoped to glean/How happy days are made to be' (lines 8–9), but he concludes about Mankind that

> 'They cannot change the Frost's decree,
> They cannot keep the skies serene;
> How happy days are made to be
>
> Eludes great Man's sagacity
> No less than ours...'
>
> *(Hardy, 'The Caged Thrush Freed*
> *and Home Again', ll. 13–17)*

To Hardy's mind all living creatures are the pitiful and helpless victims of the same misshapen set of circumstances—a view which owes a great deal to his acquaintance with Darwin's theories. He often expresses the feeling that Man is wrong to imagine he is somehow 'above' the beasts: another example of this sentiment is 'An August Midnight'.

In this poem the writer is sitting at his lamp when his thoughts are interrupted by the arrival of 'A longlegs, a moth,... a dumbledore' and 'A sleepy fly' (lines 4 and 6). The poem ends:

> —My guests besmear my new-penned line
> Or bang at the lamp and fall supine.
> 'God's humblest, they!' I muse. Yet why?
> They know Earth-secrets that know not I.
>
> *(Hardy, 'An August Midnight', ll. 9–12)*

But although the poem's primary function is to remind us that
there is less difference than we may suppose between
ourselves and the beasts, the last line reintroduces the idea of
separation by hinting that the insects may possess a form of
wisdom—'Earth-secrets'—that their human observer does not
share. Not that they suffer less—they 'bang at the lamp and
fall supine' with endearing and pathetic clumsiness—but
possibly they are able to endure their sufferings more stoically.
The unheroic abruptness of their actions suggests a complete
absence of self-delusion, and thus an implied comparison with
the poem's human audience, which by and large seems incapable of acting and suffering in the same straightforward and
uncomplaining manner.

The same implied comparison also emerges in lines 11–12
of 'The Caged Thrush Freed and Home Again':

> 'Alas, despite their mighty mien
> Men know but little more than we!'

The difference between men and thrushes is not—as we would
like to suppose—that men are better able to control their own
destinies, but that men put on airs whereas thrushes do not.
Yet the fact of difference remains: Hardy's thrushes seem far
more sprightly and clear-headed about life and its drawbacks,
far less afflicted with false hopes and unreasonable longings,
than is generally the case with his human beings. In 'The
Darkling Thrush', one of his most famous poems, Hardy
takes the comparison a step further: the thrush of the title
seems able to rise above the dreariness of his circumstances
and find hope in spite of them, unlike the pessimistic narrator
who observes him:

> So little cause for carolings
>   Of such ecstatic sound
> Was written on terrestrial things
>   Afar or nigh around,
> That I could think there trembled through

His happy good-night air
Some blessed Hope, whereof he knew
And I was unaware.
(Hardy, 'The Darkling Thrush', ll. 25–32)

Almost in spite of himself, Hardy seems to be reverting to a toned-down version of the Fall-myth. His conscious intention may be to demonstrate that the natural world and the human world are both in the grip of a single set of circumstances, but the old habit of holding up Nature as an example to Man dies hard, and of course to use the natural world in this way is to imply that Man is the less virtuous of the two. Once this implication is felt, the dividing-line between the human world and the natural world quickly becomes re-established.

This pattern, of the separatist vision reasserting itself despite growing general familiarity with evolutionary theories and geological timescales, seems to have held good for modern British poetry as a whole. The controversies of the nineteenth century have certainly had profound effects: they have made it impossible, or helped to make it impossible, for writers to assume that they share with their audience a common ground of conventional religious belief; they have made available a historical overview that spans millions rather than thousands of years, encompassing eras both prior to Man's appearance and subsequent to his extinction; and they have led to an increased awareness of the amorality of the natural world. But they have had surprisingly little effect on the prevalence of either the Fall-myth or the separatist world-view that supports it. Paradoxically, despite the fact that the amorality of the natural world is now generally accepted, Nature is still held to be more virtuous than Man. The post-Darwinian image of Nature has become involved with the post-Freudian view of the human mind, with the result that Nature's refusal to abide by the laws of conventional morality has come to symbolize an enviable lack of inhibition. In this way Nature's amorality has actually come to be interpreted as a form of virtue.

The symbolic link between the natural world and the human unconscious plays an important part, as we have seen, in the primitivist philosophy of Ted Hughes; it also underlies the treatment of landscape in Seamus Heaney's earlier collections; and the forging of such a symbolic link illustrates the way in which evolutionist ideas have been reshaped to new purposes, to the point where evolutionist language is now often deployed in contexts from which the evolutionist perspective is entirely absent. Hughes's remark (quoted in my earlier chapter) that the human race represents 'an evolutionary dead-end', whereas the natural world is 'the draughty radiant Paradise of the animals', is a case in point. Hughes seems to believe that there are 'right' and 'wrong' courses for evolutionary development to follow, and that the path Man has chosen is one of the 'wrong' ones. He is inserting the term 'evolutionary' into a discourse about moral choices and spiritual values, in a manner which any true evolutionist could not fail to recognize as inappropriate. The most fundamental tenet of the 'natural selection' argument is that the evolutionary process is self-correcting: any form of development must be judged purely on the basis of whether or not it succeeds. Questions of moral right and wrong do not apply. Rational thought, therefore, should not be condemned as an 'evolutionary dead end' any more than should the ability to fly, or to lay eggs, or to climb trees; and of course the idea that the natural world is a 'draughty radiant Paradise' from which Man—and Man alone—has been excluded is completely at odds with the evolutionist perspective. But this confusion of ideas exemplifies the manner in which British 'nature poets' since the nineteenth century have absorbed fragments of the scientific world-view without adopting that world-view as a whole.

III

The persistence of a myth is never an accidental phenomenon: it indicates the fact that the myth expresses a deeply-rooted and widely-shared perception about human life. The persistence of the myth of Man's separation from Nature indicates that there must be a sense in which this feeling of separation is fundamental to our perceptions of our place in the non-human universe.

It seems to me that our inclination to separate Man from Nature must be closely related to our inclination to separate the mind from the body. Psychologically, it is almost impossible for us to reconcile our personal experiences of mental and spiritual self-awareness with our observations of external objects. In other words, we find it terribly difficult to think of ourselves as mere physical things—mechanisms, albeit complex ones—when our experiences of life are made up of unmechanical thoughts and feelings. These thoughts and feelings do not seem to be restrained or controlled by physical laws in the same way as our bodies—they do not seem to belong in a mechanistic universe—and we make sense of this situation by supposing that our existence must be made up of two components, a material body and an insubstantial mind or spirit. We also extend this binary system outwards, by dividing up the external world into human and non-human elements, which differ from one another (we suppose) in the respect that the human world is 'free' to make its own decisions and choose its own course, whereas the non-human world is governed by mechanistic laws.

Of course, the dividing-line that separates human from non-human often throws out a loop and takes in some unexpected terrain. We are as disinclined, for example, to see our beloved pets as mere mechanisms as we are to see ourselves in those terms. In effect we think of them as honorary members of the human race. At times this honorary membership may stretch beyond pets to trees, other plants, the weather and even our cars. Conversely, we make it easier for ourselves to maltreat, manipulate or ignore our fellow human beings by mentally relocating them on the far side of the human/non-human dividing-line. But none of these eccentricities alters our belief in the existence of the dividing-line itself.

We divide things up in this way, not because we have consciously made up our minds to do so, but because we have unconsciously recognized that we must. We need to believe in the life of the spirit because we cannot explain our own thoughts and feelings to ourselves in physical terms; but we also need the mechanistic view of life, because it enables us to analyse, manipulate and exploit the external world, as we must if we are to survive in it.

In order to rise above the level of mere existence, we must separate ourselves from the non-human universe and learn to view it critically. Likewise, we must separate ourselves from the flow of time in order to project our ideas and desires into the future, so that objectives which cannot be achieved at once no longer have to be abandoned entirely. By these means, the inner life of the spirit can establish a degree of control over the external world of physical things. But there is a price to be paid. It seems to us as if we have called time and the mechanistic laws of the physical world into existence by learning to recognize and control them in this way. Our attempts to free ourselves have had the effect of making us acutely aware of the walls of our prison. We have abandoned the mindless, timeless and seemingly trouble-free state of our infancy—a state which we assume to be still enjoyed by the denizens of the natural world—for the sake of the cares and responsibilities of 'independent' adult life.

Paradoxically, the values of the two categories often seem to reverse themselves. We begin to envy the non-human world—the world of things and soulless mechanisms, where freedom of choice does not exist—for its spiritual purity and untroubled serenity. We are all too aware of the shortcomings of the life we have fashioned for ourselves, and we cannot help noticing that the non-human universe does not seem to be flawed in the same way. One of the most noticeable differences between man-made environments and natural ones is that the man-made environments are forever going wrong, falling to pieces and piling up detritus, whereas the natural ones seem to renew themselves effortlessly, day by day and year by year, and to consume their own waste in the process.

And from a moral point of view, as I remarked earlier, we pass judgement on the works of Man in terms that we would never dream of applying to the works of Nature, simply because we assume that Man is morally responsible for his own actions, whereas Nature acts under compulsion (or in accordance with God's laws). If an animal behaves in a manner which seems 'cruel' or 'indecent' to our human eyes, we assume that it does so because it 'knows no better'; whereas we find it difficult to absolve human beings of responsibility for their actions in the same way. Of course, we do prefer the behaviour of some non-human things to others: we prefer the rabbit to the hyena, the whale to the shark and the bee to the blowfly. But even the most disgusting animal is rescued from the full force of our moral censure by virtue of its inhumanity. The vulture, waiting pitilessly for the moment when a dying animal can no longer defend itself, is less horrible to contemplate than a human being behaving in the same way. And because of this double standard, the human world often strikes us as morally depraved, whereas the natural world seems incorruptible.

All this is simply another way of saying that with one part of his mind Man regrets the self-awareness which makes him conscious of his own fallibility and fearful of his own death; he envies the apparent unconscious contentment of the non-human world; and often he turns towards that world with a sense of release, simply because it is different from his own creations, and therefore offers him a moment of escape from his own problems.

Of course, we should not lose sight of the fact that the

unconscious and mechanistic life of Nature is a form of Hell as well as a form of Eden. Absence of choice may mean absence of error, but it also means absence of freedom. One reason why we separate our minds from our bodies and the human world from the natural world is that we wish to protect ourselves from the tyranny of a purely physical universe. Our impulse to rebel against God's will cannot be dissociated from our desire to overcome the tyranny of physical existence itself—to conquer disease, old age and, if it were possible, death too. Of course the struggle is ultimately a futile one, but perhaps it is part of our inheritance as human beings.

Writers who complain that Man's separation from Nature has gone too far sometimes seem disinclined to spell out what might be the consequences if the process of separation were put into reverse. Modern life in the 'developed' countries of the West is characterized not only by the television, videos, plastic wrappers, fast food and disposable goods which we can all more or less agree to despise; nor by the washing machines, cars, fridges, vacuum cleaners and electric mixers that give our everyday lives their comfortable shape; but by efficient lighting and heating, by fresh running water and good sanitation, by hospitals, drugs and antibiotics, by longer life-spans, by low infant mortality rates, by readily-available contraception and by plentiful supplies of cheap and varied food. Few people, if any, would be prepared to give up all this for the sake of a more 'traditional' and 'natural' way of life.

All the same it would be wrong to imagine that our feelings towards the countryside and the natural world are governed by mere ignorance and nostalgia. Our desire to overcome the tyranny of physical existence is tempered, as I hinted before, by an awareness that the battle can never be won. At some point we will all be obliged to submit ourselves to the superior strength of the physical world, and for this reason we cannot help feeling from time to time that instead of struggling against the inevitable we would be better off facing up to it and trying to come to terms with it. It is partly as a result of this feeling that we imagine the natural world to be more virtuous than our own, and life in the country to be more virtuous than life in the town. There is an apparently stoical acceptance of physical laws and limitations which prevails in the natural world; and people who live in the country, being closer to Nature, often strike us as less preoccupied with the vanity of human affairs than people who live in the town.

Whether this sequence of ideas culminates in a scientifically accurate representation of Nature, or of the relationship between Nature and Man, is certainly open to question. Nevertheless, it does seem to possess a psychological validity of its own. Until human psychology itself changes, perhaps our sense of separateness from the natural world cannot be entirely exorcized. Perhaps it is only by ceasing to be himself than Man can cease to be an outcast from Eden.

IV

In tracing the Eden-myth back to its psychological roots, it is not my intention to suggest that the myth is immutable. All great myths are dynamic: they change as circumstances change, they can be told in new ways when new needs arise, and they can also be interpreted afresh by people with fresh ideas and questions in mind. Our attitudes towards the landscape are changing already as a result of the environmental crisis, and undoubtedly that change will become more profound as the crisis deepens; and then the Eden-myth itself, as a result, will either be reworked, or played down in favour of some other story.

So far as our literature is concerned, it seems likely that poems about the landscape will become increasingly laden with scientific or pseudo-scientific language and concepts in the years to come. One of the most noteworthy features of the environmental crisis and its effect on public consciousness to date, has been the way in which it has begun to force the non-scientific community to recognize that the scientific world-view is of vital importance to their everyday lives. In the course of the twentieth century, those of us who are not scientists have gradually become more and more inclined to take the products of scientific thought for granted, yet less and less capable of understanding how they function. Without cars and fridges, antibiotics, and information technology, our lives would collapse—yet very few of us could explain how these things work, even in broad terms.

But thanks to the environmental crisis, the world of science and technology is gradually re-entering the domain of public consciousness. The concepts, terminology and arguments with which environmentalists equip themselves when they seek to defend or disseminate 'green' ideas are inevitably scientific or pseudo-scientific in nature; and as public aware-ness of the environmental crisis has grown, so public awareness of certain apsects of the scientific world-view has grown too. One need only call to mind a few phrases such as 'global warming', 'ozone depletion' or 'acid rain'—phrases that would have been greeted with almost total incomprehen-sion only a decade or two ago—to realize the extent to which the environmental debate has raised public awareness of certain scientific concepts. Of course the awareness produced in this way is often vague and pseudo-scientific, based as it frequently is on casual reading, listening and conversation rather than on careful study; but the fact remains that the environmental debate has already had a noticeable effect on the language and concepts in everyday use. This effect can only become more marked as time goes by; and eventually it is bound to change the way in which poets describe the land-scape.

I am not suggesting, however, that we can expect our poets to begin spouting environmentalist arguments or scientific theories. They will certainly not be very successful as poets if they do. A poem which merely regurgitated scientific facts and theories in a poetic form would be of little use to anyone, except perhaps a physics teacher searching for a new way to hold the attention of his pupils. If a poet is to bring a new system of ideas to life in his poetry, he must digest it so thoroughly that it becomes part of his own way of seeing things. Therefore what we can expect from our poets, as the environmental crisis continues to push scientific considerations to the forefront of their minds, is not an increasingly precise use of technical terms or an inclination to regurgitate scientific theories, but an increasingly pseudo-scientific mode of discourse, where scientific terms, ideas and concerns are 'poeticized', blended with other material, and reshaped until they suit the poet's own intentions.

Alongside this increasing awareness of scientific ideas it seems likely, as I said at the beginning of this book, that in the landscape poetry of the future more emphasis will be placed on the interdependence between Man and Nature, and less on their separation. But this is not necessarily to say that the Eden-myth will have to be jettisoned. It is true that the myth emphasizes Man's separation from the natural world by telling us how he came to be cast out from the divine-but-mindless harmony of Eden; but it also tells us that the human race can never be completely detached from Nature, because it is central to God's scheme of things. After all, Adam was created in God's image, he was entrusted with the task of naming all living creatures, and he was put in charge of God's special garden:

> And God said, Let us make man in our image, after our likeness: and let them have dominion over the fish of the sea, and over the fowl of the air, and over the cattle, and over all the earth, and over every creeping thing that creepeth upon the earth.
>
> *(Genesis 1:26)*

> And the Lord God took the man, and put him into the garden of Eden, to dress it and to keep it.
>
> *(Genesis 2:15)*

> And out of the ground the Lord God formed every
> beast of the field, and every fowl of the air; and
> brought them unto Adam to see what he would call
> them: and whatsoever Adam called every living crea-
> ture, that was the name thereof.
>
> *(Genesis 2:19)*

It may seem that this anthropocentric view of creation
ought to have been more thoroughly exploded by now than
any other aspect of the Eden-myth. Modern science has
certainly discouraged us from complacently imagining
ourselves to be enthroned at the hub of creation. Darwinism
has taught us that the human race is only one species among
many; and modern astronomy has shown us that our world is
nothing but a tiny speck in one outflung arm of a galactic
whirlpool, while our whole galaxy in turn is merely one point
of brightness in a stupendous sea of darkness and light. The
universe, we are told, existed for unimaginable periods of time
before our solar system appeared; but even if we ignore those
lost aeons, and think only of the years which have passed since
life first appeared on our own planet, Man is still virtually a
newborn infant by comparison with the other life-forms which
surround him. From this perspective, the idea that everything
was created for our benefit seems simply laughable.

Yet from a psychological point of view, it is of course undeniable that we stand at the centre of things as we see them.
And, in terms of the modern environmental crisis, we do seem
to have been entrusted with the care and upkeep of Nature.
The fate of numerous species, and perhaps even of the whole
biosphere, is now in our hands. Furthermore, although some
modern scientific theories seem to militate against anthro-
pocentrism, there are others which seem to reinforce it. The
following passage, for example, occurs towards the end of
James Lovelock's book *Gaia*:

> If we are a part of Gaia it becomes interesting to ask:
> 'To what extent is our collective intelligence also a

part of Gaia? Do we as a species constitute a Gaian nervous system and a brain which can consciously anticipate environmental changes?'

...The evolution of *homo sapiens*, with his technological inventiveness and his increasingly subtle communications network, has vastly increased Gaia's range of perception. She is now through us awake and aware of herself... It may be that the destiny of mankind is to become tamed, so that the fierce, destructive, and greedy forces of tribalism and nationalism are fused into a compulsive urge to belong to the commonwealth of all creatures which constitutes Gaia.[3]

My knowledge of modern science is partial at best, but so far as I can make out the latest 'buzzword' in scientific thinking is holism. If science was once about chopping things up into smaller and smaller pieces in order to see how they were made, there is now a corrective emphasis on the idea that the parts of a machine (or a living system) cannot be properly understood if they are separated from one another, but only if they are considered together as a functioning whole. So far as environmental studies are concerned, the holistic view of life on our planet urges us to recognize that the human race itself is a part of the living system, which Lovelock calls Gaia. It makes no sense to spend our time analysing how the natural world would function if Man were absent, and then bemoaning the difference his presence has made. Man is as much an integral part of life on our planet as any other species. But once the human race is allowed back into the picture, there is a tendency to dominate. Lovelock would like us to be fused into the Gaian body, but not just as another part. He sees us as the brain.

Lovelock's anthropocentric view of Man's place in the Gaian system may not be particularly well thought-out: he obviously enjoys putting forward provocative ideas, without necessarily having considered all the consequences, and he does this with particular abandon towards the end of his book. All the same, his inclination to place the thinking and observing human mind at the very centre of things is not as scientifically eccentric as it might seem. One of the side-effects of holistic theory is that it has encouraged scientists to reconsider the relationship between the observer and the thing observed. The old-fashioned scientific view that the observer must be completely detached from the subject of his inquiries seems to be breaking down, and in its place there is a growing feeling that the results of scientific experiments are always to some extent determined by the way in which those experiments are set up. This does not mean that the results are invalid: it means that there is an interaction between the inquiring mind and the area of reality on which its thoughts are focused. The scientist *creates* reality by asking questions about it. If he asks his questions in one way, he will discover reality of a certain type; and if he asks them in another way, he will discover something quite different.

In the world of quantum physics it seems that, by setting up an experiment in two different ways, scientists can arrive at two different sets of results which cannot logically be reconciled with one another. If photons are measured in one way they behave like particles; if they are measured in another way they behave like waves. The implications are mind-boggling— and they are also profoundly anthropocentric. The following extracts comes from John Gribbin's excellent book about quantum physics, *In Search of Schrodinger's Cat*:

> Is it possible that the nucleus, the positron and the neutrino did *not* exist until experimenters discovered the right sort of chisel with which to reveal their form? Such speculations strike at the roots of sanity, let alone our concept of reality. But they are quite sensible questions to ask in the quantum world... If we cannot say what a particle does when we are not looking at it, neither can we say if it

exists when we are not looking at it, and it is reasonable to claim that nuclei and positrons did not exist prior to the twentieth century, because nobody before 1900 ever saw one.[4]

Later in the same book, Gribbin describes the theories of a scientist called John Wheeler, who believes that 'observer participancy' may actually be fundamental to the existence of the universe in which we live:

> Never afraid to make the grand intuitive leap... Wheeler goes on to consider the whole universe as a participatory, self-excited circuit. Starting from the Big Bang, the universe expands and cools; after thousands of millions of years it produces beings capable of observing the universe... By observing the photons of the cosmic background radiation, the echo of the Big Bang, we may be creating the Big Bang and the universe.[5]

Are we really calling the fundamental elements of our world into existence, by giving them names and inventing experiments which can detect them? Could we even be creating the universe itself, by probing backwards in time to its origins? These are extraordinary questions to be emerging from modern science, because until very recently the scientific world-view has always seemed to start from the assumption that the world we perceive really does exist, that its life is independent from ours, and that it can be objectively analysed and measured and manipulated. In short, scientists have always seemed to believe in the absolute solidity and self-contained truth of the external world. But now it is beginning to seem that the external world may not be solid after all— or that the internal and external realms may not be as separate as we thought—and that there may be more than one truth. Perhaps certain things do not exist unless we make them real by observing them; or perhaps they exist in more than one form, until we nail them down by measuring them in a particular way.

New though these thoughts may be to the scientific establishment, they are not particularly new in the field of philosophy; and if we look again at the Eden-myth, we will see that they have long been acknowledged as what Jung would call psychic truths. In Genesis, God brings all living things to Adam to see what he will call them, 'and whatsoever Adam called every living creature, that was the name thereof'. What is the significance of this impenetrable piece of circular reasoning, if it does not refer to the power of the human mind to fix reality by categorizing things and giving them names? And is not the anthropocentricity of the Eden-myth—its insistence that Man is made in the image of God, and that he has been given power over all living things—another way of emphasizing the same thing? The Biblical authors knew all about the power and independence of the natural world; they also knew about the frailty of human life; in fact they probably perceived both of those things more clearly than we do ourselves. But they also knew that Man belongs at the centre of the universe of his own perceptions: to put him anywhere else would be a nonsense. They knew that to each of us, as we become aware of the external world, everything seems newly-created, and created for our benefit. And they knew that reality is at least partly what we make it. They understood the power we gain over things by giving them names.

But the anthropocentric view of things is only half the story. The scientist who seeks to persuade us that we are creating the universe by beholding it needs to answer one fundamental question—why, if we have created it, does the universe refuse to co-operate with us? Why is it so often awkward and unpredictable, and sometimes downright hostile? The Eden-myth is particularly wise on these points, because its fidelity is not to this or that theory of existence, but to the actual experience of being alive. Against the feeling that we have been placed at the centre of the world is set the feeling that we have been dislodged from that central position, and expelled from Eden. Against the idea that we were created in God's image is set the idea that we were made from dust, and must therefore return to dust in the end. And against the notion that Man was given power over all living things in the world is set the notion that he has been cursed, and that the ground sprouts thorns and thistles to torment him.

In fact, if modern science sometimes encourages us to believe that Man creates the universe by observing it, then the Bible warns us against a complacent acceptance of this view. In the Bible, after all, Man is not the creator: that role is reserved for God. Man is created in God's image, but as soon as he succumbs to the temptation to become godlike himself, disaster befalls him. Man's proper role is one of stewardship— 'And the Lord God took the man, and put him in the garden of Eden to dress it and to keep it'.

Perhaps it is this aspect of the Eden-myth which will come to the fore as the environmental crisis deepens. Today, even more than when the myth was first written down, it is impossible to deny that the role of stewardship has been thrust upon us. It is no longer an option for us to solve our problems by standing back and leaving Nature alone. In order to live in the world we must interact with it, and the real choice before us is whether to interact deliberately or haphazardly. We must somehow learn to look after the garden of Nature without overstepping the mark, interfering too much, and thus compounding the troubles of our fallen state.

Perhaps in the future, as a result of our increasing involvement with the care and maintenance of our planet, we will be nostalgic for different things. In years to come, when men look back to Eden, they may no longer see it as the place where they lived at one with Nature, because separation from the natural world will no longer be an issue; instead, they may well think of it as a place where their responsibilities were not so great, and where Nature could still be relied upon, in general terms, to look after herself.

NOTES

1. Keith Thomas, *Man and the Natural World* (Allen Lane, 1983), p. 122.

2. Carl Jung, *Answer to Job* (trans. R. F. C. Hull; New York: Bollingen Foundation, 1958; New Jersey: Princeton University Press, 1969; first published as *Antwort auf Hiob*, Zürich, 1952), pp. xi–xiii.

3. James Lovelock, *Gaia*, pp. 147–48.

4. John Gribbin, *In Search of Schrodinger's Cat* (Corgi/Wildwood House, 1984), p. 162.

5. *Ibid.*, p. 212.

Select Bibliography

This bibliography is by no means an exhaustive guide, either to my own reading for this book, or to the published works of my five poets, or to relevant books of criticism. Nevertheless, I hope that it may serve as a useful general list for scholars and other interested readers.

All books listed were published in London unless otherwise stated.

Philip Larkin

Poetry

The North Ship (Fortune Press, 1945; Faber, 1966)
The Less Deceived (Hessle: The Marvell Press, 1955)
The Whitsun Weddings (Faber, 1964)
High Windows (Faber, 1974)
Collected Poems, ed. Anthony Thwaite (The Marvell Press/ Faber, 1988)

Novels

Jill (Fortune Press, 1946; Faber, 1964)
A Girl in Winter (Faber, 1947)

Other writings

All What Jazz? (Faber, 1970)
The Oxford Book of Twentieth Century English Verse (as editor; Oxford: Oxford University Press, 1973)

Required Writing (Faber, 1983)

Selected Letters of Philip Larkin 1940–1985, ed. Anthony Thwaite (Faber, 1992)

Books about Philip Larkin

David Timms, *Philip Larkin* (Edinburgh: Oliver & Boyd, 1973)

Simon Petch, *The Art of Philip Larkin* (Sydney: Sydney University Press, 1981)

Andrew Motion, *Philip Larkin* (Methuen, 1982)

Anthony Thwaite (ed.), *Larkin at Sixty* (Faber, 1982)

Terry Whalen, *Philip Larkin and English Poetry* (Basingstoke: Macmillan, 1986)

Salem K. Hassan, *Philip Larkin and his Contemporaries* (Basingstoke: Macmillan, 1988)

Janice Rossen, *Philip Larkin: His Life's Work* (Hemel Hempstead: Harvester Wheatsheaf, 1989)

Andrew Motion, *Philip Larkin: A Writer's Life* (Faber, 1993)

R. S. Thomas

Poetry

The Stones of the Field (Carmarthen, 1946)

An Acre of Land (Newtown, Montgomeryshire, 1952)

The Minister (Newtown, Montgomeryshire, 1953)

Song at the Year's Turning (1955)

Poetry for Supper (1958)

Judgement Day (1960)

Tares (Hart-Davis, 1961)

The Bread of Truth (Hart-Davis, 1963)

Pieta (Hart-Davis, 1966)

Not that He Brought Flowers (Hart-Davis, 1968)

H'm (1972)

Young and Old (1972)
Selected Poems 1946–1968 (Newcastle upon Tyne: Bloodaxe, 1973)
What is a Welshman? (1974)
Laboratories of the Spirit (Basingstoke: Macmillan, 1975)
The Way of It (Sunderland, 1977)
Frequencies (1978)
Between Here and Now (1981)
Later Poems 1972–1982 (Basingstoke: Macmillan, 1983)
Ingrowing Thoughts (Bridgend: Poetry Wales Press, 1985)
Destinations (1985)
Experimenting with an Amen (Basingstoke: Macmillan, 1986)
Welsh Airs (Bridgend: Poetry Wales Press, 1987)
The Echoes Return Slow (Basingstoke: Macmillan, 1988)
Counterpoint (Newcastle upon Tyne: Bloodaxe, 1990)
Mass for Hard Times (Newcastle upon Tyne: Bloodaxe, 1992)
Collected Poems 1945–1990 (Dent, 1993)

Other writings

Selected Prose, ed. Sandra Anstey (Bridgend: Poetry Wales Press, 1983)
Neb (an autobiography in Welsh; Gwynedd, 1985)

As Editor

The Batsford Book of Country Verse (Batsford, 1961)
The Penguin Book of Religious Verse (Harmondsworth: Penguin, 1962)
Selected Poems of Edward Thomas (1964)
A Choice of George Herbert's Verse (1967)
A Choice of Wordsworth's Verse (1971)

Books about R. S. Thomas

Leonard Clark and R. George Thomas, *Andrew Young and R. S. Thomas* (Longmans, Green & Co., 1964)

W. Moelwyn Merchant, *R. S. Thomas* (Cardiff: University of Wales Press, 1979)

A. E. Dyson, *Yeats, Eliot and R. S. Thomas* (Basingstoke: Macmillan, 1981)

Sandra Anstey (ed.), *Critical Writings on R. S. Thomas* (Bridgend: Poetry Wales Press, 1982)

J. P. Ward, *The Poetry of R. S. Thomas* (Bridgend: Poetry Wales Press, 1987)

Charles Tomlinson

Poetry

Relations and Contraries (Aldington: Hand & Flower Press, 1951)

The Necklace (Oxford: Fantasy Press, 1955)

Seeing is Believing (New York: McDowell, Obolensky, 1958; Oxford: Oxford University Press, 1960)

A Peopled Landscape (Oxford: Oxford University Press, 1963)

Poems: A Selection (with Tony Connor and Austin Clarke; Oxford: Oxford University Press, 1964)

American Scenes and Other Poems (Oxford: Oxford University Press, 1966)

Penguin Modern Poets 14 (with Alan Brownjohn and Michael Hamburger; Penguin, 1969)

The Way of a World (Oxford: Oxford University Press, 1969)

Written on Water (Oxford: Oxford University Press, 1972)

The Way In and Other Poems (Oxford: Oxford University Press, 1974)

Selected Poems 1951–74 (Oxford: Oxford University Press, 1978)

The Shaft (Oxford: Oxford University Press, 1978)

The Flood (Oxford: Oxford University Press, 1981)

Notes from New York and Other Poems (Oxford: Oxford University Press, 1984)

Collected Poems (Oxford: Oxford University Press, 1985)

The Return (Oxford: Oxford University Press, 1987)

Annunciations (Oxford: Oxford University Press, 1989)

The Door in the Wall (Oxford: Oxford University Press, 1992)

Eden (poems and graphics; Bristol: Redcliffe Press, undated but probably 1985)

Collaborations

Octavio Paz, Jacques Roudbaud, Edoardo Sanguineti and Charles Tomlinson, *Renga* (France, 1971; USA, 1972; Harmondsworth: Penguin, 1979)

Octavio Paz and Charles Tomlinson, *Airborn/Hijos del Aire* (Anvil Press, 1981)

Translations

Versions from Fyodor Tyutchev, 1803–1873 (Oxford: Oxford University Press, 1960)

Castilian Ilexes: Versions from Machado (with Henry Gifford; Oxford: Oxford University Press, 1963)

Ten Versions from Trilce (with Henry Gifford; Cerillos, NM: San Marcos Press, 1974)

Translations (Oxford: Oxford University Press, 1983)

Other writings

The Poem as Initiation (New York: Colgate University Press, 1968)
Some Americans: A Personal Record (Berkeley and Los Angeles, CA: University of California Press, 1981)
Poetry and Metamorphosis (Cambridge: Cambridge University Press, 1983)

As Editor

Marianne Moore: A Collection of Critical Essays (Englewood Cliffs, NJ: Prentice-Hall, 1969)
William Carlos Williams: A Critical Anthology (Harmondsworth: Penguin, 1972)
William Carlos Williams: Selected Poems (Harmondsworth: Penguin, 1976)
The Oxford Book of Verse in English Translation (Oxford: Oxford University Press, 1980)

Books about Charles Tomlinson

Kathleen O'Gorman (ed.), *Charles Tomlinson: Man and Artist* (Columbia, MO: University of Missouri Press, 1988)

Ted Hughes

Poetry

The Hawk in the Rain (Faber, 1957)
Lupercal (Faber, 1960)
Wodwo (Faber, 1967)
Crow (Faber, 1972)

Season Songs (Faber, 1976)
Gaudete (Faber, 1977)
Cave Birds (Faber, 1978)
Moortown (Faber, 1979)
Remains of Elmet (Faber, 1979)
River (Faber, 1983)
What is the Truth? (Faber, 1984)
Flowers and Insects (Faber, 1986)
Wolfwatching (Faber, 1989)
Rain-Charm for the Duchy (Faber, 1992)
Three Books (Faber, 1993)

Poetry for children

Meet My Folks (Faber, 1961)
The Earth-Owl and Other Moon People (Faber, 1963)
Nessie the Mannerless Monster (Faber, 1964)
Moon-Whales and Other Moon Poems (New York: Viking, 1976)
Under the North Star (Faber, 1981)
Moon-Bells and Other Poems (Bodley Head, 1986)

Stories

How the Whale Became (Faber, 1966)
The Iron Man (Faber, 1968)
Tales of the Early World (Faber, 1988)
The Iron Woman (Faber, 1993)

Other writings

Poetry in the Making (Faber, 1967)
Shakespeare and the Goddess of Complete Being (Faber, 1992)
Winter Pollen (Faber, 1994)

As Editor

A Choice of Emily Dickinson's Verse (Faber, 1968)
A Choice of Shakespeare's Verse (Faber, 1971)
The Rattle Bag (with Seamus Heaney; Faber, 1982)

Books about Ted Hughes

A. Bold, *Thom Gunn and Ted Hughes* (1976)
Keith Sagar, *The Art of Ted Hughes* (Cambridge: Cambridge
    University Press, 1978)
Ekbert Faas, *Ted Hughes: The Unaccommodated Universe*
    (Santa Barbara, CA: Black Sparrow Press, 1980)
Stuart Hirschberg, *Myth in the Poetry of Ted Hughes*
    (Portmarnock, Co. Dublin: Wolfhound Press, 1981)
Keith Sagar (ed.), *The Achievement of Ted Hughes* (Manchester:
    Manchester University Press, 1983)
Thomas West, *Ted Hughes* (Methuen, 1985)
Craig Robinson, *Ted Hughes as Shepherd of Being* (Basingstoke:
    Macmillan, 1989)

Seamus Heaney

Poetry

Death of a Naturalist (Faber, 1966)
Door into the Dark (Faber, 1969)
Wintering Out (Faber, 1972)
North (Faber, 1975)
Field Work (Faber, 1979)
Selected Poems 1965–1975 (Faber, 1980)
Station Island (Faber, 1984)
The Haw Lantern (Faber, 1987)

New Selected Poems 1966–1987 (Faber, 1988)
Seeing Things (Faber, 1991)

Other writings

Preoccupations (Faber, 1980)
Sweeney Astray (Faber, 1983)
The Government of the Tongue (Faber, 1988)
The Cure at Troy (Faber, 1990)

As Editor

The Rattle Bag (with Ted Hughes; Faber, 1982)

Books about Seamus Heaney

Blake Morrison, *Seamus Heaney* (Methuen, 1982)
Tony Curtis (ed.), *The Art of Seamus Heaney* (Bridgend: Poetry Wales Press, 1982)
David Annwn, *Inhabited Voices: Myth and History in the Poetry of Geoffrey Hill, Seamus Heaney and George Mackay Brown* (Frome: Bran's Head Books, 1984)
Neil Corcoran, *Seamus Heaney* (Faber, 1986)
Elmer Andrews, *The Poetry of Seamus Heaney* (Macmillan, 1988)
William Cookson and Peter Dale (eds), *Agenda—Seamus Heaney Fiftieth Birthday Issue* (Agenda, 1989)

General

Theodor Adorno, *Aesthetic Theory* (Frankfurt: Suhrkamp Verlag, 1970; London: Routledge & Kegan Paul, 1984, trans. C. Lenhardt)

Kenneth Allott (ed.), *The Penguin Book of Contemporary Verse 1918–60* (Harmondsworth: Penguin, 1962)

A. Alvarez (ed.), *The New Poetry* (Harmondsworth: Penguin, 1962)

Jay Appleton, *The Experience of Landscape* (John Wiley, 1975)

John Barrell, *The Idea of Landscape and the Sense of Place* (Cambridge University Press, 1972)

——*The Dark Side of the Landscape* (Cambridge: Cambridge University Press, 1980)

John Barrell and John Bull (eds), *The Penguin Book of English Pastoral Verse* (Harmondsworth: Penguin, 1974)

Joseph Warren Beach, *The Concept of Nature in Nineteenth-Century English Poetry* (New York: Russell & Russell, 1966)

Calvin Bedient, *Eight Contemporary Poets* (Oxford: Oxford University Press, 1984)

John Berger, *Pig Earth* (Chatto & Windus, 1985)

Hugh Brody, *Living Arctic* (Faber, 1987)

Martin Buber, *I and Thou* (first published in Germany as *Ich und Du*, 1923; New York: Charles Scribner's Sons, 1958)

Rachel Carson, *Silent Spring* (Boston, MA: Houghton Mifflin, 1962; Harmondsworth: Penguin, 1965)

Kenneth Clark, *Landscape into Art* (1949; John Murray, 1976)

Robert Conquest (ed.), *New Lines* (Macmillan, 1956)

——*New Lines 2* (Macmillan, 1963)

Charles Darwin, *The Origin of Species* (1859)

Donald Davie, *Purity of Diction in English Verse* (Chatto & Windus, 1952; Routledge and Kegan Paul, 1967)

——*Articulate Energy* (1955; 1965; Routledge & Kegan Paul, 1976)

——*Thomas Hardy and British Poetry* (Routledge & Kegan Paul, 1973)

——*The Poet in the Imaginary Museum* (Manchester: Carcanet, 1977)

——*Collected Poems 1971–1983* (Manchester: Carcanet, 1983)

Martin Dodsworth (ed.), *The Survival of Poetry* (Faber, 1970)

William Empson, *Some Versions of Pastoral* (Chatto & Windus, 1950)

Richard Feynman, *QED: The Strange Theory of Light and Matter* (Princeton, NJ: Princeton University Press, 1985; Harmondsworth: Penguin, 1990)

Boris Ford (ed.), *The New Pelican Guide to English Literature: The Present* (Harmondsworth: Penguin, 1983)

R. F. Foster, *Modern Ireland 1600–1972* (Allen Lane, 1988; Harmondsworth: Penguin, 1989)

R. F. Foster (ed.), *The Oxford History of Ireland* (Oxford: Oxford University Press, 1989, 1992)

P. V. Glob, *The Bog People* (trans. R. L. S. Bruce-Mitford; Faber, 1969)

Robert Graves, *The White Goddess* (1948; 1952; Faber, 1961)

John Gribbin, *In Search of Schrodinger's Cat* (Corgi/ Wildwood House, 1984)

Michael Hamburger, *The Truth of Poetry* (Weidenfeld & Nicolson, 1969)

Eric Homberger, *The Art of the Real* (Dent, 1977)

W. G. Hoskins, *The Making of the English Landscape* (Hodder & Stoughton, 1955)

Gabriel Josipovici, *The Book of God* (New Haven, CT: Yale University Press, 1988)

Carl Jung, *Modern Man in Search of a Soul* (1933; Routledge, 1961)

——*Answer to Job* (trans. R. F. C. Hull; New York: Bollingen Foundation, 1958; Princeton, NJ: Princeton University Press, 1969; first published as *Antwort auf Hiob*, Zürich, 1952)

——*Psychology and Western Religion* (Routledge, 1988)

P. R. King, *Nine Contemporary Poets* (Methuen, 1979)

D. H. Lawrence, *Apocalypse* (1931; Harmondsworth: Penguin, 1980)

James Lovelock, *Gaia* (1979; Oxford: Oxford University Press, 1987)

Bill McKibben, *The End of Nature* (Penguin, 1990)

Blake Morrison, *The Movement* (Oxford: Oxford University Press, 1980)

Blake Morrison and Andrew Motion (eds), *The Penguin Book of Contemporary British Poetry* (Penguin, 1982)

Paul Muldoon (ed.), *The Faber Book of Contemporary Irish Poetry* (Faber, 1982)

Elaine Pagels, *The Gnostic Gospels* (Weidenfeld & Nicolson, 1979)

——*Adam, Eve and the Serpent* (Weidenfeld & Nicolson, 1988)

Thomas Pakenham, *The Year of Liberty* (Hodder & Stoughton, 1969)

John Press, *Rule and Energy* (Oxford: Oxford University Press, 1963)

——*A Map of Modern Verse* (Oxford: Oxford University Press, 1969)

Myra Reynolds, *The Treatment of Nature in English Poetry Between Pope and Wordsworth* (New York: Gordian Press, 1966)

Michael Schmidt and Grevel Lindop (eds), *British Poetry Since 1960: A Critical Survey* (Manchester: Carcanet, 1972)

Rupert Sheldrake, *The Rebirth of Nature* (Rider Books, 1990)

Robin Skelton (ed.), *Poetry of the Forties* (Harmondsworth: Penguin, 1968)

A. C. H. Smith, *Orghast at Persepolis* (Eyre Methuen, 1972)

C. K. Stead, *Pound, Yeats, Eliot and the Modernist Movement* (Basingstoke: Macmillan, 1986)

Stanley Stewart, *The Enchanted Garden* (Wisconsin: University of Wisconsin Press, 1966)

Keith Thomas, *Man and the Natural World* (Allen Lane, 1983)

James Turner, *The Politics of Landscape* (Oxford: Blackwell, 1979)

Barbara Ward and René Dubos, *Only One Earth* (André Deutsch/Harmondsworth: Penguin, 1972)

Gilbert White, *The Natural History of Selborne* (1788)

Raymond Williams, *Culture and Society* (Chatto & Windus, 1958; Harmondsworth: Penguin 1961, 1963)

——*The Country and the City* (Chatto & Windus, 1973)

William Carlos Williams, *In the American Grain* (New York, 1925; New York: New Directions, 1956)

Index

319